What People Are Saying about *Charming Impossibles*

"Susan E Foster's insight and humanity illuminates the warning signs of abusers who are dangerous to men and women's survival, compromising their children's well-being. With profound wisdom, she reveals the pain of betrayal and offers solutions that can protect families before it's too late. I am grateful that Susan has taken on the mission to help thousands by sharing her personal journey."

—Paige Flink, CEO, The Family Place, Dallas, Texas

"My former head coach Tom Landry would always preach to his players about work ethic and character. Susan E Foster epitomizes those traits. Her inspiring story is a must-read. I am particularly appreciative of how she highlights former pro football colleagues valiantly standing up against domestic violence."

—Mike Renfro, former NFL Wide Receiver,
Dallas Cowboys and the Houston Oilers

"This beautifully written book presents excellent examples and meaningful stories that reveal how complicated and real this matter continues to be. From personal experience, I can attest to the importance of being proactive and strong. *Charming Impossibles* bears a crucial message that a lot is at stake: women need to think with their heads, not with their hearts."

—Jana Cole Bertrand, author of *Beware the Red Flag Man*

"With what Susan went through and how she was able to pull it all together is admirable. It took courage and strength for her to share her personal journey of survival and faith in order to help others. I'm not ashamed of the fact that I was once an addict. I persevered and overcame, and so has Susan."

—Isiah Robertson, former NFL great,
Los Angeles Rams; Six-Time Pro Bowler

Charming IMPOSSIBLES

How Ordinary Angels Help Free the Hopelessly Stuck

SUSAN E FOSTER

Clovercroft Publishing

Charming Impossibles

©2020 by Susan E Foster

Published by Clovercroft Publishing, Franklin, Tennessee

Edited by Gail Fallen and Sandra G Willis

Copy Edit by Gail Fallen

Proofread by Gail Fallen and Tammy Kling

Cover and Interior Design by Suzanne Lawing

Front Cover Design by Suzanne Lawing and Nelly Es

Printed in the United States of America

978-1-950892-32-7

This book was written by Susan E Foster in her personal capacity. The personal accountings, opinions, and views expressed in this book are the author's own and do not necessarily reflect the views of the Tarrant County Hospital District d/b/a JPS Health Network.

Author's Note: This book was written by Susan E Foster based on true stories. Some names have been changed and some stories altered. The personal accountings, opinions, and views expressed in this book are the author's own and do not necessarily reflect the views of any other individual or entity mentioned in this book. Stories mentioned are common or classic to what many experience. Situations described in this book that may be similar to those of others is a matter of pure coincidence.

Dedication

*To my parents, thank you for your powerful
unconditional love and for teaching me how to listen
by sharing your faith using so few words.*

*To my four children, you are my inspiration.
Keep shining your bright, beautiful light.
I love you and look forward to all of us being together
again on the other side of this life.*

Introduction

Have you ever met someone so captivating and alluring that they were the center of attention in every room? I have. But at home, behind closed doors, out of the eye of others, he was entirely different. He was charming on the outside, but at home with his own family, he was a different kind of charming: he was a tormentor. Reflecting on my own journey navigating, sieving, and dealing with this type of confusing personality, I wondered how many others there are out there. How many people are walking around looking dynamic and charming to the world yet are double-faced tyrants at home with their families? How many people were suffering in confusion and silence under the confusing, chaotic domination of another such individual? I suspect there are more than we know.

I wrote this book for them. If you are one of them, I hope you can hear my story and see that not only is it not normal to suffer the way I did, but most importantly, I hope you can learn from the mistakes I made while living in fear. I hope to encourage those who need to leave, to do so. You deserve more. You're worth more. You do not need to stay with someone who is charming, yet impossible. I also wrote this for the fortunate outsider who never has suffered like this. I hope you grow in understanding the potential role you may play in all this without even knowing it.

* * *

They are everywhere.

I call them "Charming Impossibles." They could be in your family; in your neighborhood; at your office, schools, and place of worship; or even leading your political and social movements. They might include your mother, your father, or your spouse or in-laws. They are acquaintances, strangers, and friends. They are managers and agents of superstars.

Abusive people are great pretenders, masters in not revealing their true insincerity, hiding behind a big smile, or manifesting self-superiority. They are masters at appearing caring and kind as they manipulate anyone in the path toward their objective: *control and domination.* The spectrum ranges from mean girls and bullies on the playground to the Hannibal Lector and Ted Bundy types, with most falling somewhere in between. Charm is their convincing lure and invisible mask. Impossible to *satisfy* is their secret weapon or intentional method of control. Their approval strategically remains just beyond reach. This empowers their manipulative strategizing as they move "goalposts" when need be. By never allowing their Target to achieve their elusive approval, they insidiously maintain power and control.

The other portion of humanity is people I call "Kinfolk," as we are truly all related. Among these Kinfolk are jerks: mean-spirited, challenging people and lovely, wonderful, beautiful people. What separates Kinfolk from Charming Impossibles is that they want to feel loved and valued. They desire peace. Among Kinfolk is a shared desire for joy and well-being for others and for themselves. Abusers know this and are good at playing to the basic human needs of Kinfolk by brilliantly appearing caring, magnetically luring trust and support from key people in their sphere of influence and, more importantly, from the sphere of influence surrounding their Target, their victim of choice. In politics, those who fall prey to such tyrannical charm are referred to as "Useful Idiots." For those who fall prey to such charm in the domestic and business world, I call them "Enablers Unaware," as these folks keep the Charming Impossible empowered to continue abusing the Target, causing their Target to remain "Hopelessly Stuck."

According to the NCADV (the National Coalition against Domestic Violence), one in four women and one in seven men in the United States have been victims of severe physical violence (e.g., beating, burning, or strangling) by an intimate partner in their lifetime.[1] One in three girls will be sexually or emotionally violated by an abusive person they know and/or trust before the age of 18.[2] Those numbers are derived from instances of abuse reported to police and mental health authorities; however, many experts believe that numerous cases of abuse go unreported. It is believed that if all cases of innocents being abused were reported, perhaps as many as half our population has personally been victim of some form of mental, physical, or emotional abuse.

What complicates the situation is the chasm of misunderstanding that exists between those who have suffered childhood trauma, an abusive spouse, boss, or spiritual leader from those who have not. Unless you've endured it personally, it's nearly impossible to understand or truly comprehend. Responses, fears, reactions, and defensive decision-making resulting from physical, sexual, mental, emotional, or spiritual abuse are unique to responses of unwarranted meanness or harsh treatment from someone else in the other 95 percent of our communities. It's different. There are lots of mean, unethical, vicious jerks among the Kinfolk. You may have been the subject of their cruelty. And please hear me when I tell you that while I'm sure it hurt, it did not wound your spirit like the destructive attack of a Charming Impossible. What sets Charming Impossibles apart is their insidious skill of intended targeting and diabolical planning. They intentionally strike where they know their Target is most vulnerable while controlling who sees only their charm. They simultaneously chip away at their Target's support system while systematically winning over the devotion of that same system to themselves, eventually isolating their Target completely.

Charming Impossibles choose their victims for positive and nurturing energy on which to feast. In order to feed off their Target's power, these abusers maliciously attack the Target, triggering an intentional and completely different kind of self-doubt, confusion, and loss of sense of self that only these abusers are capable of causing. It is through this process, the abuser derives satisfaction. They are emotional leeches that suck the very life out of their victims for pleasure.

Charming Impossibles target and strategically choose those who believe everyone has "good" in them. Abusers choose those who believe and trust in the power of love. They choose good, healthy people. Charming Impossibles present themselves through a façade of charm with a hidden undercurrent of intentional control and manipulation. They are phony yet brilliant pretenders who attack to dominate certain Targets and pull invisible strings through deceitful charm, orchestrating multiple other people's lives. Their cunning manipulation of others feeds their craving for control. In a way, they are god over their own world stage, pulling the strings as if others are their very own marionettes. They cause others to act, believe, and do their bidding as they orchestrate from above with invisible strings we can't even see.

Beware when someone is going after your empathy or your devotion. By the simple act of listening to their whisper in your ear, pulling you away from one or turning you against another, you may have judged another precisely as planned by being manipulated by such an invisible string without even knowing it. Hopefully, I can show how anyone, and I mean anyone, can fall prey to the manipulation of Charming Impossibles. Hopefully, more of our community will begin to understand how they trigger an intentional and completely different kind of self-doubt and confusion in their victims, making them feel as though they are the crazy one in a way that those who have never been targeted don't understand. These emotional leeches suck the very life out of their victims, emotionally and sometimes physically, as well.

Childhood trauma (emotional or physical) changes the physiology of the brain. A team from the McGill Group for Suicide Studies at the Douglas Mental Health University Institute and McGill University in Montreal, Canada, aims to decipher how a history of abuse can impact key brain mechanisms, affecting mental health. In one report, Dr. Pierre-Eric Lutz and colleagues noted that in adults who went through severe abuse as children, the neural connections in an area of the brain associated with the regulation of emotion, attention, and various other cognitive processes are critically impaired.[3]

With no personal reference points, those who have never suffered abuse don't truly understand what an abused sufferer has undergone. More importantly, they are also prime targets to play yet another role for the Charming Impossible. To keep victims stuck, these sociopathic abusers spin a separate web of confusion around the victim's support network. This causes the victim to feel Hopelessly Stuck while Enablers Unaware around them misunderstand, isolate, and don't believe them.

Enablers Unaware, too, are victims of the same invisible strings controlling the Hopelessly Stuck. Before you proudly declare you would never fall prey as a victim, you might want to think again.

Victims remain Hopelessly Stuck because they feel they have no one to whom they can turn. These narcissists cleverly orchestrate how others respond to their Target by spinning stories or webs of confusion into ears of people surrounding the Target, creating a team of Enablers Unaware. Society's limited vocabulary and knowledge on this subject further exacerbates Targets feeling Hopelessly Stuck. Targets usually have limited vocabulary and knowledge, as well. Far too many of our professionals and lay people are not properly equipped with the necessary words to even discuss the diabolical deeds of these abusers adequately. In addition, the deep chasm between the haves and the have nots of personally experiencing this sort of abuse keeps us worlds apart. I know because I've lived on both sides. By sharing my story, I hope to close that divide.

Having spoken about my experience has opened doors for me to meet many women and men who have endured living under tyrannically chaotic, abusive manipulation. There seems to be little limit to what a person will do when they are obsessed with completely controlling another. No form of peacemaking or appeasement works with this type of person.

Conventional marriage counseling with couples involving a Charming Impossible is counterproductive as Targets are encouraged to explain what the abuser does that hurts or is disagreeable. That's like giving their Charming Impossible a bullet for the gun they readily have aimed at them! Family and marriage counseling with a Charming Impossible can ultimately be very harmful because better explaining to a narcissist how they hurt you assures they will revisit that wound only to dig deeper, especially if you are their child crying out for help. With their child or spouse, the abuser will convince the counselor the victim is to blame.

With conventional counseling counterproductive, victims are deeply stuck. In these cases, quiet submission encourages the same abuse as fighting back, leaving victims with the choice of "My way or the highway." Why is "taking the highway" not an easy, obvious choice? For many Hopelessly Stuck, leaving is the most traumatic, abusive, terrifying option of all. Leaving a Charming Impossible is very risky as Targets have lost businesses, suffered broken relationships, and been estranged from their children due to the sabotage of lies from another. With all this, plus a community of groomed believers trusting more in the abuser than their victims, how does one leave?

Experts say the most dangerous time in such a victim's life is right after they leave. According to Stand! For Families Free of Violence, 70 percent of domestic violence murders happen *after* the spouse, girlfriend or child leaves, which is the reason many choose a life of self-denial and stay.[4]

When a victim leaves, some outsiders are sure to judge, condemn, and side with the abuser. It *will* happen. I hope that by sharing my story, I can educate those on the outside looking in. I hope I can encourage those who are fortunate to have never been targeted by a Charming Impossible to consider the effects of the insidious web of which they, too, may be a part, unaware. You may be an outsider. You may have never been Hopelessly Stuck, but you very likely may have been entangled as an Enabler Unaware.

Society has a code of silence for victims of abuse. We are to quietly put it behind us and move forward. We are to ignore, take the higher road, and not "lower" ourselves to their level by refuting their lies with truth. Abusers groom the community around their Target. They are articulate and know just how to broadcast lies, impacting attitudes while victims are asked to quietly move on, as two wrongs don't make a right. "Don't tell" is our message not only from our abuser but from the surrounding community. This is a much bigger problem in society than any of us may realize. This code of silence empowers abusers to continue abusing, breeding more little abusers, which is where we are today: in a society full of angry, silenced victims of abuse acting out radical acts of terror like we've never seen before with the majority of society ignorant on how to even discuss abuse, raising their hands in wonderment of *why is this happening*? We are only as sick as our secrets. Truth is the answer to setting us free. Telling the truth may hurt many, initially, but not nearly as many as keeping a secret will. Secrets don't lead to healing. Truth does. Truth is the answer, no matter the fallout. Why do we, as a society prefer silence? Gloria Steinem says it so well: "The truth will set you free, but first it will piss you off!"[5]

Brené Brown, a research professor at the University of Houston and an expert on courage, vulnerability, shame, and empathy says, "If we can share our story with someone who responds with empathy and understanding, shame can't survive."[6] There it is . . . the golden nugget. Abusers and victims are both trying to free themselves from shame. Your listening ear and empathy is your greatest commodity where their healing is concerned. Whomever you listen to, responding with empathy, you give the gift of healing from shame. How do you know I am not the liar creating a smear campaign? Which one of us is telling the truth? Why should you even care? We haven't even gotten into it, and this read is already mentally exhausting, with many readers ready to put down this book. I get it! I do not know the answer to these problems nor the answer of how we can most effectively hold these abusers accountable in order to stop this madness. I hope to be part of the solution and invite you join me. By telling our story, I hope to educate others on the dilemma of this societal problem and hope to build a system of role models. I hope that by telling our story, others will find the courage to tell theirs and their communities will discover their role in how to best support them as they heal.

Together we can limit the damage done through abuse. In order to do so, we must understand it. Learning about abuse is no joyride. This isn't pleasure reading. But I believe that if you push through, you will gain insight and tools to help someone near you. I believe that after you read this, you will see abusers who were otherwise invisible to you. You will learn of someone's suffering of which you were otherwise unaware. You will know what to do. You will become part of the solution. You will become a safe place to whom someone in need can turn. Or perhaps you will find answers and healing for yourself.

Victims stay not only due to the violent nature of the beast but also for what might happen to the children in the court system. Charming Impossibles do not co-parent, they counter-parent without concern of damage to the children as long as they hurt the Target. Not only are their Enablers Unaware surrounding the victim in naïve support of the abuser, they unwittingly are often the cause for children of Targets to remain Hopelessly Stuck as well.

Too many have said to me, "This doesn't happen in my neighborhood, in my church, in my social circle, or in my school. . . ." I believed that too. For so long, I thought I was the only one. It was through others sharing the kind of car in which they drove off, the kind of home they left, or the type of church they attended that I was convinced I wasn't alone. Therefore, I share those details of my life story hoping to break through the misconceptions.

Abuse starts subtle and small and is twisted into blame of the victim by the abuser. For years, I didn't see the emotional abuse for what it was. Until the physical abuse turned into big, ugly bruises that I hid, I didn't fully grasp the emotional torment I also hid, even from myself. When I began to hear my abuser tell me my problem was that I had never really been beaten up, that's when I knew. It was the subtle consistency of his chipping away at me, slowly, steadily growing worse, with acts of kindness mixed in that kept me confused. If only I had recognized this much earlier. Abusers escalate. They don't start out in severe ways. But they rarely change, and they all pull from the same list of tactics.

Fortunately, there is hope. We are never alone. As you will see in my book, there are many sincerely loving, truly good people placed on our paths in this life.

I believe most people are good. Some of these good people are strategically placed on our path for a specific purpose. I call these people placed along our journey "Ordinary Angels." To see them, we must blindly take steps. We must also anticipate them. They appear when we least expect it. They often come when we are most discouraged, which is why we must keep walking. I can't wait to introduce you to my Ordinary Angels. I hope that by meeting some of the extraordinary Ordinary Angels along my path, you will be even more encouraged and inspired to finish strong the journey that lies before you. You are never alone.

We all play the different roles of these characters throughout our lives. Playing the role and being the character are two completely different phenomena. Moreover, just as one man's trash is another man's treasure, some true Charming Impossibles have played the role of an

Ordinary Angel. This is why there's so much confusion in knowing what and whom to believe, especially when considering custody battles. It's a messy, dark world out there. But the smallest ray of light brightens up complete darkness. Charming Impossibles do not reinvent themselves. There are certain tactics they all use. Once educated on how they operate, I've seen Hopelessly Stuck, Enablers Unaware, and others recognize Charming Impossibles for who they truly are, disabling their power and control in their own lives.

So why did I stay 21 years?

For me, there was more to it than leave or stay. It was that deep within, where there was hope that no matter how dark and harsh it was, the hope reached deeper still. It was a belief deep within in the power of love and commitment combined with faith in God. It was belief that God could and would soften, change and make better, make straight the crooked path. There was a hope that good would eventually come out of the bad and right all the wrong. There was the knowledge that God could, so maybe He would, turn this ship around and get us on a smooth course. It was faith, hope, and love that kept me there.

We aren't quitters. We don't give up. We are *fighters*.

I was standing on faith that God would heal, standing for our family, standing to keep sacred a covenant that I sincerely meant when I made the promise for better or worse. What can I expect from God if I break a covenant with Him? One doesn't just walk out on that. I stood strong, hoping and praying until every ounce of hope was completely drained. Then I prayed again and again, still standing, because what if faith, hope, and prayer *do not* bring healing? Then where would I turn?

1

Chapter One

Never admits to being wrong
Avoids accountability and emotions
Rages when someone challenges them
Childish when they don't get their way
Instills doubt in their victims
Stonewalls during conflict
Slanders you in a smear campaign
In denial and gaslights you
Subjects you to the silent treatment
Tears you down and creates love triangles.
—SHAHIDA ARABI, @selfcarewarrior, selfcarehaven.org

"Gaye, someone needs to know where I am," I whisper into my cell phone to my sister-in-law in a shuddering voice.

"Susan, are you all right?" she asks.

"Seth just informed me that he's taking me to get demons prayed out of me!" I tell my brother's wife. "Listen, I'm here at our river property, and Seth is acting very odd. My God, he's losing his mind. He just told me he is taking me to get demons prayed out of me in the morning."

Shaking, hidden behind the tree trunk of our pecan grove, deluding myself that he couldn't see me, I summoned up the courage to make this one call.

"What? What are you talking about?" she asks, grasping for understanding. I couldn't imagine.

To have demons prayed out of anyone was ridiculously radical and certainly not practiced in our church family or by anyone I knew personally. I explained that he just told me about a book he had read. It was about a man who prayed over men in prison, delivering them from demons. And Seth became inspired to have this man pray over me.

After contacting this man's office, Seth was recommended to someone who recommended someone else, and so on, until he reached this couple who agreed to meet with me about my *problem*.

"Where does he come up with this stuff?" she said, asking the obvious. "What does he hope to accomplish from all of this?" she continued, questioning his crazy madness.

"I don't know. I just want someone to know where I am right now. I'm scared."

"Let me stay on the phone with you. This sounds *crazy*," she said.

Strangely keeping at a distance, Seth crept in and lurked around the trees like a wily coyote, watching me from afar as I talked on my cell phone. His distant silhouette in the moonlight seemed the perfect backdrop for starring in what felt like my own horror picture show.

"No. I have to go, now." I hesitated. "But please call and check in on me in the morning. Just make sure I answer."

* * *

Earlier that evening, my three kids and I were working late at our river property. (My other daughter Audrey was off at college.) Having worked all day on our river property, we were exhausted and ready to go home. With paint brushes washed, paint cans stacked, and tarps folded and put away, we were finished and eager to wash the paint from our hair, hands, and faces, and we were especially looking forward to getting into clean clothes.

Seth showed up to assess our work, insisting that we remain and work more, assigning yet another project on the cabin windows. We were tired and it was getting late. I insisted we save that for another day. His behavior was dark and agitated as if he was seeking a battle.

Concerned for all our safety, I convinced him to let the kids go on home as they had school in the morning. I would stay to do the extra work, but they needed to get on home. The kids piled in the car quickly and scrammed down our caliche driveway with my 16-year-old, Winston, at the helm, trailing a dust cloud behind.

Then, in the dark, as I stood alone with him in our pecan grove on the river, Seth informed me of my early morning appointment to have demons delivered from me.

"We will be leaving early tomorrow," he commanded. "Be ready by eight o'clock."

In the shadow of a majestic pecan tree towering over our green, lush river-bottom pecan grove, my senses were heightened. I could smell burning wood from a distant neighbor's chimney. The sounds of falling leaves touching the ground, squirrels and lizards rustling, fish fluttering, turtles diving, and the river's gently flowing sounds all seemed amplified around me. My overly acute senses heard echoes of water streaming in the near distance over the dam, splashing against the riverbank of our property line while flowing on down. Longing for the river to take me with it, wanting to be anywhere but there, I stayed.

The next morning, on the way to get demons prayed out of me, I asked Seth, "What are you hoping to accomplish through all this?"

"I want my rightful authority over my family back," he explained through gritted teeth, further accusing me of having usurped his leadership by leading our children astray with my rebellion and disobedience. With Scripture, he had stripped me of rights to myself and given all the power over the family to himself as priest over our home. I was to follow him and teach my children to do the same. Agreeing to disagree was rebellion. We were to walk in complete harmony, following him implicitly. Anything less was disobedience and rebellion. With any sign of such rebellion, if even in thought or opinion, we would pay dearly through his covertly underhanded, manipulative ways. Having been treated like an appendage or possession whose purpose was to convert all my wants, desires, and likes to his, a reintroduction to me was required. *Who am I, anyway?* I was beginning to ask. *What are my likes and dislikes? What do I believe?* I had lost all sense of self, but a renewed eagerness to rediscover the real me was emerging. Seth was pushing all of us over the edge, feeding our growing resistance, which led to his big idea of taking me to have demons prayed out of me.

* * *

One very late evening, I lay in bed next to my husband after "listening" to a familiar, several-hour rant as he berated me. The whole time, I lay there singing a song in my head, obstructing every word, envisioning phrases passing from his mouth directly to God, bypassing me. When he finally tired himself out, I said something that caused him to realize I really wasn't listening to him and that he had not had his desired impact on me. Then he opened the gates of my mind and said, "I can't believe I haven't been able to break you yet."

Until that point, I did not realize he was consciously trying to break me. Even still, the obvious wasn't completely convincing. I may have been emerging but remained deeply buried under layers and years of manipulation and deceit. Breaking me *was*, actually, his cognitive intention. His appetite for control required me to be broken by *him*? What was once a covert effort on his part had become entirely overt. I was beginning to wake up and he knew it. His beliefs were that I was to die to my rights, I was to die daily (according to Saint Paul in

Scripture) that the Lord may live. Because he was one with the Lord, according to his own interpretations, I was to die to my wishes that his could flourish and we could "become one." His children were also to think, like, and dislike according to his mandate, which was, in essence, according to the Lord, in his opinion. My encouraging them to think for themselves was teaching rebellion. His crazy, conflicted spiritually evil web of marriage, love, and control was unraveling. The growing intensity of his physical abuse was causing me to finally begin mentioning it to others. He was losing control. *How the hell did I get here?*

This crazy nightmare had to come to an end.

* * *

Imagining the rundown rickety home or building we were going to and the wacky, snaggle-toothed witch lady with teased hair answering the door, I envisioned a filthy, messy, chaotic, crazy place littered with filthy plates, used paper towels, and torn, frayed furniture. With nothing but road noise and a radio my mind wouldn't hear, I pictured blue peeling paint rotting off siding adorned with flickering neon signs. Having no idea where we were going other than north of Austin, my imagination ran wild. Visions of *The Exorcist* came to mind. Does he envision my head turning on my neck full circle like an owl, with green goo running out of my mouth? *How on earth did my life come to this?* I wondered. *What am I doing in this crazy, crazy mess?*

* * *

Waiting for the private electric gate to open, I peered through the wrought-iron fence to see an earth-toned, stucco Mediterranean-style luxury home that looked like one I might expect to find in North Dallas's finest neighborhoods. The gate opened as Seth punched in a code. While Seth parked out front, I wondered what these people have been told about me. I began to ponder as we opened our doors and walked across their slate-colored tiled driveway approaching their beautifully landscaped oversized entry, billowing bright multicolored flowers and creatively designed manicured greenery stretching across the grand façade.

Seth rang the doorbell; it chimed like a grandfather clock inside. I looked everywhere but at him.

The large wooden double doors opened. The man wore khakis and a blue button-down oxford shirt. His wife came to his side. Conservatively dressed in nice slacks and a simple sweater, with the manners of an elegant, proper lady, she offered me a gentle smile as we were graciously invited in. We were guided into their elegant living room, where I sat on the far end of the golden velour couch as far opposite of Seth as possible, taking in the smell of a cinnamon spiced-apple candle.

Leaning away from Seth, hovering over the arm of their luxurious overstuffed couch arm, I learned through quick introductions that the man of the house is a professional engineer. No chatter from me. No interest in small talk or introducing myself. Not rude. Not friendly. I vowed to speak only if asked to. Saying as little as necessary, I politely co-existed.

Once pressed to participate, I suggested to Seth, "How about you tell them what you have done to me?"

Glaring over at me, scowling as if to say *How dare you*, Seth sarcastically replied, "You mean about the time I slapped you?"

"That would be a good start," I replied, shrugging in matter-of-fact agreement. Evidently, I had finally come to a place where hiding his actions no longer was stronger within me than suffering the consequences for revealing him.

Scanning me through squinted eyes, he slowly turned his attention back to our hosts, relaxing his facial muscles into a pleasant crested smile. Tossing his hands up as if to brush it off, Seth told the couple he slapped me, explaining he was willing to do whatever necessary to keep my disobedience in check. They didn't react and encouraged him to continue.

"Go on . . . tell them the rest," I encouraged him with a shrug, half rolling my eyes, still clinging to the armrest, still leaning far from him.

Suddenly, his countenance completely lightened, and scooting enthusiastically to the couch edge, he began to tell them *everything*.

Stunned that, for the first time, all of his physical abuse was public and confessed by his own admission, I could hardly believe my ears. Simultaneously, another conversation echoed in the background of my mind. While they talked as if in a silent movie, I replayed in my own mind what I'm hearing him say. It was if two conversations were taking place at once. He actually described to them everything he had done to me. And he did it enthusiastically, with a smile, quoting his Scriptures backing up his actions, truly believing these people were in utter agreement with him. I was stunned, shocked. *He really believes this!*

He told them how he grabbed my neck and threw me down in our RV, how he threw me against the wall and to the floor, pulling a fist when I refused to agree with him (insisting rather that we agree to disagree), how he slapped me, pulled me by my hair from one room to the other, and punched my thigh and kicked my shin, leaving bruises . . . big ugly bruises.

My own little conversation was going on in my head as I listened to him tell them everything he had done to me. *He is willing to tell them this?* He was telling *them* that he would stop at nothing and was determined to stop all my rebellion and disobedience for the sake of our Lord and our children? He enthusiastically continued to share what he did, assuming their listening represented their approval and agreement.

Up until this moment, I had alluded to my physical abuse with only a rare few, never in full disclosure. Strangely, I was afraid of it, afraid to talk about it. This was the first I heard *him* put words to the abuse. Words that invaded my self-protected, self-built mental sanctuary where I apparently had convinced myself that he didn't really realize what he was doing at the time, evidently having *further* convinced myself that he did these things unbeknownst to himself. *How stupid of me.* And, even more bizarre, it was something I did in my head that I didn't realize until that very moment, listening to his full confession. I simply could not fathom he did these things to me while lucid, coherent, and himself. *It was him all along. How foolish of me to think otherwise!*

His vice was never the influence of drugs or alcohol but rather his "self-righteousness." It was his calling as "head" and "priest" of his home. It was his understanding of how I was to submit to him completely because, in his mind, my obedience to him was unto the Lord.

In his world, for me to be obedient to God, all I had to do was be obedient to *him*, with no right to correct him and no rights to myself, my own opinions, or thoughts; therefore, for me to agree to disagree was rebellion and worthy of physical assault. Such "disobedience" threatened his "headship" and our "holy oneness." Anything less than completely united was not tolerable because we could not tolerate two heads. After all, by marriage we had become one. There was no room, no tolerance for any division; we were to be completely united and he was always right unless God told him otherwise. Correcting him was entirely left to the Lord and was not tolerated from me.

My life was very simple. All I had to do was follow and agree in everything.

* * *

My brother and I grew up Episcopalian, where church was a never-miss family affair of enjoying fellowship with friends over donuts and coffee. It was wholesome stability, more social than religious. My parents' weekly commitment proved grounding. In our adult years, my brother and I became involved in fundamental Bible churches where "personal relationship with God" was taught. This was a new and genuinely meaningful experience for us.

My husband grew up Southern Baptist. I do not hold the Southern Baptist or any other church we attended responsible for what he chose to believe. However, I have a clearer understanding of where he came from after recently reading an op-ed written by former president Jimmy Carter entitled "Losing my religion for equality." In this opinion piece, he explained he was leaving the Southern Baptist Church because "Women and girls have been discriminated against for too long in a twisted interpretation of the word of God."[1] He went on to say, "The truth is that male religious leaders have had—and still have—an option to interpret holy teaching either to exalt or subjugate women. They have, for their own selfish ends, overwhelmingly chosen the latter."[2] As global leaders brought together by former South African president Nelson Mandela, Jimmy Carter wrote of their declaration to other world and religious leaders: "The justification of discrimination against women and girls on grounds of religion or tradition, as if it were prescribed by a Higher Authority, is unacceptable."[3]

As a married couple, Seth and I participated in many Bible study group discussions, and more often than not, no one agreed with my husband. That didn't matter to him. In fact, it only proved to him his devotion to God was stronger and more superior to theirs. It was as though his steadfast commitment to what he believed the Bible meant was above anyone else's opinion, and I was to submit to *his* understanding of its truth. In our Bible study and churches, "Wives submit to husbands" (see Ephesians 5:22–24, KJV) and "Husbands are to love wives as Christ loves the Church" (see Ephesians 25) were the verses and expressions commonly discussed around the subject of marriage. This notion always had as varied an interpretation as the number of people discussing it. Seth's radical belief grew subtly, remaining hidden from most as was his campaign of slowly chipping away at me. I was losing myself one layer at a time.

To his request that I blindly follow and subjugate myself to him, I would ask him "Why, then, have I been given a brain, tastes, and likes and dislikes if I am supposed to submit all my opinions, likes, tastes, and dislikes into agreement with yours?" Perhaps unwisely, I would bait him even further. "How is it that you feel I am to function as an appendage of yours? I am a person, an individual with my own independent thoughts." To which, toward the end of our ordeal one day, I finally realized his intentions when he said, "I can't believe I haven't been able to break you yet." The realization this has been the intention from the beginning was only beginning to sink in. He *meant* it.

And there it was. He actually *said* it. I *felt* like he was trying to break me, but I didn't believe it to be true. *Was my brain like a horse's? With horses, you have train both sides. Do I compartmentalize information? Does only part of my brain comprehend certain pain and trauma? Does not all of me understand or even recognize it? What is wrong with me?* I wondered.

Feeling as though numbing Novocain had been applied to my many layers of pain, I imagined my brain disassociated from my many traumatic encounters with him in an effort to cope. Perhaps that's why I assumed he disassociated himself from his traumatic actions taken against me. Up until that moment, realizations, confessions, traumatic actions, or words did not resonate in my mind as they should have for the cowardly, deliberate lies and manipulations that they were. My brain was in such a coping mode, I evidently could not recognize the reality of all the pain and confusion for what it was. Those realizations began to penetrate as I sat there hearing him boldly confess what I thought he didn't realize. While it may only have penetrated my immediate layer and while the real me was still buried under many layers, I finally was awakening.

How the hell am I here in this crazy nightmare? How did I wind up here in this living hell? My brain, my conscience, me. Responding to trauma and pain, without asking my permission, my own body buried me a little deeper underneath. *At least, that's what this feels like. My*

God, I have heard about this sort of brain malfunction associated with trauma.

But I didn't think it could happen to me.

I guess this was why I didn't argue with his denials of doing the very things he did. *Healing. How deep below the layers is true healing then? Would it come in layers too? I just wanted to rip off every layer right then. I wanted to find myself! My God, what have I done with me?* It would be a long process. But first, I would need to get out.

* * *

The conversation I was having with myself, the realization of what I was hearing Seth admitting at face value, was interrupted when the man stood to his feet and turned to Seth with a pointed finger, telling him he was a narcissist, had a personality disorder, a religious spirit, a controlling spirit that he once controlled but that now controlled him, that he was delusional and a sociopath. His problems were pathological, this man said to him. The man said that clearly nothing Seth said of me was true. He could see it in my demeanor and how I responded or didn't respond to what he said.

Finally, that truth made it straight down to me, passing through all the layers. My deepest fear was confirmed when this couple advocated for *me*. Not him. Without me saying a word, they supported *me*. I got it. I *heard* it and while I was empowered by their trust in me, the implications of this truth required me to leave him, leave my marriage covenant, and leave hope for healing our family behind. No matter how hard he tried, he was losing his power to turn others against me. He was revealed. It was now too dangerous to stay.

* * *

Lashing out in anger, Seth stood nose-to-nose with the man in full-throated retaliation, turning on both of them, questioning their credentials, refusing their having any authority to tell him *anything*; therefore, accepting nothing they had to say about him. It was then that the man pointed to his door, ordering Seth out of his home. The lady nervously fumbled for her phone, saying to me, "Please give me your number." Frantically, I recited my phone number as I was rushed out the door.

Seth was thrown from their house . . . and me with him, essentially. What else could they do? I couldn't stay with those people. My children were at home. *Of course, I must go with him*, I thought. *But oh my God, what's going to happen now?*

Locked inside my husband's Mercedes, I didn't say a word as Seth and I sat in their driveway just outside of their locked front door. In an almost lucid moment, he said, "I know three adults are saying I am the one with a problem." Then he turned to me and asked, "Do you really think *I* am actually the problem?" Much to my surprise, he seemed to be genuinely lucid and open-minded.

I said, "Yes, they're not the first who have said these things to you." I reminded him that we had been to another counselor recommended by our pastor because our situation "required a professional."

"That professional, too, declared you a narcissist," I continued. "And you questioned his credentials, as well, never to return to him."

Highway noise penetrated the stony silence until he started gripping the steering wheel in an agitated manner, his face wincing as he hovered forward and said, "No, no! I am like Walt Disney. I have ability to *see*! I have *vision* that average people can't recognize or comprehend. I am not the problem!"

Oh dear, I thought, *I hope he wasn't going to take me on another one of his maniac drives.* He'd do that every now and then when mad. With the whole family in the car, he'd drive at ridiculously high speeds, weaving in and out of traffic as we remained silent. It was so scary. We all learned with Seth, if we asked him to stop anything, it only encouraged him to do more of what we asked him not to do. But to my surprise, as I held my breath, he drove relatively calmly.

I'm not sure which of us was worse off. This was sickening. We were hung over on our own disgusting overdoses of insanity, and our children were suffering for both of our irresponsible, illogical delusions, dysfunction, and weird interpretations of faith. Finally, one of us was awakening. I may have drunk the juice, but its power was finally wearing off. I was coming to and determined: my children and I were getting out.

The next morning, I heard from the wife. "We are concerned your husband is dangerous. We are concerned for your safety. Please do not let him know that we contacted you."

She went on to explain, "In our twenty plus years of ministry, your husband is the first client my husband has refused. After discussing your case with our ministry partners, we have been instructed to stay away. We want nothing more to do with your husband. Again, we are very concerned for your safety," she reiterated.

Awareness of his efforts to destroy me still fresh in my mind, accepting that he consciously and intentionally berated me/us intending to break us, I wrestled with the ramifications. His charming side had no relevance. In his own flustered, agitated, and disgusted words, he said, "I can't believe I haven't been able to break you yet." He *meant* that. He also meant it the several times he had said, "You know what your problem is? It's that you have never really been beat up."

Over the four previous months, I had heard this from him several times. Staying any longer clearly meant I would soon discover what he truly meant.

Descending in slow motion, seeking emotional comprehension, my memory journeyed back to our time in Greece after a donkey ride up a winding cobblestone road to a monastery. As I purchased local handmade treasures in the monastery gift shop, the ladies across the counter said, "You are such a lucky lady; look how he looks at you. He is *so* in love with you," they said. "You are so blessed."

Yes, he was convincing. To me, too.

Then my mind went back to "I can't believe I haven't been able to break you yet."

Break you . . . *yet*. Were his charming moments completely, utterly phony? I struggled with myself. Could one ever be in love and want to break you at the same time? *Intentionally?*

He is intentional. He knows he is doing this. He is trying to do this. He has been trying to do this. To break me is his objective. I sat there and absorbed what this meant, considering all the happy memories that seemed veiled in counterfeit cloud cover. We didn't get here overnight. After all, it didn't start like this. It cleverly and intentionally evolved through confusion, manipulation, and lies that would take years to sift through.

Wanting so badly to understand my husband, please him, and make him happy, believing that if I tried hard enough, I could, I lost myself.

Some people don't *want* to be happy: Whether they realize it or not, they are more comfortable feeling angry, disappointed, or mired in some other negative emotion because it keeps them in control. They are more comfortable in an argument than in peacefully getting along. They will create chaos or stir up a fight to avoid the discomfort of joy, peace, or happiness, as those emotions don't provide the controller their need for power over another. Equality in a relationship is threatening because they believe their partner wants power over them. A relationship is a battlefield to them. They believe their partner will overcome them if they don't overcome their partner. So they fight continuously to always be in control, winning against any and every perceived threat.

It's true that happiness is a choice. But it's also true that you must *want* to be happy. This is not the universal desire I thought it was. Not everyone is comfortable feeling happy. Happiness and joy are not the common goals I assumed they were. Some prefer to create whatever negative situation best suits their need for power and use manipulation over another ultimately for control. This was a fascinating discovery for me that I realized entirely way too late.

At first, I did not realize that Seth and I were really not even working toward the same goals. I really didn't understand that this guy I married really and truly did not care if our relationship was fun and enjoyable. In fact, he was irritated that "fun" and getting along was so important to me. He actually had fun arguing his case about how wrong my priority for fun and getting along actually was. There I was, beating my head against the wall trying to achieve peace and harmony, when that was not his objective at all. Our objectives in life were polar opposites causing me to wonder what was wrong with *me.*

This is what overshadowed all those moments, stealing the missing joy I couldn't explain. No wonder I struggled to feel joy in all the seeming goodness. Rather than being the accused ungrateful and selfish one, it became clear that during my struggle, in the midst of the nice trips, fancy clothes, and beautiful homes, he had been trying to *break* me while accusing me of ungratefulness.

Seth went out of town the next day. And that's when I made the right choice to leave.

* * *

With one away in college, two in high school, and one in the eighth grade—all were finally 14 years old or older (what I believed to be the age the courts allow children to decide for themselves with whom they want to live, which I now know is not necessarily true). My understanding, however, about their age gave me confidence to make a move if my children were ready. And I believed they were. *How did a strong, confident, educated person like me end up in this mess? Why didn't I do something sooner? Why did God allow this? What's wrong with me? How could I be so stupid?*

Wrought with shame and embarrassment, I was absolutely sick with myself. And most importantly, I wondered, *What have I done to my children?* I thought my choice to stay was best for them. That's why I stayed. *Was I a fool? Was I so wrong?* I was absolutely disgusted and angry with myself and more determined than ever to get a divorce . . . and get it *fast.*

Predetermining a likely response from him about our leaving was like expecting certain responses from calling a cat. *How would he react?* He was so unpredictable.

But it no longer mattered. I was left with no other option.

We had to leave.

* * *

A Note from the Future

I didn't know then how long it would take to get a handle on my fear. Fear and confusion remained my constant companion long after leaving.

Yes, we were leaving a very difficult situation. But we would soon learn we were also trading one terribly traumatic challenge for another. Little did we know how caught up in his web of confusion we still were. It took years of being away from the chaos to truly see the craziness for what it was and to mend the damaged layers deep inside us.

Even long after cutting off all communication with Seth, it would take years for us to unravel and escape the emotional stronghold he had over us. Leaving was a long process that required patience with ourselves. We wanted to quickly heal, but healing came long after lots of twists, turns, and what seemed like a never-ending tumultuous journey.

Leaving, as it turned out, was the easy part. But making it on our own was tantamount to moving a mountain. Making it was our *only* option.

We simply *had* to make it, because returning to Seth was never a consideration.

* * *

Six years later, as I was scrolling through my cell phone, a name surfaced, drawing my attention. It was the contact information for the woman to whom Seth had brought me to have demons prayed out of me. I called her, and much to my surprise, she answered.

"Hello?"

I told her who I was and asked if she remembered our visit when Seth brought me to them for deliverance of demons.

"Oh, yes, I remember it well," she said. We visited awhile. I told her I was writing my story and asked if she and her husband would read my account of our visit to confirm that I was recalling it correctly. They were honored to read it and confirmed my account was accurate. But they also explained, "We are not exorcists, just so you know. I don't know how he found our name, but we do not know anyone who wrote a book to the description of what Seth claims he read that inspired him to seek such deliverance for you. We cannot imagine who would recommend us to him. How he found our name remains a mystery. We are Christians, and we pray for people. After you left, we and our team prayed for your safety and for your wisdom. I am thankful you managed to get out of that situation safely." She went on to say, "If you are ever in this area, please call us. We'd love to meet you for coffee."

I replied, "I look forward to that visit. Thank you."

* * *

The affirmation of this couple witnessing my then-husband's own confession, and later confirming my account as accurate, gave me great courage to move forward, to trust in myself again and to write this book. Therefore, they are significant people on my path. To me, they are Ordinary Angels. As the life cycle would dictate, I wouldn't hear this confirming encouragement until six or seven years later. Blind to this affirming truth, I soldiered on.

Sometimes, things come full circle, but not in the timing or order we would like. I'm glad I moved forward blindly with or without confirmation. While I'm equally glad I didn't stay another day, I'm also glad I didn't leave any earlier, as it would have been exchanging one set of challenges for another. And I have to caution you: For some readers, I predict that many of you won't make it through all the coming chapters. It will be too much. This coming "too much" in the chapters ahead is what we are asking another to potentially face when posing the question "Why don't you leave?" Or telling someone "Just leave." By sharing my story, I hope to expose the multilayered challenges in that simple solution: "Leave."

Leaving is not so simple.

* * *

Today, there are many more organizations and resources set up to help people who are in situations like I was. I encourage anyone who may be contemplating this step to contact an organization long before leaving. Establish a relationship with experts who will help you develop a plan. They offer a host of resources. Had I known of the help available before I left, I would not have burdened my friends and family so heavily. What my friends and family did for me, organizations can do for others. And, by sharing my story, I also hope to encourage donating to organizations that help women, men, and children leave the abuse they face. I hope that bringing awareness to this still-hidden epidemic may help effect positive change.

2

Chapter Two

No one can stop the blessings that are meant for you. It always ends up backfiring for envious people who try to thwart others, because the pure-hearted operate from a place of authenticity which cannot be diminished in the long run. Their ability to create and recreate is limitless, and so is their abundance. Meanwhile, naysayers and saboteurs eventually face the karma of their actions—and live a life of meaningless hatred of the people they tried to belittle.
—SHAHIDA ARABI, @selfcarewarrior

While backing a U-Haul truck down our meandering driveway, majestic oak limbs screeched along its tall sides. With each twist and turn, this freedom machine forced itself back, daring any branch to slow me down. Oak arms crushed beneath the tires. Leaves, twigs, and fallen branches were ignored as I redirected my three teenagers' attention from the mess to quickly packing everything they wanted . . . because we were never coming back.

Safely tucking my phone down my pocket after leaving a message for my brother Arthur, I see Marshall through the front door windowpanes reaching for his waterfall painting, an eight-year-old's master-piece. His painting, a real treasure of a gift, at least to his mom, was significant as it was the first time that I had experienced fidgety, young Marshall sitting still and losing himself in creative bliss. It was the first of hopefully many more creations.

Standing on a table, he couldn't reach it. *How many other treasures will we leave behind from this life, from this marriage of 21 years?*

Stalling, transfixed at my bedroom threshold, deeply breathing in courage, releasing empowerment, I proceeded. Pulling open dresser drawers, unsystematically dumping socks, shorts, and undergarments into laundry baskets, spare boxes, and opened blankets for bundling, I forged ahead. Arthur learned of my tumultuous marriage when I had last visited his home. The truth could not bear hiding any longer as it revealed itself through a painful anguished release I was not prepared to share. It poured out of me without permission or care for its conse-quence. It simply would not stay hidden any longer. Without any con-sent of my own, my painful truth finally released itself from within my hiding place to my brother. He knew my pain. He knew the struggle.

Vibrating chimes resounded from my pocket, quickening my heart rate. I checked my caller ID before answering.

"Hello?"

"I'm on my way." I heard my brother's calming voice. "As soon as I heard your message, I got in my truck. I'll be there in a few hours."

"Thank you," I said gratefully, collapsing the phone back down my pocket.

With the setting sun rose a fog of anxiety. What if my husband came home? That fear too debilitating to consider, we picked up the pace and moved things faster.

Darkness brought nervousness. I had not told anyone else what we were doing. No one knew. Like worker ants, we just kept moving, saying very little. Fear was beginning to choke my very breath. I called to see where Arthur was.

"I'm fifteen minutes away!" he said.

Like a ray of light breaking through our nervous haze, Arthur's arrival reenergized us. With him came a second wind of comfort and faith that we could do this.

Arthur moved us at a much more rapid pace, throwing clothes in unorganized piles, packing furniture furiously, stacking our possessions one on top the other as if they were toy blocks. Effortlessly, he eased our panic by filling our truck with lamps, blankets, side tables, armchairs, and beds until every gap was filled.

Finally, the truck was full and we were ready to leave. Forever.

I walked through the house one last time. To me, it's still the most beautiful home I've ever seen. I loved its soft French yellow grandeur. It was a grand house. One we never really could afford. We were "all hat and no cattle," as they say in Texas. With this charade in which I participated and upheld in an "if-you-can't-beat-'em, join-'em spirit," we accentuated the appearance of worldly success far beyond our reality. Appearances were so important to both my husband and his father that Seth's father contributed largely to the down payment by giving Seth just shy of two hundred thousand of recently inherited dollars, a fourth of which would pay off our river property, but that was evidently too practical a choice that would not accomplish the intent of the gift.

I have my suspicions of what the true motivation was behind the sudden urgent purchase of my lovely dream home. It involved a phone call from a relative of theirs announcing they purchased a new, very expensive luxury home. To which my thought immediately went to *Oh boy, I bet I'm about to get the house of my dreams!* Would they allow Seth, the favorite "golden boy son" to be outdone? I didn't think so. In fact, the purchase happened so fast, I've often wondered if we actually closed on our house first.

Inside, wrought-iron railings trimmed a gorgeous winding white-marble staircase. Family photos cascaded down the wall along with artwork from foreign countries of memorable trips that, for me, were hopeful furloughs from our day-to-day marital war of dysfunction turned merely subdued dysfunction due to accompaniment of co-travelers. Minimized abuse that lay just beneath his surface was ever-present even on vacations, leaving behind our dark shadows that still linger on the banks of notable historic rivers and at other foreign historical points of interest commonly reproduced on canvas. I gazed up to grand open spaces and down toward our not one, but two large oversized Persian rugs that were purchased by Seth during a spending frenzy, depleting within a year his recently inherited money that could have all but paid off, in full, our river property with money left over or to perhaps purchase this grand glorious home. While he was running through the money, I took Seth to a car lot to look at a used Volkswagen I found for Audrey, who at the time was working towards her driver's license. That day, we came home with a bright, shiny brand new XJ8 Jaguar.

Recognizing the absolute absurdity of purchasing that home, I chose to revel and enjoy every moment in it. I loved living there and am grateful for the experience. Surrounded in beauty gave me some reprieve. Each child having their own beautiful space was nice. Finally, we were out of the flood-zone river property that was a continual unfinished project. Had Seth been willing to sell it, our grand home would have been affordable. My suggestion of which was not only declined but also came with dark vengeful threat that he would *never* sell it. This, by the way, is a common response of this personality type: *I'll do the opposite of what you want.* It was a response to which I had grown accustomed. A change of mind did come later with the downturn in the economy, at which time we did put that river house on the market, but to no avail.

Living with properly hung towel racks and well-finished trim were small things that gave me great pleasure after years of living in the middle of an unfinished home flood project. Not sure how long he could continue this balancing act of two mortgages we definitely could not afford long term, I embraced and enjoyed every ounce of pleasure I could, knowing it would eventually come to an end. I took great pleasure in sharing it, remembering enjoyable years of entertaining large crowds and hosting intimate gatherings. Huge tall ceilings with clouds painted above on a sky-blue background accented ornate fire-places standing guard in several rooms. Big bold Corinthian columns supported the French-style architecture inside and out. Its beauty helped me endure. The house had provided enjoyable moments of sharing by hosting debutante parties and symphony board meetings, but my favorite events were the wedding and baby showers and the graduation teas.

Prior to the money evaporating, I deposited some into all four of my children's savings accounts that my parents opened for them when they were babies. Each account held holiday money gifts my parents gave them over the years along with their own hard-earned money. Each birthday, Christmas, or other monetary gift they received was carefully considered, usually involving the child choosing to spend some of their money while saving the rest. As my father did with me, I took them into the bank to make their deposits, teaching them the value of a dollar. Each account had grown, averaging $5,000 or more, which was how they planned to purchase their first car by themselves. Sophia worked extra hard at building up her savings, collecting cans from the river to sell, hosting lemonade stands, and creating her own dog walking business. For extra savings, Winston watered a neighbor's grass and fed dogs while they were away. As he grew, he worked as a lifeguard at the local water park. With Seth's inheritance money, we wrote checks left and right to everyone but the bank and the IRS, and I was hoping to save, at least a little.

Unfortunately, as was the case with Seth and his father, money was for spending and buying. With them, money was not for saving, not for paying debts, and later I would learn, not for paying taxes, either.

Be extremely wary about lending money or putting your name on a loan with a Charming Impossible. They are silver tongued, well able to sell an idea when borrowing money. And they will be every bit as silver tongued at placing blame and responsibility on someone else when they can't pay it back.

Due to their pathological fiscal irresponsibility, we were continually at financial risk. Had they spent their money wisely, we could have afforded what we had. Watching our funds dissipate, I took the liberty to splurge on myself before our world came crashing down. At the passing of my mother-in-law (five years into our marriage), my father-in-law gifted me her full-length white mink coat, ordering me to never alter it. Before the funds ran out, I did something I wanted to do for sixteen years. I had the mink cut into a short vest, something I could actually wear. Sick to my stomach with worry of repercussions, I wore it in front of them. Nothing was ever said. This mink vest was an expression of my surviving confidence and independence in spite of their commands and denial of my rights.

With the manic cycle affecting our finances, I did take charge over areas that involved our children. One precautionary measure was my goal to pay our children's school tuition in two payments. I'd pay one sum covering the beginning of their school year through January so I would know what monies were available for Christmas. The other sum would cover January to the end of school year. This was an effort to see that their education would not be disturbed. Eventually, the inevitable happened. We ran out of money, causing our children the trauma of getting kicked out of their school. Changing schools during their high school years, going through the difficult process of making new friends while their longtime friends from their private school looked on confused by our unexplained financial crises, created an emotional mess. Our children and families of their friends could not possibly have understood our sudden lack of money after observing our frenzied high-end lifestyle of spending. The sudden depletion made no sense. Bringing us to desperate financial crisis, Seth depleted each of our children's savings accounts, even going into their bedrooms, taking what little money they had stashed in their piggy banks.

Our financial ruin was a torn scab covering much deeper darkness. A dark secret we could no longer hide.

It was time to say goodbye.

Inside, tiny little mosaic-like pieces of me remained. With my little parts connected yet disassembled, I felt like a distorted Picasso-like painting. Could I ever really mend? Would the true me ever surface from all my emotional rubble? I remained buried inside myself, trapped within what felt was a stranger. I had to be rebuilt.

3

Chapter Three

The narcissist has trained the entire family, by example, how to treat you. Once you have been labeled as the bad one, you are fair game for siblings, spouses, relatives, even family friends to pick on you.
—The Black Butterfly, Freedom From
Narcissistic and Emotional Abuse

The Narc creates the 'Golden Child' and the 'Scapegoat Child,' treating one with favor while the other gets blamed for everything. When these children grow up together, the golden child thinks the Narc, as a parent, was great, whereas the scapegoat child becomes the truth teller. As a result, the scapegoat child is isolated from the family and hated because they tell the truth and refuses to lie about what the Narc is and does. Here's the rule in Narc led families: ANYONE who speaks the truth is the enemy because they refuse to remain silent about the Narc abuse and pierces the bubble of silence surrounding the Narc.
—The Black Butterfly

A child that's being abused by its parent doesn't stop loving its parent, it stops loving itself.
—Shahida Arabi, PsychAlive.org

"My last day of driver's ed was Friday. See my certificate? I got this, Mom! I can drive," declared Sophia.

"Sophia! That's only a permit," I said. "You are required to have an adult with you."

"Mom, I'm fine!" Sophia reassured me. "I can do this."

With Sophia's driver's education course certificate still wet with ink, Sophia convinced us of her ability to drive the loaded SUV a four-hour trek north, extending past two o'clock in the morning. We were out of reasonable options and time. It was already so late. We wouldn't get to my brother's home until after two o'clock in the morning. She said she could do it.

Marshall, our 14-year-old, rode with Sophia, holding Napoleon, our black and white miniature Papillon, in his lap. For the time being, we had to leave our Great Dane, Duchess, behind. Leaving extra food and water and with no time to waste, we each hugged our beloved Duchess. With each stroke of her shiny black coat, expressing pain in our hearts for leaving her behind, numbed by the urgency of time, we drove off, leaving her standing on the very edge of our property, watching until we were no longer in sight. Off we went. Away from our home, our friends, our life. . . .

We were dismembering ourselves, forever.

In a caravan, we drove into the deep unknown. Arthur, from the U-Haul truck window, waved us on down the driveway through the neighborhood gate entrance to a mysterious new life. Winston, at 17, drove Arthur's truck; Sophia, who just turned 15, drove the Excursion; and I commanded the caboose in the Jaguar.

Our caravan began the long drive back to my hometown where I was reared and to old friends I had known since the third grade.

Driving alone, my mind went back to the memories leading up to this day.

* * *

These are very difficult memories to share. My kids and I decided to share only a few, and certainly not the worst, to hopefully help others not suffer the misunderstanding and loss we have. Telling what psychological warfare looks like falls short of showing it, which is why we are willing to show a brief peek into just a small part of our reality, a reality that anyone suffering at the hands of a Charming Impossible is experiencing. When recovering Targets get together, we astound one another with the similarities in our stories. What we are about to share with you is commonplace and is all around you, well-hidden (as was ours) because that's what we, as Targets, do. We hide it until we can't take anymore and our hope is completely demolished. My children and I share nothing out of the ordinary to other victims of this sort of abuse. These abusers are a "type." There are terms and definitions to describe and explain their abuse. Had I educated myself, I would have seen it. In educating others, I hope to help free more who are Hopelessly Stuck.

A common tactic among Charming Impossibles is what many professionals refer to as "smear campaigns." Abusers publicly smear their victims with false accusations and subtle, twisted half-truths, projecting their own wrongdoing onto their Target. This essentially renders their Targets defenseless with confused "informed" onlookers who usually represent the Target's otherwise supportive friends and oftentimes family. With no one to whom they can turn, they become Hopelessly Stuck. Theresa Little of The Family Place in Dallas likens this tactic to character assassination or identity theft, explaining that through this process, the abuser steals, redefines, and spreads an identity of another passing it for others to spread.

Little explained it to me this way, "A Target's identity is not only stolen, but the process to get it back is a process much like losing a credit or Social Security card," rendering the Target Hopelessly Stuck.

You see this in politics daily. One broadcasts blame on someone for something; the accused retaliates, taking to the airwaves to explain the misleading allegations; then the original accuser issues a rebuttal, leaving the listening news audience more confused and divided as the two sides duke it out, getting nowhere. It's brilliant; the true liar draws the victim-Target into the mud with them so they both get dirty: Viewers have no idea who to believe.

Charming Impossibles don't mind the mud and feel empowered watching their Targets get muddier as they work their way out. A direct confrontation is a no-win scenario if you're a Target of such a liar.

Some Charming Impossibles work covertly, whispering their twisted lies in people's ears one or two at a time, while others broadcast to the masses through social media or email blasts. This is why so few Targeted by this tactic speak out. It's also why so many become psychologically isolated and explains why they are Hopelessly Stuck.

There is an unwritten code of silence where victims are concerned. The cycle goes something like this: "Why didn't you say something then? Why are you leaving now? If it was so bad, why did you stay? Why are we talking about it now? When are you going to put it behind you? Why can't you just get along with them now? It takes two. I don't believe you."

This cycle leads back to "Why didn't you say something then?" and the cycle continues.

At the point of leaving an abuser, the Target is in an extreme state of trauma, with only shallow layers of enlightenment, while the abuser is eloquently aware and prepared with a brilliant dissertation, the smear campaign. By the time a Target escapes or leaves the abuse, the abuser is many steps ahead, prepared with all necessary accusations mixed with just enough half-truths, appearing reasonably self-assured as compared to the completely dismantled Target who, by that time, is nearly destroyed.

After 10 years of silence and enduring a smear campaign that still continues, at the risk of being accused of a smear campaign of our own, we have chosen to arise from years of silence to tell our truth. For far too many it is "same song, second verse," as the story we share is typical. By sharing our story, we hope to bring about awareness and ignite much-needed conversation surrounding the quieted subject of emotional abuse. Talking about abuse does not suggest lack of forgiveness. Quite the contrary, talking about abuse acknowledges it and prevents it from continuing. Talking empowers the Target to forgive the abuser for who they truly are rather than forgive the allusion of whom they were believed to have been.

* * *

After we left, Winston was homesick, missing his friends. Agreeing it would be helpful for him to be with his buddies, Winston drove down for an enjoyable weekend with his friends, his support system. It was like old times for him, providing him some semblance of normalcy within his trauma. Upon his return from that visit, I could visibly see that maintaining those relationships would be critical to his moving forward successfully.

Immediately upon Seth hearing from others that Winston returned to his hometown for a visit without acknowledging his father, Seth put the smear campaign into motion, one that is active to this day. It involves numerous emails to parents of our children's friends, entire newsletter lists of our two former churches, various other friends, random political and spiritual leaders (whom he did not even know personally), friends of my brother, and members of his family and mine. His accusations against us were successful in securing some sympathizers while causing many of Winston's friends to pull away.

Winston felt the first effects of it the second time he went home to visit his friends. They were noticeably cold and more distant. For Winston, those relationships have never been the same since the slandering emails and accusations from his own father began.

Young Targets suffer irreparable emotional loss due to these kinds of shenanigans. I hope to one day help restore some of those friendships lost in the aftermath of my kids leaving their father.

* * *

In sharing our story, I have heard stories far more tragic than ours of the smearing that takes place on social media. Smear campaigns are successful only when others listen and respond. Hopefully, awareness of these common practices will enlighten potential Enablers Unaware from succumbing.

Leaving was only the *beginning* of removing the scales from our eyes. Because of what it takes to survive abuse, Targets require a long debriefing process to actually see the level of abuse they suffered and survived. Limited communication skills leave younger Targets even more defenseless in understanding—much less explaining—what happened. Even an adult fresh from such a situation isn't fully aware of what they left until long afterward. Winston didn't know how to talk about it, nor did his friends. His friends remain an important part of his life. I hope they can one day reengage.

* * *

After the smear campaign geared up, one woman called saying she didn't know *what* to believe. Not wanting to engage in "he said, she said," I asked her to sort it out for herself. To me, the audacious and extreme statements of a father about his own children were evidence enough of selfishness and direct sabotage; I couldn't imagine anyone giving his words much credence. What kind of decent father *does* that? Quite frankly, four teens, one in college, during their most "don't tell me how to think or feel" periods of adolescence don't just walk away from *everything*. I may be influential, but for one mother to turn four teens against their dad and convince them to leave their friends, youth group, homes, and basically their whole life's foundation states the obvious. Four teens willing to leave *all* that they left behind reveals just how painful their situation truly was for them.

An old proverb (its source unknown) says, "Make sure everybody in your boat is rowing and not drilling holes when you're not looking." This process quickly taught me who my real friends were . . . which comes with disappointment and wonderful surprises. Seeing our world of "friends" sifted right before our eyes was fascinating, some-times shocking and hurtful, but more often enlightening as precious unexpected people surfaced in support. These moments revealed love and devotion of others we otherwise would have not realized.

Most contacted me saying they saw right through it. Others fell silent as they pulled away. Seth copied me on many of his slandering email attacks in an effort to lure me into bickering with him publicly. I ignored the bait. In a follow-up email, Seth interpreted for his audi-ence that my non-response reflected admitted guilt. I stayed silent. To some, my refusal to engage in that forum was interpreted as self-con-demnation. But every situation is unique. For us, we didn't see any other option. Our true friends stuck with us, and Ordinary Angels awaited our arrival along the path moving forward. If you give a Charming Impossible plenty of rope, he will eventually hang himself, unfortunately not after creating even more damaged lives in his wake.

* * *

Following almost every interview she conducts, Oprah says that once the cameras are off and the conversation is over, she is always asked this one common question in some form: *Was I okay? Did I do okay?* Every president, superstar, business genius—everyone—asks for validation. She goes on to say that in every exchange, we as humans have a need to feel heard, understood, and seen.[1] We need to know, *Did what I say mean anything to you?* This is the basic core need of a child with parents, of a boss or business partner, of a young wife with her new husband, or of a spouse. It's in these little exchanges when we are vulnerable, exploring unknown territory. Even as successful adults in other areas, we seek validation of a certain person we trust and desire to please. If, in these little vulnerable exchanges, the person you're seeking validation from is a Charming Impossible, they will slowly, subtly chip away at your core. Their most destructive work is never done in hitting, punching, or loud arguments. It's in those little intimate moments of vulnerability unique to you, that many times only they know of, that they inflict devastating emotional wounds. With this explanation, some will still say, "What do you mean? What did he do that's so bad?" How does one explain this? My only answer is to share our story.

* * *

"I hate him," Marshall, my then 12-year-old son, said.

"Oh, be careful of hate," I cautioned him. "Hating leaves your own soul bruised and does nothing to him."

"Why is he so mean?" Marshall continued.

"Hate is how he got where he is," I replied. "He has enough self-hate for all of us."

"Then why does he always brag about how holy, righteous, and good he is if he hates himself as you say?" he asked.

Marshall was my little truth seeker, always seeking to understand and know the truth.

"I don't think he hates himself at all," he argued. "He loves himself . . . *a lot*!

"I see what Dad is doing," Marshall firmly decreed at the ripe young age of 12. "He gets us to work, promising us things, but he never follows through," he continued, listing off all his father's broken promises. "I see how he works, and I'm going to tell him."

"Oh God, no, Marshall," I said in what I hoped was my best persuasive manner. "Marshall, please don't. You are not able to handle the backlash that will come from it. I *agree* with you but keep it to yourself, for now. It is not safe for you to confront him like this. You're too young. Trust me."

Marshall had no idea all that I had protected him from emotionally. I would often say to my husband I shouldn't have to be my children's PR agent to their own father. Seth was continually coming to me with complaints and accusations he wanted to confront them about. I'd manage to divert his attention or take the blame for their perceived infractions, enticing him to hurl his insults at me instead of them.

The most insidious tool an abusive parent uses to prop up their feeble ego is their own child. Their full knowledge that the innate, innocent trusting nature of a child longs to believe the love and intentions of a parent are good, true, sincere, and worthy of trust is the very vulnerability they feast upon rather than protect. As a cat plays with their food, a "bully" parent toys with the need their children possess to *feel* loved by them. Children are pawns to use and manipulate, as their bullying ego hungers for empowerment. This abuse will continue as long as the child allows it, even into adulthood. Therefore, children of these toxic parents are at risk of substance abuse, suicide, and other mental and physical health issues. Likewise, children of abusers are also some of the most intuitive, aware, wise, and emotionally intelligent adults around.

* * *

Upon my realization there was no stopping Marshall, I said, "If I can't stop you, I'm going with you."

"Fine," he said. His determination obviously had the best of him. "I'm going now."

And with that, he briskly walked past me down our winding staircase with his small shoulders squared like a soldier going into battle. On the way, I shared with his sister Sophia what he was doing.

"Oh, no . . . Mom!" she said, as she, too, tried to discourage him. Determined, with his mind made up, Marshall marched on.

Narcissistic parents have an ego fragile as a bomb. They rarely admit wrong even when faced with facts and damning evidence. In fact, being faced with the truth of their wrong will likely set them into a rage. For the sake of appearances, they may offer a disingenuous acceptance of some small, insignificant infraction as if to say, "See, I admit wrong when I *am* wrong." They never stop lying and often resort to what I have since learned professionals refer to as "gaslighting." They guilt trip and twist the truth, forcing the victim to apologize to the abuser for that which the "toxic" is guilty. And that was the exact sick, twisted response Marshall received from his father that day. It brutally undercut Marshall's trust in his own reality and sense of self.

Throughout the couple of hours during which Marshall was made to stand while his dad sat tearing down his young son's worth and value, accusing him of being spoiled, lazy, and unappreciative rather than owning his accused habit of broken promises made to the kids as reward for their work, Sophia stood outside the window, showing her brother support. With their father's back facing her, she stood looking into Marshall's eyes. Seth twisted the truth about himself, projecting his own guilt upon Marshall, accusing him of being selfish, ungrateful, disobedient, and rebellious, topping it off with "You are a loser," demanding Marshall apologize, admitting the guilt of which he himself was guilty. I finally called him off.

Marshall's direct confrontation with truth birthed a quiet raging flame that would not ever be extinguished.

"That's enough!" I said, ending the tirade. Seth's willingness to end it at my request without any backlash against me suggested he knew he had crossed a line.

"Marshall never fully recovered from that episode," Sophia would later say.

She was right. Years later, Marshall revealed he could never get out of his head that his dad called him a *loser*.

"I see a champion in you. Who do you see?" I would often say.

"You say that to all of us," he'd say, repelling my compliment.

"That's true. But I say it for four very different reasons," I'd insist.

Talking truth, love, and affirmation of Marshall's thoughts, feelings, and observations, I tried to steady him emotionally from his own father's blow.

Now once a Charming Impossible dumps their dark accusatory anger on another, they become "light." They become giddy, fun, and enjoyably light-heartedly charismatic. This is what Seth did after dumping rage and other emotional venom upon any one of us.

Following the episode with Marshall, Seth gathered the family for fun at the basketball hoop. Marshall was deeply emotionally wounded. The projection and twisting of half-truths is designed to cause victims to second-guess themselves, creating a lack of trust in their own intuition. It utterly breaks them. And that's exactly what happened to Marshall that day.

While Marshall spun in mental anguish, with no time to process, Seth required him to join the family in a "fun" game of basketball, expecting laughter and fun from all, taunting and teasing anyone who was not "showing" feelings of being "happy." Very similar to a scene in the movie *The Great Santini*, it was as though he was playing out his inspiration from a VHS he brought home for us to watch years prior. "The character in this movie reminds me of me," he admitted, comparing himself to Santini for all of us to hear.

Thinking at the time that it was a lucid moment of self-realization and hope for change, I now deduce it was more a warning. I only wish I had listened. Like all of Santini's family members, we, too, learned how to go along with plastered smiles on our faces because faking it was better than the alternative. If he was in a good mood, we all were supposed to be. If he was mad, he'd be sure to make us mad too.

In *Confessions of a Sociopath*, M. E. Thomas explains how Charming Impossibles don't feel as others do. They learn how to act as though they feel by watching others.[2] We learned how to perform the emotions he wanted to see in us to temporarily appease him. Fortunately, he couldn't see through our smiling performance, although we all clearly did, eyeing one another and encouraging each other along until the charade was over.

Eventually, we'd go into our separate rooms to unravel the chaos: how we truly felt, what we really thought, and what was actually happening . . . and why. But before we had time enough to process it, much less discuss it, Seth would create more drama. It could be anything from the crisis of not purchasing the right toilet paper to using the wrong spoon to stir the contents of a saucepan. "If I want anything done right around here, I have to do it myself!" was his war cry. And just like that, we were off one crisis and on to the next. Having multiple mixed-up episodes of drama and twisted accusations all at the same time was our crazy, mixed-up, insane life behind beautiful doors.

Following Marshall's devastating emotional blow from his father, I began getting calls from the school counselor as Marshall developed behavioral issues we had not previously seen, further exposing the emotional wounds from that fateful day. Those behavioral issues at school were just what Seth needed to hammer down more on the audacity of his son confronting *him*, our great family leader, the priest of our home, he who could only be reproved by God himself.

With Seth's fragile ego now challenged by his own son, our home life grew continually darker. Narcissistic sociopaths go for the jugular when threatened by a *minion* stepping out of line, even when that "minion" is their own child. Seth was losing power over his family. His control and dominion had been (in his mind) brazenly challenged, so he cowardly attacked his youngest son. Marshall cracked open a hornet's nest, bringing on himself full-on vengeance. Seth continued his campaign to reclaim dominion over his family by making an example of Marshall, threatening anyone else from attempting to step out of line as he did. One such punishment for getting in trouble at school was making Marshall sleep with the dogs.

Yes, you read that correctly.

Marshall's realization of the discrepancies in his father came at a huge cost to all of us, especially him. At 12 years of age, my son would have to sleep outside with the dogs, in the cold, for a week. Walking away from him, leaving him alone nightly, crying alone, left a deep scar in both our hearts. We each cried silently, separately, privately . . . and alone. More often than not, the tears never even came. Too accustomed to the belittling for crying (because tears were made fun of), we cried dry tears.

"The dogs are kind, Marshall," I would remind him. "They are beautiful and loving. The only one true monster is the beast living inside: your dad."

Defending my children directly to their dad only brought on more verbal abuse toward *them*. Running to their defense only caused a torrential outpouring of wrath and rage . . . upon *them*.

"You are 'mama's boys,'" Seth would relentlessly tease my sons. "You poor little babies need your mommy to defend you. Waaahhh!" He'd laugh and taunt them like a schoolyard bully.

This cyclical torment that periodically surfaced with growing, compounding vengeance was cause for me to rip myself from my son's side each night, leaving him outside in his sleeping bag with Duchess, our Great Dane. It wasn't so much the act of making Marshall sleep outside as it was the insidious nature of how he was ordered outside, stripping away at Marshall's worth, suggesting he didn't deserve to sleep in the house, digging at his sense of self-worth rather than a poor choice in actions. My efforts to divert abuse or defend the children became risky for all of us. Realizing any effort to protect them would only bring on even more taunting from their dad toward them, I said, "Let me know when you are ready to leave, Marshall. Let's get out of here!"

"I'm seventy-five percent ready," he replied after sleeping several nights outside.

"Let me know when you are one-hundred percent. I'm ready to leave when you are, but I will not leave one of you behind. Just say when you're ready."

* * *

Recent new studies show that ADHD in children is often rooted in axiety and anger.[3] Therefore, when ADHD is suspected or diagnosed in children, many schools and medical professionals are looking into what is causing the anger before prescribing medication or other therapies. Anger is a secondary emotion to a primary emotion (such as hurt) and often presents itself in learning disabilities. Marshall suffered learning challenges and was diagnosed with ADHD. He took medicine for one month, but didn't like the side effects. Marshall was angry, very angry.

Abuse causes a rewiring in the brain. Marshall had all the signs of PTSD. At the time, I didn't know that. It was only later that I learned this from a counselor.

* * *

After this episode with his father and several visits to the school counselor, Marshall emotionally shut down. He closed himself off to everyone as if he had made a pact with himself not to talk . . . at *all* . . . about *anything*. I asked my then 13-year-old to read a book on anger and write about it. Hoping to help him not only understand himself, I hoped it would help him express himself and relieve the ticking time bomb he'd become. Marshall, my child who hated reading and rarely wrote, to my shock, actually read the book and filled an entire lined notebook page with words in pencil. This is what he wrote:

It makes me angry to read this book because I don't want to have to read about anger that makes me more mad, and if I'm angry when I do homework, I won't be able to do it or I will do bad and make a bad grade. I can't read when I'm angry! One of the reasons I have rebellion is because when I was little, anything that happened I kept and 1 little thing that hurts will hurt 3X more now. There are five steps to rebellion and they are being hurt in your heart, bitterness, Anger, stubbornness and rebellion, and all three steps lead to now from the past. I have been angry for a long time and I have wanted to kill myself, but my friends called me and changed my

life and they told me how it would change theyre [sic] life dremat-
icly [sic]and I really didn't want to hurt my best friends. I wanted
them to feel that I care about them and that I loved them. I love all
my friends and if we fight I will always get back with them.

Making friends didn't come easy for Marshall. From kindergarten
through adulthood, even into his professional life, he'd come to me for
advice on how to go about making friends. When he was young, his
anger would get in his way. In his adulthood, he simply didn't know
what was acceptable. Consequently, he suffered tremendous loneliness
all his years of growing up. In his scrapbook, I found a card I colored
with his markers stating, "Be patient, God has special friends for you."

At 20, working with men older than he, he'd discover they'd verbally jab at each other with friendly teasing, bantering back and forth
in "man talk," the way many men do. It's a fraternal male bantering in
friendly jest that he didn't understand.

"C'mon, Marshall," they'd egg him on, inviting him to jab back.
"C'mon, Marshall, give it back to us," they would say, basically inviting
him into relationship, friendship.

"Mom, should I?" he asked me one day. "Should I really jab back at
'em?" he asked. "I don't know what to do."

Marshall had come to me his whole life for advice on friendship.
He didn't know how to joke around with a bunch of guys because the
only teasing in our family was directed from Seth toward one of us
. . . and it was "fun" only to one: Seth. And Seth would not tolerate the
least sarcastic comment, even if it was said in jest. He was heavy on
doling it out, and it always led to hurt. In our home, teasing was yet
another form of abuse. That is why Marshall had no concept of how to
interact with those adult men in friendly back-and-forth banter.

For Marshall to have finally developed a network of friends he
mentioned in his note was huge in his life. He wanted and longed for
friends of his own so badly and was finally developing a support group
all his own at a critical time in his young life.

In March 2010, those same kids mentioned in his note contacted me to have a surprise birthday party for Marshall in our home. This was a first! I had never experienced him having such a beautiful support group of friends, nor did I know these kids or their parents, as Marshall had attended a new school that year. They were nice, what I had always hoped for him. They, along with a couple of their moms, brought a cake, streamers, posters, and food, complete with a plan on how to surprise him. It was precious, meaningful, and very significant in his time of great pain. To peel him away from that was tough to consider.

Not even a month later, on April 1 of that year, we left. Pulling himself from that group of budding friendships was deeply, deeply wounding and a great case for why abusers should be jerked from their homes rather than victims having to flee. An emotional wound from leaving friends was as deep, if not deeper, than those he suffered from leaving his father. Marshall had already shut down from facing his father and, after leaving all his friends and support system in addition, Marshall went mute. For a while, Marshall completely turned off. He couldn't talk. He could barely speak a complete sentence, even to me. His wounds ran so deep.

I later learned this is what Charming Impossibles do. It's part of their crazy, chaotic cycle. It's classic. Evidently, they can transfer their darkness onto someone else in order to lighten themselves. And this is what happened almost every time with Seth, no matter which of us was his chosen emotional dumpster. This specific episode with Marshall, however, became pivotal in our family. Things changed after this. Everyone had become of age and was able to see, recognize, and disagree with what was going on. And we became very concerned for Marshall, our youngest and most vulnerable, developing what a retired abuse counseling expert from The Family Place in Dallas years later called the strongest "trauma bond" she had ever seen in her career.

Sandy was a counselor willing to see us as a family. Because we were all adults, most counselors insisted on seeing us individually. As a family going to counseling together, we learned that trauma bonds form when the victim develops a twisted attachment to the abuser, first accepting blame, then being accused of enjoying it.

Uniquely, our trauma bond as mutual victims linked us together. Sandy explained to us how we were linked by a chain that most likely saved us as well. "All Seth wanted," she said, "was to snatch just one of you into his clutches. Just one was all he needed.

"This should be a case study," she added. "In my thirty-seven years of practice, never have I seen a more insidious, manipulative shredding and stripping every fiber of your foundation out from under you."

She was especially intrigued how he used our faith to sabotage us. Her validation that faith held us hostage rather than set us free (as further confirmation that our trauma bond saved us), helped us during the long journey ahead requiring diligent unraveling so that we could each be free to live our own lives. Unfortunately, I didn't learn about all this until much later.

Not all of Seth's self-loathing was turned upon Marshall. The others had an equal share. We all did. I was continually cleaning up his emotional messes with all four of my children on top of my own. He was tireless in his destructive rampages. He never seemed to rest from the outpouring of abuse. And yet we couldn't see it because he mixed in delightful unexpected surprises like a family meal at a favorite seafood restaurant or a "fun" adventure ride in the evening fog on our horses. His constant pounding at one of us was relentless, but so were his fun family nights watching the National Geographic Channel. Also mixed in were exotic family sailing trips in the Virgin Islands. Our experiences were all over the place. From the outside looking in, one could easily wonder about what on earth we could complain. Of course, we were constantly reminded of that, and our blessings were certainly many. It was confusing.

And yet, the kids' achievements, including straight As or scoring a highest personal best in basketball, were not only *not* celebrated, they were met with scorn, as he raised the bar even higher.

"Straight As?" he'd say. "Really, I'd be impressed if you graduate a semester early. In fact, if you do, then. . . ." This is where he'd insert one of his infamous broken promises, something they really wanted. Unfortunately, they also knew it was a promise he never intended to fulfill. Rather than praise, he would set an even higher goal for them to achieve, an impossibly higher standard levied by "his highness," with yet another false promise of a gift they had already learned would never be fulfilled. The impossibility of his new requirement would be his safe "out," excusing yet another broken promise. Their achievements were almost always greeted with ridicule, with them falling just below his lofty standard. And as he'd move the goalpost once again, the cycle would continue: He'd dangle elusive false hope for his approval . . . approval that was always just beyond their reach. This is how he'd crush their moment of celebration or expected joy. Why? Because the ego of a Charming Impossible cannot allow anyone to outperform them, not even their own children.

As if his disappointment in their achievement wasn't enough, we'd then be forced to listen to him as he served us his self-righteous self-admiration, bragging of unmatched prowess in high school sports or however he chose to show himself up against his own child's less-than-approved performance. Yes, he competed with his own children, making sure that in comparing each of their accomplishments to his own, he was the winningest, savviest, and smartest when he was their age. This is classic narcissistic, sociopathic behavior. Equally classic is how Charming Impossibles sabotage holidays and special events with chaos, angry outbursts, or some other kind of drama--anything to ruin a special occasion.

Charming Impossibles have a standard for themselves that is completely unique to the standard they set for everyone else. They provoke their Target to retaliate to their abuse so they can turn and accuse them of the very act of abuse the victim just suffered at their hand.

"Come on, hit me back," Seth would say to me after assaulting me. Just once was all he needed. He wanted to exploit my retaliation to others as if he were on the defense. He wanted to be able to say that *I* hit *him*. But I never, ever did, knowing exactly what he was doing in trying to provoke me.

Sadly, he was more successful at this with the kids. When the kids were in elementary school, he'd tickle them. It always started out with laughter. Once they asked him to stop, he'd tell them, "You like it, you were just laughing, after all," as he amped it up. When they demanded he stop, he accused them of being disrespectful. This led to them crying and yelling, "Stop!" resulting in him yelling back, "Don't yell at your father! That's disrespectful! Now I'll keep tickling till you wet your pants," he would threaten, laughing at them.

When they were finally mad enough, they used force, hitting him, which was his objective from the beginning. Then he could justify hitting them back. The kids would be screaming and crying. "You started it!" he'd then accuse his young children as if he himself was a five-year-old. "I was just trying to have a little fun," he'd say, shuffling off disappointed as though he were the victim, leaving his kids feeling guilty as though *they* had done something wrong.

Tickling is also a tool abusers use to get their hands all over the children. It gets children used to being touched in usually untouched places. It can have insidious purposes where Charming Impossibles are involved. Tickling can be a terribly confusing, twisted form of abuse.

Anyone who believes it costs nothing to be nice has not been in a relationship with this type of character. Likewise, recommending better communication or telling them what hurts only enables abusers to hit where it hurts most effectively. This breed of toxics live in an emotional muddy cesspool. They long to bring their victims in to get muddy with them. With Charming Impossibles, *healthy* disagreements are nonexistent. Normal standards for healthy relationships only hold Targets hostage even more deeply.

Many grown children ask why their mothers or fathers, whichever was the case, were like doormats, being run over by the other "overbearing" parent. When Audrey was in high school, she wondered this as well, accusatorily stating, "You never stand up for yourself," expressing warranted disrespect toward me, asking, "Why do you willingly put up with *that*?"

As she was certainly aware of her father's unwarranted, degrading attacks toward me, I responded, "Well, okay, now that you see it, I will show you why I haven't stood up to him in front of you."

I immediately began standing up to him, countering his attacks in front of the children rather than behind closed doors so they could see how ugly it would truly get. Carefully choosing wise words and a proper tone, standing for right and correct treatment without provoking him even further, I stood up to him intentionally, respectfully using self-control for them to "see." The stormy backlash began almost immediately, resulting in Marshall and Audrey growing more vocal in their resistance toward this fresh revelation of their father. Winston and Sophia, suffering deeper wounds from previous encounters with him, quietly stood on the outskirts, dodging emotional shrapnel. Before long, Audrey called a truce.

"Please stop," she said. "It just makes things worse for all of us." She not only understood but also grew to respect my passive choices.

* * *

Abusers make sure that most people around them do not see anything but their charm. I've heard "experts" say that one would see the signs of an abuser, that there are patterns and evidence and "tells."

To them, I say, "Tell that to the wife and daughter of the BTK killer who, for most of their lives, had no idea . . . or tell the overcrowded courtroom of Ted Bundy's family and friends advocating for him, vouching for his character. They saw no signs of these brutal killers' atrocities to the degree they were willing to stand up in their defense, vouching for their character." They reserve their dark side for only but a few, which is why the masses struggle to believe the "wild" stories of abuse that later emerge from the victim(s).

Even within families, one child can experience a completely different upbringing from another. By participating in casting disbelief or belief, you may be an active Enabler Unaware to someone Hopelessly Stuck. I hope to encourage anyone aware of such situations to voice your opinions carefully because words and attitudes of others do matter in these situations. In these situations, onlooker's empathy is their greatest commodity because giving empathy towards one is to judge the other. Targets interpret judgment of others as shame, blame, and cause for remaining hopelessly stuck.

Too many counselors and "experts" have no real knowledge of how neighborhood narcissists and sociopaths operate because narcissism and the tactics narcissists use are often not taught in psychology courses. Just because they have a license, a PhD, or a certain title does not mean a counselor has a clue about these people. Do not assume counseling or legal professionals have working, experiential knowledge of these characters. If you are dealing with a Charming Impossible, choose counselors and seek advice wisely. Experience with an abuser can be radically unique from one person to the next, depending on how and why the web is spun.

An extreme case is the BTK killer. According to his daughter and wife, he, evidently, was a wonderful father and husband, yet he brutally tortured and killed over 20 plus women. Many around this man never saw any evidence that he had such darkness in him. It's perplexing. We see these people on *20/20* and *Dateline* regularly. People can carry out the most evil of acts and yet be surrounded by crowds of supporters vouching for them.

* * *

When the abuser is a parent, that is a child's normal. They don't know what is normal and what is not. When the toxic parent seems so committed to—and respected in—the church, this adds to the confusion. Church people don't see the abusive behavior in action, so why would they think otherwise?

As my children aged, Seth started dropping the F-bomb, a word that had not been allowed or acceptable in our home. Directing it at the kids and me, he regularly began cussing, to which we never did reciprocate as we were well trained that he had a different set of rules than the rest of us.

Not long before Audrey graduated high school, Seth was yelling at her about something, dropping the F-bomb throughout his rampage, when she finally had had enough. Retaliating by dishing right back at him what he so liberally doled out, she bit his bait. She cussed back at him, firing his choice words right back in his face as he had done to her. Audrey was immediately slapped so hard, she fell to the floor of her bedroom.

Masterfully, Charming Impossibles tell on themselves *only* when they know the story will or may get out. They strategically choose whom they tell, to whom they want present, when they tell, and how they will spin the story. Most importantly, when a Charming Impossible knows something about them is going to be said, they want to say it first so as to control how it's presented.

These clever orchestrators are the people who lie awake at night devising evil. It had become my practice to always expose Seth's abuse to someone. He knew I would talk about what had just happened to Audrey. Therefore, soon after the incident, Seth told a man, in my presence, about slapping Audrey. This was a man in whom I had previously confided. In self-righteousness, Seth cleverly recounted the incident about "his rebellious teen-aged daughter," prefacing his account with "the societal problem with teenaged girls these days," getting the man to agree with him, discussing how he would not tolerate blatant, foul, cussing-in-your-face disrespect from a teenaged girl with *that* attitude. Once his targeted audience was shaking his head in full agreement, Seth then offered how he was even willing to "slap his own daughter for her own good."

With that subtle twist of the story, I watched the countenance of that man's face change, dismissing any outrage due to how my "disrespectful teenager" was falsely accused of behaving. While Audrey was the victim, her disrespectful, immature father behaving like a foul-mouthed bully confused yet another Enabler Unaware, winning them over without them even knowing it. My presence, and the fact that I remained silent, not contradicting the story, confirmed it. Or so it would seem to an outsider.

"Why didn't you say something then?" is the most commonly asked question to victims of ongoing abuse. Only another abuser or one ignorant as to how Charming Impossibles operate with their Target would ask such a question. It is an uneducated and offensive question for one who is Hopelessly Stuck. To have disputed Seth at that moment was a decision layered with possible backlash and danger, most of which would unfold at home behind closed doors. There was also the risk of providing an opportunity for Seth to twist me into the mix, accusing me of what was already being spread: "Susan is encouraging rebellion and disobedience in our home."

Imagine if I had defended Audrey at that time. Seth would have come unleashed with more twisted lie-truths. The list is long with what could have gone wrong. But one thing is for certain: Nothing would have gone well or right had I stood up to him at that moment. That, I know.

This is how Charming Impossibles get away with their abuse, keeping their Targets silenced and Hopelessly Stuck. Just a slight twist in the telling keeps the truth buried. And if I were to go back to that man later to try to explain what had really happened, he would have most probably thought *I* was the manipulator, trying to spin the story while Seth wasn't there to defend himself. I, therefore, remained silent.

* * *

While off at the University of Hawaii, with a massive ocean and time zone separating her from her father, Audrey would take his calls. No longer was I able to shield her as I had when she was growing up. She would get him full dose. Once his wrath would reach the level of his spiritual ranting cadence, she would lay down her phone, walk away to visit with friends, and return sometime later to hear he still had not broken his rhythm. She would set the phone down again, only again to return to hear him still in full force. Eventually, he would tire himself out, and she would offer a couple "hmm-mms" and "okays" before the call finally ended, with him completely oblivious to her ignoring his lengthy monologue that he considered a conversation.

He had become a self-proclaimed priest of one—*himself.* He was a leader without a following. We were treated as though we were lucky to have his incredible leadership. While he tried to keep us a step behind, we began to gain ground on him. Hence, we endured more and more of his self-righteous self-adoration, the litany of his biblical rights to reign over us, enduring, watching, and listening to his red carpet performances of imparting unto us his sage wisdom from the Bible or his favorite devotional . . . with him fooling no one but himself.

* * *

In Scotland, a new bill was passed criminalizing psychological domestic abuse. Special online and face-to-face training is now required for judges and sheriffs. Around the world, all counselors, educators, clergy, and legal counselors should choose such training, as well. In Australia, some communities offer shelters for abusers as an innovative way to counter domestic violence. Rather than uprooting the entire family, the abuser is forced to leave. The world seems to be awakening to this epidemic. We have a long way yet to go, but change is coming. I hope to be a part of expediting that change.

* * *

"Are you ready to leave?" I asked. "Let's go. Let's get out of here," I continually told my children following one of these episodes. I felt my children were getting closer to the inevitable fact that we had to leave. This would've been a much easier decision had their father's dark cycle not been countered by an equally dynamic and charismatic light, fun cycle that always inspired more hope just when we were giving up. But one day the stars aligned, and all four were ready go.

We were actually leaving.

* * *

Turning into my brother's neighborhood brought me out from my deep thoughts. Shortly after two o'clock in the morning, Gaye greeted us at the front door. Leaving our caravan of vehicles parked lining their street, Gaye ushered our tired, weary souls upstairs where she had fresh sheets on the beds and pallets on the floor. As I gratefully climbed in bed, Seth's words rang in my ear: "If you ever leave, I will not financially support you. I'll stop working before I give you any money."

Always working for himself, he didn't have a regular job where his wages could be garnished. Having not worked in 21 years other than as a substitute schoolteacher and too tired to worry about tomorrow's troubles, I collapsed, knowing those worries would await my much needed night's sleep.

4

Chapter Four

Friendship isn't about who you've known the longest.
It's about who came, and never left your side.
—UNKNOWN

A good friend knows all your best stories,
but a best friend has lived them with you.
—*Unknown*

You are not my friend, you are my sister."
—SUSAN E FOSTER

There is a supernatural energy shift that occurs when girlfriends come together. Life alters and makes way for our power when we unite. Together, we problem-solve. When it's for one of our own, we move mountains. That's what began to happen the first morning of my new life.

With the morning dew and sunrise returned the looming fear. With my head still on the pillow, lying in bed upstairs in my brother's home, looking up at the ceiling, wondering how to face the first day of our new life, I was bombarded with a list of issues needing immediate attention. I was contemplating, *What do I tackle first?*

Suddenly, the doorbell rings and I hear my sister-in-law greet a familiar voice. Walking down the stairs, I saw a great big bright-eyed smile on Gina's beautiful face. My best friend since the age of 12, Gina, was standing at the foot of the stairs holding three steaming to-go cups of coffee, smiling. "I thought you might like a fresh Starbucks," she said, adding, "Welcome home!"

Home . . . I *was* home, in my hometown where I had family and hometown friends. I had not felt home since I married. The *me* they knew had become someone in my past life. It felt good, soothing, to be with people who knew the *me* I lost. They knew me before all this trauma began. And there stood my lifelong best friend.

We were two of a group of soul mate friendships, some of which went back to third grade and beyond. We went through the adolescent stage, the disco dancing, and what was supposed to be *fun* "Teen Dance Nights." Gina could move to the groove of the *Saturday Night Fever* soundtrack. I, on the other hand, was ridiculously stiff and awkward, turning down any invite to the dance floor, watching her blissfully twist and twirl from the sidelines.

Determined that would never happen again, Gina stood me before her mirror with the *Saturday Night Fever* record playing, teaching me all her great moves in the privacy of her bedroom. The next Teen Night Dance, I was out on that floor. If she had a finger pointed up in the air with a hip swung out, I did too; if she twirled, I twirled, and we laughed hysterically at each other as I finally learned to make it out on the dance floor on my own.

Fast forwarding past all our weddings and into motherhood came the crises that rocked all our worlds. Gina's 10-year-old daughter, Tara, contracted an amoeba-borne illness while swimming in a lake.

Nothing prepares a parent for the loss of a child, nor friends on how to console one so brokenhearted. Our friend group rallied around

Gina, consoling her, sharing her grief and tears, totally unsure of what to say. How does one console the yearning heart of mother for her child? Gina had always been our leader. She organized our first pep squad, served in almost every student leader position, and excelled in academics and sports. Now she would lead us in dealing with a mother's greatest loss.

Not sure how I could be a support for her, during a momentary break of our deep, communal rushing flow of sobs, I risked asking a seemingly inappropriate question: "What are you going to wear to the service?" Four wide-eyed sets of eyes looked at me shocked and appalled, as if to say in disgust, "*Susan*? Seriously, you're asking this *now*?"

"Well," I said, having started it, "what look shall we go for?" running with the question I always asked her for any and every event. Bringing our *normalcy* to this traumatic moment would either feel good or really bad. Knowing this was going to be the most crowded funeral service I'd ever attend, I waited for her to respond. Shaking her head, cracking her first smile, Gina breaks the gasping in of air with her reply: "Susan, you know me so well."

Temporarily tossing the mascara-laden tissues to the trash, we all pile in a car to take Gina shopping. *Sometimes, the answer is a new pair of shoes* has long been my personal mantra, and I continue to stand by it today. Bombarding a local boutique, we five usher our friend cloaked in the balm of "grief shock" that numbs the coming flood of unbearable pain to find that perfectly put-together outfit.

Tara's funeral left us forever altered. It was our first loss of that magnitude. The loss of a child is a loss all its own. It was deep. It was dark. It didn't leave. Not for a long, long time.

In grief counseling, Gina later learned that when life's path takes you on a sudden drop into a dark, deep abyss, not all your friends meet you down there. Oftentimes, the ones you least expect are there to greet you, softening the blow, while others stay at the top looking down, just waiting for you to come back up. Sometimes, you are never able to make it back to them.

A crisis comes in many layers. It either attracts or repels the people you love. The pain is multilayered, as well, because every kind of loss involves more than just one person. Even within our group, some of us picked up where others dropped off.

It happens.

* * *

January 2, 2010, almost three months before my children and I packed up to leave, my other very best friend since the third grade rushed us back into the next of our greatest crises. Nell was the friend that would say, "We're going to do *what*?" when presented with one of my wild, exciting adventurous ideas to which all my other friends, possessing too much common sense, would boldly refuse. Nell, however, was the one upon whom I could always rely. She faithfully joined me on many escapades, exploring many outlandish ideas, including an exciting high school senior trip to go on a road trip without a plan.

"Let's just take off and see where our adventure leads!" was my bright idea for two young teens, never giving the question of safety a single thought. Fortunately, an Ordinary Angel swept in, diverting a few episodes of what could have turned terribly dark.

Eight years after Tara's passing, and three months before my crisis was in full bloom, our second daughter of the group went to heaven at the precious young age of 15. What started as aches and pains in her wrists and ankles turned into fainting spells, visits to multiple children's hospitals, and more and more blood work, with no conclusive answers. This was Alex, Nell's otherwise healthy, vibrant, sassy little high-school teenaged soccer player, the baby of four beautiful girls.

There Alex lay in the same ICU as Tara once had. Visiting Alex was Gina's first time to return since the passing of Tara. And going down the familiar corridor brought forth daunting, challenging, ever-raw stuffed memories. As she forged ahead to support Nell, our friend who was no stranger to life trauma, I worried about both of them pulling out of this one. Nell survived losing her mother at the age of eight; being shunned by her cantankerous, crusty, harsh father; divorcing from a tumultuous marriage with four little girls; and now add *this*?

Her list of traumas, at the time, included all that we had collectively been through and more. With Hollywood beauty and Diana-like grace, she faced her life from the outside-in, looking like a beauty queen on the outside while fighting vicious depression within. Losing Alex would take her depression to new heights.

Our hope rested in her wonderful, amazing second husband, David, whom she and we all love and appreciate. It would be a heavy load for him, but we would be there to support him as he carried the mother lode. It would take her family, all of us, shock therapy, psychotherapy, medication changes, drinking with her, overlooking her drinking alone, girls trips, and, of course, *shopping* to see her through. Nothing was too much for us. We took turns with each other through the ugly. Infidelity, financial crises, and more couldn't break the bond of all our friendships; in fact, it made us stronger.

Crowded around Alex's graveside, huddling and hugging beneath a cold, overcast Texas January gray sky, another storm cloud loomed, threatening to erupt. Lost in grief with and for Nell, Gina whispered to me, "Susan, I don't know what to say," allowing a different set of tears to flow freely down her cheeks. "I'm scared for you to return to him," expressing herself more boldly in response to the massive hematoma covering my shin beneath my pant leg.

Knowing my husband recently kicked me, she begged, "Please stay here," as they all turned toward me in unison.

"I drank the juice," I responded. "I let all this happen. It's all on me. I have been so stupidly blind, believing all his fundamentalist lies, and I must fully own this predicament I'm in.

"Please don't bother Nell with this," I asked of them all. "Please take good care of her, because I can't. I'll figure something out for me,"

I said, assuring them. "I am going back for my kids. I'll figure a way out."

Walking away from my trusted group of friends shrouded in grief, tears, and fear for two of their own, I could see Nell in the distance, hovering over her daughter's white casket, offering a final hug to a cold box. From the grassy, crowded hillside of mourners in black, I drove myself back to what would be my closest encounter with hell.

Not even three full months later, I awaken in my brother's home to find Gina greeting me at the foot of the stairs.

* * *

How is it that so many memories flash through our minds in seconds? Carefully taking a cup of steaming coffee from Gina, I held and hugged my dear, precious friend. This was my *girlfriend* who I was bonded to like a sister. Gina, Gaye, and I made our way around Gaye's kitchen table, sipping coffee, energetically discussing my game plan. It's powerful what happens when women are given the task of attacking a crisis. A few women, coffee, pen, and paper, and things begin to turn around. Actually, *they* discussed, wrote lists for themselves and for me, as *I* sat watching in a fog. Oh, the power of *two* women, *two* friends, and *two* sisters coming together for another.

Following the echo of a discussion in which I witnessed rather than participated, from my trance I hear Gaye declare, "Perfect!" writing the final to-do on her list, raising her pen to Gina like a glass of champagne.

"Susan, you go to the local public school and let's meet back here tomorrow," they said. "We'll run our errands and make our designated calls. We've got this!" they reassured me and each other with a nod and a raised eye.

My attention remained focused on the kids. "Please do not answer your phones," I directed my children, "not until we have a plan. If your dad calls or texts you, do not answer. Forward all his messages to me."

There were two months of school left. Jerking one eighth grader and two high-school kids out of school with only two and a half months of the school year left was problematic. They needed to get into school.

After meeting with counselors from several local public schools, I was told that my children would have to wait and finish their semester the next school year, as students were preparing for finals. Essentially, I was told by one counselor that my children would have to repeat the whole year because the courses they need to complete would not be available until the second half of next year. This came as a devastating blow. These kids had had enough setbacks in life; surely, there was another answer.

The next day, Gaye, Gina, and I reconvened at Gaye's kitchen table.

"My pastor has offered free tuition for all three kids to finish out the school year in their small private church school," Gaye gleefully announced. "And The Tara Sawyer Foundation will buy your children's uniforms!" Gina exclaimed. Gina's family foundation, The Tara Sawyer Foundation, was formed after the tragic loss of her 10-year-old daughter, Tara. Gina and her family turned their tragedy into an opportunity to help others.

Life has a way of circling around. Now her tragedy was helping me through mine. It was a humbling, perfect plan. My kids would be attending the same school with their tenth-grade cousin, Cole. They were very excited about going to school with Cole. I could hardly believe this was happening. We were *doing* this.

From stress, I was losing my memory. I couldn't remember anything I had just said, was having trouble thinking clearly, and kept repeating myself. All the needs were so great and so much. I coped from one moment to the next, thankful for family and friends helping me make decisions, keeping us moving forward.

With the kids settled in school, we focused on finding a home. Fear loomed over all my activities, knotting and tangling my intestines in anticipation of what would happen when Seth realized we had left. *We left. Oh my God, we left. I can't undo this now. We are in this for the long haul. We gotta make a go of this.* I couldn't begin to wonder *how* I would be able to do this.

Hoping not to unload the truck twice, I wanted to look for an apartment right away. Gaye drove me around. We looked at so many places my eyes were crossing, and nothing seemed quite right. Mainly, I had no idea how I would pay for this, so what was I *thinking*? I had been a stay-at-home mom for 20 plus years. I needed a job, but we also needed a *place*. We sure couldn't stay with my brother forever. Still, in faith, I looked.

Just as Gaye and I were headed home, discouraged and tired from not having found any good options, Gina called Gaye. "John found Susan the perfect place!" I hear over Gaye's car speaker. John, Gina's husband, was looking at properties between their home and Arthur and Gaye's home so that I'd be nestled safely between them. Gina recited the address to Gaye, and Gaye drove us straight there. It was a lovely three-bedroom duplex with a tiny fenced-in side backyard, perfect for our dogs.

Never having lived on my own, I couldn't imagine how I was going to do this. I went from my father's care directly into marriage, something I discouraged all my children from doing.

"Prove to yourself you can make it on your own," I'd encourage them, hoping they'd never face the self-doubt with which I was struggling. Doubt though I did, I forged forward. I *had* to. It simply had to work out.

Feeding off the confidence of Gaye and Gina that the duplex was the right choice, wide-eyed, I agreed. Arthur made financial arrangements for me with our dad. My dad was willing to help any way he could even though he had long since been retired and had limited resources barely enough for himself.

After school, we helped unload the U-Haul at our new home. Friends of friends came to help. Perfect strangers were offering all sorts of services and personal items, surrounding us with positive energy, feeding us hope. Gina's Bible study group lined up deliveries that included casseroles, paper towels, toilet paper, and other necessities. A fog of surrealism embraced us as we kept moving forward relying on friends and strangers.

"I want to talk to Jeff," I told Gina one morning. "I am going to call him."

My friendship with Jeff went back to the first year I moved to Texas the summer before the third grade. He lived down the street and around the corner from me. Jeff became part of the motorcycle gang with whom my brother and our neighbor Sandy rode. Jeff was always nice to me in those rare times I convinced my brother to take me tagging along with them. Jeff and I remained friends over the years. I *needed* Jeff.

"You know, Susan," Gina said, "I think it would be best if he hears about this from Seth."

Though Jeff was a childhood friend of mine, he was also a family friend of Seth's through his brother. Gina knew Jeff from high school. She also knew how very special Jeff's friendship was to me, so I heeded her suggestion. After all, I had not talked to Jeff in many months. I decided she was probably right and let it go.

Early next morning, I was awakened by the ring of my phone.

"Wut are ya doin', Chic?" Unmistakably, it was Jeff's regular post "Mr. Orange County" salutation. It had been years since he was a professional bodybuilder, but he retained that beach-dude lingo for moments like this.

"Jeff! I was hoping to hear from you."

"Hey, man, I called lookin' for ya yesterday when Seth answered the phone. He said you left. Where are you? What's goin' on, man?" he asked.

"You called looking for me yesterday?" I inquired, seeking more.

"Yah, man, I ran into an ole buddy of ours while shopping for cuff links on the internet. Turns out, I bought 'em from ole Thompson. Remember him?"

The coincidental series of events that led to him reconnecting with an old mutual friend made him think of me, so he called. Out of the blue. That's how he'd occasionally call over the years just to catch up.

"You okay?" he asked, "What d'ya need?"

After filling Jeff in on what was happening, he said, "I'm here for ya, man. Let me know how I can help."

This sort of thing started happening more frequently. Another family friend from whom I had not heard in months called. People wanted to help. Little surprises were being left on my doorstep. Refrigerators, beds, and washers and dryers were offered, delivered, and installed. Friends were telling me to just go shopping and pick out whatever I needed and bill them for the expense. My three closest childhood friends combined resources for a cash gift. It was humbling being the recipient of so much.

Taking it all in, I watched it happen through tears, fear, and awe. I was so needy. People were so beautifully giving. We were making it. The kids were going to school and making new friends. But while we were making it, I knew Seth wouldn't stay away indefinitely. The thought of his sudden, unexpected appearance continually haunted us, causing anxiety for us all.

Upon his return to our vacated house, Seth threw himself into writing us accusatory, vengeful, non-stop text messages and emails. He'd leave numerous voicemails, spewing anger and resentment. Not knowing what to say, we remained silent.

Another friend called. "Hey, I just found a note on my desk that reads, *Susan left Seth and Seth called looking for her.* You are the only Seth and Susan I know. Is this you?"

It was Isiah Robertson calling. He was a former LA Rams retired football legend and very close friend of my mother. My mother worked at Isiah's drug rehab center, House of Isaiah, for over 15 years. She always said her happiest days, second to the years when my brother and I were young and hanging around her ankles, were the days mothering "the boys," as she referred to the men at House of Isaiah.

Isiah and "the boys," as she called them, were all she talked about. She deeply, deeply loved them.

"Yes, it's me," I confirmed.

"What are you doing now?" he inquired following my brief update.

"I don't know, Isiah," I answered. "I, I . . . have no idea."

"How can I help you, Susan?"

After offering a list of services to help me, he said, "How about you come assist me with a Super Bowl event?" Isiah was the president of the Dallas chapter of retired professional football players. "Come get involved with our retired professional players organization. It'll be good for you. I'll call you later with details," he said. "You will meet some great people that may lead to an opportunity for you, and we could use your help."

His call led to my regular involvement with the players for the next couple of years, and I developed some wonderful friendships. His call also gave me renewed hope and a sense of direction. It was as though my mother was orchestrating from up above.

5

Chapter Five

Mother's love is peace. It need not be acquired, it need not be deserved. Motherhood is the greatest thing and the hardest thing. Sometimes the strength of motherhood is greater than natural laws.
—UNKNOWN

A mother's love for her child is like nothing else in the world. It knows no law, no pity. It dares all things and crushes down remorselessly all that stands in its path.
—AGATHA CHRISTIE

You ask how I am so strong. It's because of my mother's powerful love.
—SUSAN E FOSTER

Isolation caused by Charming Impossibles comes in many forms. First, they require extreme loyalty. By causing emotional "wedges" between the victim(s) and their support system, usually their families, these relationship wreckers begin to break down the Targets' otherwise stabilizing and affirming forces by not being able to get along with them. In order to mold their Target, those who affirm and unconditionally accept the Target must be removed in order for the toxic to acquire their intended complete domination. The impossibility for the toxic to get along with the Targets "difficult" family is usually their first line of business. This causes the Target to have to choose between their two loves. In a crafted sort of tug of war, the toxic interprets for the Target how the family is at fault, demanding loyalty and commitment to their new union as a couple. This is what happened to me with my mother, first, eventually spreading to my entire family and most of my friends.

Seeking peace at home, the Target almost instantly gives into the demands of the toxic, leading the Target and their entire loving family into the harrowing decent of confusing accusations and chaotic division. This eventually leads to the intended isolation of the Target, oftentimes utterly destroying the once beautiful, peaceful, loving family. With amazing finesse, one toxic can come out of this scramble unscathed, leaving an entire innocent victimized family bloodied and accused of outrageous nonsensical guilt.

Abusers groom their victim for deeper control by strategically getting sideways with the victim's mom, dad, brother, sister, or best friend, whoever might stand in the way of the victim falling under deeper control and manipulation. In order to successfully create the "new and improved" version of their Target, they must chip away at the "old" person, essentially destroying the person their loved ones once knew. By creating strife and disagreements with the support system, they groom loved ones to stay away and victims to emotionally pull away. Charming Impossibles coerce their victims to mold themselves into the "better version" of themselves, someone who, in actuality, becomes even more willing to accept greater abuse and control.

My family was my greatest support system, which made them my husband's greatest threat and first line of attack. I had to carefully navigate my husband and his father's war against my family, primarily my mother and father, so as to protect my children. They were innocent, naïve, and beautifully trusting. They could never imagine their dad ever intentionally lying as he habitually did, especially about my parents. Lowering myself in a battle of bashing each other's family would have only led the children into watching a confusing, nasty battle neither of us would win. I trusted truth would prevail, hoping that by my walking in integrity and honesty, my husband and his father would be exposed for their lack of those characteristics.

Believe it or not, this actually *worked*. But it came long after many relationships were severely damaged at a brutally high cost.

My strongest bond was with my mother, my best friend, my confidante. As youngsters, my brother and I spent many of our preschool days entertaining the elderly while our mom led sing-alongs at a nearby nursing home. There, she regularly volunteered, cutting and styling hair, offering the ladies permanents. Other days, we accompanied our mother as she took her elderly friends bowling at the local bowling alley. With a cane in one hand and a bowling ball in the other, they'd shuffle up to the spot, roll their ball, and laugh in delight. She was a fun-loving most beloved Bluebird leader, a comforter to the hurting, encourager extraordinaire, and the neighborhood kids' driver, transporting motorcycles and bikes to competitive events, packing everyone and all she could in our blue Dodge station wagon. She was a fun-loving, toilet-paper wrapping kind of mom that my friends came to visit . . . whether I was home or not. She was effervescent, full of unconditional love, and she welcomed every kind of person into our home.

My mother and I also spent hours, days, and many lunches shopping the malls. She and my grandmother taught me about finer fashions. When I'd fall in love with a dress out of our price range, she sewed one for me. My mother lovingly made me beautiful dresses with exquisite attention to detail, matching plaids and using only the finest fabrics. We had great fun together.

Everyone loved my mother. Her favorite sidekick was Gina's mother, Frances. What are the odds that mothers of two best friends become *besties*, too? My mother would later buy a lake house beside Frances's, and she helped Frances open the best little gift shop in that town. How I grieve the loss of my children sharing what should have been joyful years with two of the sweetest, most loving grandparents, my mom and dad.

Underneath my mother's joy and love loomed a battle with depression. She kept it well hidden from me until my older years. In my high school years, I began to see it more and recognized the toll it took on my father. My father's rock solid optimism and dependability created a strong sense of security at home. My father taught kindness, lived out patience, and always preached, "Think positive, Susan!"

While my foundation was strength and security in the home, my father's lack of emotional availability caused me some doubt about his undying love and devotion for me during my early years, the opposite of which he would later prove abundantly true. Until that realization, I sometimes misunderstood his emotional stoicism. That created unnecessary doubt in my perception of his understanding and approval of me. This left me lacking confidence, particularly where boys and men were concerned. I never was quite sure what to expect in the way of love from a man. That vulnerability I would later share in a rare moment with my toxic—and it would repeatedly be used against my father and me throughout my married years.

Both my parents willingly shared pain from their past, a pain I did not understand, because my parents gave Arthur and me abundantly above and beyond what they felt their upbringing may have lacked. Therefore, we only knew support, love, and provision. I always knew I was loved, but I didn't feel my dad really *knew* me, creating a dilemma of if you don't *know* me, can you really *love* me? My parents provided financial security, protecting us from worry or fear. Bad things didn't seem to happen . . . to *us*, anyway, feeding a naïve, childish delusion within myself that bad things, therefore, couldn't or wouldn't happen to me. They never did in my young life, so why would they later was my logic. This also fell in line with my "think positive" influence. It seemed to work. I became quite the believer!

Our grandparents were active, vibrant, positive forces in our young lives, taking us to museums, teaching us sewing and woodworking, and instilling a high standard of kindness in each of us. Never did I see my grandfather pass someone ringing the bell for The Salvation Army or handing out tokens for a charity that he didn't reach in his pocket to give. Our grandparents' playfulness once involved performing a Native American rain dance, bouncing around one another with my mother's feather duster in hand. As a family, we enjoyed laughter and love.

Eventually, my "Think positive, Susan!" dad was broken due to the blindsiding betrayal of a friend involved in a business deal. It was a blow from which he would never fully recover. From that blow he began to show signs of "skipping" in his mind. It was slight but noticeable. He never again had a lilt in his step. He let that beat him. Once I was away at college, he started drinking a little bit at night. His night drinking soon started much earlier in the day, which led to dozing off to sleep earlier. He was a quiet, sweet man even if he was drinking. The example he set taught me that giving up is never, ever an option. Watching his vibrancy deteriorate, I determined I'd rather go down swinging, fighting hard and believing, than giving up.

In retrospect, I now realize my husband and father-in-law together directly attacked my mother vehemently. She bought too many toys from the dollar store for our young children, she shouldn't have offered the kids candy; whatever she did, it was wrong, a bad example, or some other random offense. Their accusations that my father wasn't a good leader and my mother was disobedient along with the drinking and depression were the proof my husband and his father used to convince me that I had a skewed view of what a healthy family was. Their accusations against my parents were endless.

Pushing my mother away in compliance to my husband and his father, thinking I could prove my devotion by *temporarily* alienating her, nearly destroyed her. The more I pushed her away, the more he demanded. Convinced I would eventually win his trust, I kept pushing her away, breaking her heart. Lost in this battle of tug of war between my husband and mother, I determined that I had to choose my husband with the intention of reestablishing my relationship with my mother once things settled down. But things never did settle down. He made sure that every time we got together with my family, an argument between the two of us soon broke out.

"See, we get along fine until we get with your family and friends," he'd say.

It was easier to stay away from friends and family, easier to be with his family, easier to isolate. Keeping the peace, I let all my people go. It took me years to catch on to the fact that he was creating strife on purpose, by design.

Had I known I married the man who would ride over me like a propeller-driven boat, chopping me to shreds, leaving behind a wake of broken, destroyed relationships with family and friends, I would have declined the invitation to meet him, an invitation his father so graciously offered. His father selected me and used me to pressure him. It's all clear, now, why Seth would tell people we were "arranged" and that his "father fell in love with her first." For him, that was true. He didn't choose me. His dad did. Seth, I would later learn, was in a relationship with an older woman he loved. Withholding approval of her, his dad insisted Seth meet me, a girl he met when I modeled for their family- and friend-owned dress line. That business was yet another business and friend relationship that was eventually destroyed in the aftermath of Seth's father's wake of destruction.

In marrying Seth, I overlooked red flags, trusting not in my gut but in his knowledge of Scripture, the history of Bible study leaders in his family, and his having grown up in this biblical discipline that was relatively new to me, I succumbed. Likewise, he succumbed to his father's wishes. We both compromised in marriage.

Eventually, I saw the pain I caused my parents. Admitting my painfully poor choices and the damage I caused to my loving, devoted mother and father, family, and friends whom I abandoned, rejected, and wrongly accused, I hope to help others avoid my mistakes and comfort those who are suffering as family of Targets. I hope to open the eyes of blind victims to never isolate your loved ones for anyone. No marriage covenant should rip you from relationships with those you love and who love you. My parents were kind to Seth and all his family. There is no truth in the terrible things written by Seth about them over the years in multiple mass emails. I'm grateful for this opportunity to share how truly beautiful they actually were. My brother and I feel blessed to have had them as our parents.

If your spouse can't get along with your family, that's *their* problem—not yours—to sort out. Don't go to bat for them. Make them fight their own battles and stand against your family and friends on their own if they feel so compelled. By doing their dirty work, valiantly defending them, as I did, you cycle yourself deeper down into their control and manipulation.

When a loved one marries and suddenly can't seem to get along with their loved ones with whom they otherwise enjoyed a healthy relationship, a Charming Impossible is likely involved. If someone is torn between a spouse and their loving family, study up on how narcissists operate in marriage and relationships, learn their tactics, recognize which ones are being used, and get help . . . privately, at first. Marriage and couples counseling does not work with these characters. They will manipulate and twist and turn their whole mess on you and your family. They do not own wrongdoing and are brilliant at convincingly blaming others.

* * *

How did I allow myself to hurt those whom I love and who loved me? I believed my husband and father-in-law loved me. I believed they had my best interests at heart, and I had a marriage covenant to make good on. On one hand, I wanted to "improve" myself; on the other hand, I wanted to be accepted. It was confusing. Some of the changes I really liked. I liked how much more physically fit I was with him, but I didn't like how he felt entitled to use this improvement to pick apart my physical appearance. I liked his interest and influence in what I wore, but I didn't like that he only complimented me when I wore what he picked out.

Our pattern became one of him establishing the standard, pointing out my need for improvement, and me dutifully working to achieve his approval, sucking me into a natural progression in every area—physically, emotionally, spiritually, philosophically, and politically—until every part of me was somehow fashioned by him. By complimenting the changes in me only in areas in which he could take credit and disliking things about me, the *me* of who *I am*, I became his project as he molded me—my ideas, desires, and likes—in his own image, which paralleled the Christian teaching I learned in college. I was to be a helpmate, a submissive wife, putting my husband first and becoming one, which was new teaching for me. Desiring to have a happy, peaceful family, I succumbed.

Sound crazy? I see it all the time. In fact, I share this because of the number of mothers who come to me wounded, suffering the same pain as my mother. I hope by sharing this mistake, I can enlighten someone who is Hopelessly Stuck not to appease. It doesn't work. With each part of you that you sacrifice, they only want more. And to the hurting mother, father, family member, or friend, please remember: This is not about you. Your being "iced out" has nothing to do with what you did right or wrong. It is that you love and affirm parts of a person the Charming Impossible wants to change, manipulate, and control. Your love and acceptance is a direct threat to their power of destroying the person you know to create the version of them they want. Charming Impossibles manipulate in royalty, powerful ministers' families, political families, the extremely wealthy, the extremely impoverished, and everywhere in between. Never would I have believed that one day I would allow this to happen in my life, to my family. Regretfully, I did, deeply wounding my mother and many others.

In the beginning, friends told me I didn't even sound like *me* anymore. Even during my early married years, I remember Gina speaking on behalf of our friends, telling me that they heard my husband's voice coming out of my mouth.

To which I responded, "I know. This is a *better* me," I would concur.

"If I didn't define myself for myself, then I would be crunched into other people's fantasies for me and eaten alive."[1] This quote from Audre Lorde sums me up rather well. For me, it was "You need to call the horse trainer and tell her this . . ." or "You need to call your political friend and say it just like that; if you don't, I will . . ." But it also was "Tell your mother the way I'm suggesting, she needs to know *you* feel this way. . . ."

And just like that, I was the front man fighting all his wars while he hid, protected, behind me. I ran everyone off and away from me, just as he had planned.

If you know someone pushing or pulling away from those who love them most, they likely don't know they are the Target of a Charming Impossible . . . yet. They *will* make this discovery but most likely not until they are but a remnant of who they truly *are*.

Finally, in utter heartache, my mother told me she felt her daughter had died. Little did she know, that was my goal—to die to myself according to Paul as my husband and father-in-law were instructing. My emotional captors were filling my head with the Scripture that I should *die daily* as per the teachings of apostle Paul. If Seth and I had a disagreement, I was instructed to defer to him, like a good wife. At night, I would wrestle with myself and God, asking, *Why can't I just die? I'm trying!*

While my mother meant her stated observation as a criticism, I took it an encouraging compliment. That's how turned upside down I had become. And that's when my mom attempted to take her own life.

One day, my phone rang. It was my father. "Susan, your mother is in the hospital," he said, his shuddering voice struggling to continue. "I found her on the floor with an emptied bottle of prescription sleeping pills."

Detached from my own emotional state of being, I had to run this by Seth for feedback on how I should respond. I actually sought out his counsel on how *I* should *feel*. After all, by now, I had been thoroughly ridiculed as the cause for rage and marital distress due to my "overreacting" or not properly responding emotionally in any number of situations.

Not only was the restructuring of my whole emotional makeup in process, I was a new mother of a beautiful baby girl with a new baby boy on the way. They would be 13 months apart. At that point, offering emotional stability for my daughter was my first priority. Protecting my unborn was next. So how do I respond to my mother?

"How selfish of her," I heard my father-in-law say.

"Yes, she is thinking of herself," my husband added.

Making the mistake of trusting my husband's family, considered by many as strong, fine people of faith upon whom I could rely and be proud to be part, I tolerated their defamation of my family.

"See, this is just what we've been saying about your mother," was their explanation. *Selfish, is that how I'm to respond? Is my mother being selfish?* I wondered.

"You were unemotional." That's how Gina refers to me that day I dropped off Audrey for her to babysit while I went to visit my mother in the psychiatric ward of the hospital. "You were numb and showed little feeling."

"I know you better than you know yourself," my husband told me on the drive to Gina's house. "This is how you *should* feel," he would coach me.

Numb, I handed my precious baby girl over to Gina to babysit so that, together with my husband, I would see my mother for the first time since hearing of her suicide attempt.

My mother battled depression all my life and most of hers. She was never suicidal, however, until she lost me.

This is part of the sick, twisted risk involving Charming Impossibles. Anyone suffering from isolation abuse should research the subject and learn the tactics used against them. It took me years, but I eventually did awaken to it. I reached out to my parents, admitted what I had done, and apologized profusely, and in no time we were back to how we were. Sadly, many years of relationship were lost, stolen, never to be recovered.

Of course, my husband would use my upbringing and the fact that my mother tried to take her own life against me the rest of my married life with my children, in marriage counseling, and among friends. These perceived weaknesses and my father's drinking were used to undercut my sense of judgment when I referred to having had a stable, good upbringing. He used it to keep my parents from our children, as their instability, he said, set a poor example for our kids.

My father's drinking increased when I married, in large part due to Seth. He and his father sat from on high in judgment, watching my family spiral into painful, destructive loss.

My dad was grossly referred to as a reprobate. He was accused of not being a leader. Seth and his father also attacked my mother because she was rebellious and disobedient, an offense of which they accused most women. Quite frankly, anyone coming near either of them was smeared, belittled, and gossiped about in negative terms. Typical of Charming Impossibles, they'd smile and shake hands with the preacher after church only to get in the car to blast him with ridicule in front of the children all the way home. Charming Impossibles do this. They tear everyone down, but always behind their back, never to their face.

My children experienced this regularly with Seth and his father. We know this to be true, which is why I framed a quote from Eleanor Roosevelt boldly in our living room that says, "Great minds discuss ideas, average minds discuss events, and small minds discuss people."[2]

Again, I was constantly working to offset the influence of these two in my children's impressionable lives.

Continually battling for my children's minds with two Charming Impossibles tag-teaming against me, I was still unware of how close I was to losing my children to their influence. Besides, the lingering knowledge that my father-in-law had previously practiced civil law always kept me careful to not step too far out of line.

My father-in-law, with his big gummy smile, hid his machinations for a long while. For many years I trusted and loved him. He was much better at hiding himself because he did his dirty work through his son, much like the dirty work my husband eventually would do through me. But intuitively wanting to keep positive examples of a healthy home life in front of my children, I tried to create opportunities for them to experience the peace and respect reflected in the home I grew up in. That's why I always encouraged them to spend the night with friends when invited by nice families . . . even when I missed them and would have preferred them being with me. This happened most often with Winston. I would later learn Winston felt I didn't want him around because I encouraged him to spend so many nights away with friends. Truth is, he was my most tenderhearted and I believed his numerous invites to spend the night away were God's way of protecting him from trauma that would possibly have destroyed him. I grieved his absence and missed him terribly but thought it was in his best interest. This was an unspoken misunderstanding between us for years even into Winston's early adult years. Oh, the many layers of confusion and pain.

Fortunately, motherhood began to awaken me from the temporary spell I had been under. My allowing my husband to wash my canvas clean and paint his creation on me was one thing, but to script the lives of my children was unacceptable. To compromise respect and freedom for the individuality of my children, denying them the ability to write their own life and emotional script, was nonnegotiable.

This is when my wonderful upbringing kicked in. My life experience, full of respect toward us as children, trusting us to paint our own canvas where we were treated equally important to the well-being of our family dynamic, emerged. I would fight for my children to be gifted the same trust and respect I was given to live according to their own gifts, talents, likes, and dislikes.

Wanting them to see better examples lived out before them was important. I took on leadership roles at school so they could "see" me being respected. That's why I went on to create a variety of children and youth community programs as fundraisers for the Mid-Texas Symphony. Each program involved arts, manners, and etiquette because my kids were not learning manners and respect at home. Therefore, they would have fun learning respect, manners, and etiquette in the community with their friends . . . and me as their respected leader.

* * *

Early in our marriage, with many friends and acquaintances speaking their concern for me, I considered divorce before motherhood. During our first year of marriage, we were involved with a church where a counselor gave personality tests. Arthur and Gaye took the tests as did another married couple in our church group.

"You should do it," they all exhorted us. "It's amazing how it tells you exactly who you are!"

We decided to take to the test. The counselor, after assessing us, pulled up his chair across from me, looking straight into my eyes.

"Remember what I am about to tell you," he said, not so much as glancing toward Seth seated next to me. "Your husband has the propensity to be a wife beater."

Rolling his chair away as if to say he was finished, the session was over. We walked out with that man never speaking a word to Seth.

"I remember how mad you guys were about that," Arthur recalled. "We couldn't believe it either," he said. "It sounded so harsh."

While I do not blame my upbringing for why I got into this mess, I do credit my parents—their character, integrity, and my upbringing—for why I got out. It came together for me when I became a mother. While leaving Seth was not optional, knowing when and how to leave required outsmarting and out manipulating him.

At first, I felt so guilty about it. It seemed so vindictive and required me to go to a place I never wanted to go. I would tell him, "I resent you for the person I must become to handle you."

Apologizing to my parents and family after I realized what had happened halfway into my marriage is when I learned that in response to being refused the opportunity to lavish our kids with her overflowing love, my mother found an outlet that needed and welcomed her. The men at Isiah Robertson's House of Isaiah Drug and Alcohol Abuse Rehab Center became her second family. She always said, "When life gives you lemons, make lemonade." But her powerful love intended for my children remains one of their greatest losses. Not having my mother in their lives, the way she should have been, is one of my greatest regrets, so difficult to admit and face. It is tragic even still today.

As I came out from under their spell, Seth and his father slowly became the outsiders in my life, growing more threatened by my burgeoning independence. With this, I had to be careful. So, using their own tactics on them, I tossed them some comments indicating my alignment with them in their thoughts about my family, comments I knew they wanted to hear, but I didn't feel. Motherhood and good, fair parenting, for me, was nonnegotiable with regard to their controlling efforts.

"Don't you ever tell me again that my husband is your favorite son," I'd scold him. "And don't ever favor one of my children over another," I'd threaten.

I'd stand up for my children where I would not stand up for myself. I still don't know why.

The final six years of my mother's life were spent attached to an oxygen machine. Her final two years, she was under the Ordinary Angels of hospice care, five minutes away from our home. My father moved down to be near me so I could help. On my way over to visit, I'd play "The Prayer" by Celine Dion and Andrea Bocelli to prepare myself, wiping my eyes, replacing my tears with a smile, passing her threshold bringing joy. Sophia was there almost every day.

Hiding stress and negative energy was oftentimes too debilitating for me, resulting in my driving past her home rather than stopping by for a visit. My visits grew less frequent due to stress I could not hide that would only worry my mother. Only when I could present a joyful front, bringing a happy vibe to her world of oxygen, a Lay-Z-Boy chair, and the Cooking Channel, would I visit. Her fighting for each breath as if through a coffee straw, my guilt, or her worry overrode my choice to visit. Sophia picked up my slack, offering much joy when I couldn't. I went as often as I could.

My last years with my mother were my last years of marriage. Those last years were my most difficult for two drastically different reasons, yet I had to keep smiling for my mother, my children, and my husband, each for unique reasons. Once again, I had to deny myself my rights to emotions . . . of which I had become well accustomed.

My mother released herself for a final breath of this life and was lifted by angel wings to the beautiful heavens on Mother's Day 2009. My dad, Sophia, and I were with her. She opened her Mother's Day gifts, read all her cards, oohed and ahhed over all the love we shared, soaking it all in, and then lay her head down, closing her eyes for a couple hours before taking her final breath.

As I was seated at the cemetery with a small crowd gathered around me, Isiah Robertson rolled up in his white limousine, interrupting my mother's outdoor funeral service. Numerous men scrambled out of his car, the heart and soul of the House of Isaiah. Each walked over to stand beside my mother's casket, which was draped with a gorgeous rose spray in her favorite beloved "sunshine" yellow. Folding their hats in hands or fumbling with their hands in their pockets, shifting from side to side, each shared through tears and from the heart what my mother meant to them. These men knew my mother better than my own children knew her. Then, it dawned on me: Had she been given the proper privilege to grandparent my children, she wouldn't have gone to House of Isaiah. "When life gives you lemons," my mother always said, "make lemon *aide*." Taking something bitter, she made it sweet.

Everyone came to my home following the service. One man wouldn't come in. Through our large windows, I could see him strolling out in the hot sun in our backyard. He was a thin, elderly man who had come with Isiah.

"Excuse me," I said, leaving our guests to speak with him. "Why don't you please come in for a plate of food?" We had a beautiful spread of food that so many friends had brought by.

"Oh, no, ma'am, but thank you," he said, removing his hat at my presence, keeping his head bowed.

"Please come in," I insisted. "It's too warm out here."

"Oh no, ma'am, I can't go in *that* house," he said.

"What is your name?" I asked.

"Johnnie, ma'am," he said. "I sure loved your mother. Miss Nancy was something special," he said, shaking his head in sorrow.

"Johnnie! You're Johnnie!" I exclaimed. "My mother talked of you all the time. She told me how you regularly called her, prayed for, and encouraged her," I added, beginning to weep.

"Johnnie, she loved you. She hung on your words of encouragement and shared them with me. Please come in, sir."

Sensing his reluctance, I added, "Please come sit with us and dine with us. I can't go back in knowing you're out here, and I'm hot, so please, let's go inside," I implored him, smiling at him and giving him a hug.

Johnnie came in, made himself a full plate of food, and joined us where my mother's two families were meeting, some for the first time, to which I know my mother smiled down from above. I could only imagine the abuse he had endured from others due to nothing more than the color of his skin. We humans are sadly capable of abusing one another in so many forms.

Mentally returning from this journey of memories, I considered what Isiah was offering. Before I could continue moving myself forward with opportunities involving the NFL retired players association that Isiah was presenting me, I had to go back . . . to file for a divorce. The gripping fear of facing Seth again brought me to my knees.

6

Chapter Six

Sometimes we need someone to simply be there
. . . not to fix anything or do anything in particular,
but to just let us feel we are supported and cared about.
—Eyeore, from *Winnie the Pooh*

Maybe I'm not the only one.
—Susan E Foster

"Now, I'm not condoning divorce, you understand . . ." is the common disclaimer that pastors, clergymen, and Christian counselors give when advising but not wanting to be accountable for the advice they give. This was the same predictable intro my former Christian counselor used while adding, "But . . . if you *are* getting a divorce, who *is* your attorney?"

As I named an attorney I found in the phone book, he responded, "No!" adamantly advising, "If you are divorcing *Seth*," as if sticking a stake in the ground, "you *need* Carter Casteel," he admonished vehemently.

"Carter!" Why didn't I think of her?

"Yes!" I agreed. "I *do* need Carter."

Carter was the most powerful attorney in town. A former state representative, she had a stellar reputation that preceded her in every local courtroom but also in Dallas. Her granddaughters went through my cotillion program with Audrey and Winston. One of her granddaughters and Audrey were debutantes together. We shared a personal connection. *How did I not think of her?*

That short conversation, that powerful piece of advice, is in large part how my children and I successfully survived separating ourselves from the far-reaching, evil tentacles of a very masterful Charming Impossible. Hiring Carter was the cornerstone to my new life moving forward.

Carter Casteel and her son and law partner Barron were powerhouse game changers because Carter and Barron, as it turns out, are not only the best, they also understand Charming Impossibles. Simply due to their working knowledge of how Charming Impossibles operate, they actually knew my husband of 21 years better than I knew him myself after only having briefly met him. Their knowledge of who my husband truly is set me on a new track to recovery.

In *Above the Chatter, Our Words Matter,* author Bruce Pulver writes a profound epigraph to preface his book: "Intensely focus on the rules of the game. You are then able to decide how you will play it."[1]

Working with Carter and Barron is how the light bulb in my head began to turn on, because they knew his rules, they knew his game, and with that knowledge, they knew their strategy. This is why civil attorneys need training in these clever orchestrators of chaos and abuse.

Now, about that dance around divorce Christians perform: It is devastating, holding many Targets hostage. Anyone who knew I *needed* Carter Casteel should not only have encouraged divorce but should also have warned me of dangers in *not* leaving. This dance throughout faiths, touting covenant and marriage over abuse, entices many Charming Impossibles to join churches to become pastors and youth leaders. Abusers love the teachings of submission and covenant promises. They love the denominations that teach women and children to submit to the lordship of the men in their homes. Not only do judges, police, and legal counsel need intense teaching on how abusers operate, churches and educators need this teaching even more. In some churches, toxics have free reign with our children who are being taught to trust the leadership. Church children are taught plenty on being "innocent as doves." But they need even more teaching on being "wise as serpents."

From my experience, church leadership teaches more from a wives and children submitting perspective, neglecting the "submit one to another" verses. Many wives of pastors are, therefore, Hopelessly Stuck. I know this through a counselor who once shared that his largest demographic was wives of pastors.

"They have nowhere to turn," he said, stating what I personally realized was the obvious. Victims who are also members of churches are sometimes more Hopelessly Stuck than those outside of the church for these and various other reasons. Acknowledgment that abuse exists among their own, a challenge many church leaders and members are often not willing to consider, would be a good start. Churches have an even longer way to go than legal and protective services. I hope to effect educational change that respects their doctrine but better protects their people.

* * *

The moment I filed for divorce with Carter Casteel, I knew I was in safe hands and that she respectfully understood my situation. I still feel a debt of gratitude to her and Barron.

"I'm going with you," Gina announced when she reached me by phone. "You are not going to face Seth alone. Besides, it's not safe for you to drive in your state of mind. I'm driving," she said insistently.

"Gina, it's a four hour drive, and who knows how long court will last," I said. "It'll be a full day, possibly two."

"Fine, I'll pick you up tomorrow morning," she said. "Seven o'clock sharp. Text me what you'd like from Starbucks," she quickly added before saying goodbye.

With fresh hot coffee made to order, Gina drove me the four hour drive to face Seth for the first time since we left. With every mile south, my anxiety grew. By the time I got there, I literally hid. Fear is weird. Just being in town, I felt visible to him.

In the courthouse, I would have to see him face-to-face. The language in the divorce papers grotesquely stated that I was suing my husband. Just the sound of that was offensive and made me feel even grungier about myself.

Walking into the courtroom, taking in a very deep breath and letting it slowly flow outward with my head hung low, unable to even stand up straight under the weight of shame, I followed close behind my attorney through the courtroom double doors.

But the downward spiral of self-degradation and shame abruptly stopped when I took my seat in the courtroom. I astonishingly discovered two rows of community support, people dressed in business suits and dresses, quietly seated there to support me. Without any forewarning, they sat waiting for my entry. Some were from the symphony board on which I had served, others were from church and my kids' school. *Why would they want to be here for me,* I wondered, *when I am nothing but a failure?* I had failed at marriage, but even worse, I had failed as a mother and daughter. I felt completely unworthy to have such support. That they wanted to take time in their day to be there with me, this stupid, idiotic failure of a human being? It didn't compute.

Unforgiveness poses a potentially worse dungeon that traps and shackles its victims. I emotionally chose to hand Seth over to himself. He is his own problem. He must deal with himself and sort through his own issues. He can believe whatever he wants to believe as long as it's far from me and his children if that's their request. I just wanted out and free from him.

Me, however . . . I struggled to forgive *myself*. I could not forgive my naiveté, my stupidity, and my utter lack of judgment that had led to great pain for my children. I could not believe these people wanted to support me when I was such a big failure as a mother. Their support confused me because I felt so unworthy. Insecurity and self-defamation spoke louder to my soul than did their actions or any other kind word or gesture from anyone. Perhaps they had been reading Seth's email blasts. I'm not sure how they all knew. Comforted by their presence, nevertheless, sitting close to them, leaning into them, struggling with conflicting feelings of great comfort, utter thankfulness, and sheer fear, scared, absolutely terrified of facing Seth and a judge, I took my seat.

One of my supporters was a local elected official. She leaned forward to inform me that she could not stay, that she was late for a meeting, but that she wanted the judge to see her sitting there in support of me.

Before she left, she softly spoke from behind me, so only I could hear: "My sister was found dead, holding her Bible, seated next to her husband who was found holding a gun. They were both found dead, together, in the front seat of their running car in their garage."

Patting my shoulder, she gave me a nod of confidence and departed the courtroom through the side door.

I could hear the voice of my mother from heaven say, as she often did, "You need to pray for compassion, Susan." But this time, she was asking me to extend it to myself. I needed to accept the compassion from these dear people and to stop beating myself up if I was to ever become who my children needed me to be.

Maybe I'm not the only one, I began to ponder.

The judge called Seth to the stand three times. There was no sign of him. With the hustling and bustling of other clients with their attorneys who were working about the room, approaching the bench, going off to the side for private conversations, then going back to their seats, we waited.

Is he a no-show or simply characteristically late? I wondered.

As he reached for his gavel to adjourn, the judge stopped himself midstream, sighting my attorney rushing to the bench with her hand held high as if to yell "Stop!" as she informed the judge of Seth's late arrival.

"He's here, he's here," she pled.

Representing himself, Seth calculatingly stepped into the court-room, slowly, methodically, perfectly groomed with his shoulders squared toward us, alone, with not another soul in support of him. With apparent perfect composure and confidence, he slowly loafed down the aisle, passing me as he made his way toward the judges' stand.

"Sit up straight," Gina prompted me. "With each of his steps closer, your shoulders fall. Don't cower in his presence, Susan."

"I didn't know I was cowering," I whispered, fighting my light-head-ed impulse to faint on the floor as he walked by.

"Your whole posture changes when he's around."

She then modeled a perfectly strong, straight, determined posture, a confident expression on her face, facing forward beside me, not giv-ing him so much as a glance.

How am I so weak and unaware of myself? I said to myself as I shim-mied up beside Gina in the courtroom pew. *What happened to the confident, self-assured me? She seemed to have died a long time ago.*

With much self-discovery yet to unveil, I leaned into my posse who made a beautiful show of support. Watching my attorney and Seth talk to the judge, I wondered, Will I have to go up there?

Fighting the urge to vomit or fall asleep, my anguish ushered in even deeper panic to my already rapidly beating heart. It was as though I had just contracted the flu. I felt sick . . . terribly, deathly *sick.*

Nervous and rattled, I couldn't properly put two sentences togeth-er, much less defend myself. Feeling a failure and that my children deserved so much better, with the certain expectation any wise judge could easily see me as unfit, confronting Seth in that courtroom seemed a losing battle.

Any judge would see my weakness as compared to his seeming strength, I assured myself. *Look at him. He acts so together and composed while I foolishly struggle not to cower.* I thought to myself, *Get a grip!*

But I couldn't get a grip. A grip wouldn't make itself available.

From the pew we watched them talk among themselves, then the two turned from the judge and walked directly to me.

If only I could pass out and awaken when it's all over, I wished.

Relief by confirmation that I would not have to approach the judge's bench was overridden with sinking anxiety by directives for me to join my attorney and Seth privately.

Oh my God! We have to sit . . . together . . . just the three of us!

As I thanked my friends for being there, I realized that leaving Gina and the others was letting go of my strength source. Vulnerable, I winced as Seth engaged me in a weird, cringing side hug. The two of us were ushered into a small confined conference room with my attorney. Awkwardly, shadowing my attorney as if she were a great pecan tree trunk in our pecan grove, hiding behind her, I allowed her to seat me between her and Seth at a round table in a tight-fitting conference room.

Feeling the oxygen leave the room, I could barely breathe.

Giving us strict instructions not to talk to each other, pulling out her cell phone, my attorney made a quick call. Once she was engaged in conversation, Seth questioned me.

"Why don't we work this out ourselves? We can work this out. You just need to talk to *me.*"

Kicking me under the table, my attorney disrupted my attempt to respond while looking sternly at me with eyes that silently yell, *"Shut up!"*

Reducing ourselves from a mature married couple of 21 years to the likes of two kindergarteners who haven't figured out how to get along on the playground, we sat at our assigned seats awaiting the principal to get off her phone call. Torn on whom I was to obey, I felt even more pathetic. Had I lost all sense of self? My nerves were on edge and I was anxious to get in Gina's car to drive far away from there.

After explanations and instructions on next steps falling on my deaf ears, finally, it was over. Gina took me back to my new home four hours' drive north, plenty far away from there, where some anxiety could melt away.

I had successfully filed for divorce. It was complete. My exhausted nerves, still wired and jangling, continued to cause a sour stomach. But at least I was heading to my new home.

According to the laws in the state of Texas, I had to wait three months before my divorce could be final. My attorney assured me that it would take a lot longer than that because of our situation. We had two big properties to sell in one of the worst real estate markets in recent memory, Seth was behind on our taxes, and our financial situation turned out to be much worse than I was aware. My attorney said that not only were we in an extreme financial mess but that Seth didn't want the divorce and would fight it. She tried to prepare me for a long drawn-out three-year divorce.

What they didn't know is that *I* was emerging from the rubble within and could *not* wait.

7

Chapter Seven

*With the light of your soul, you can illuminate
the darkness of this world.*
—WE ARE HUMAN ANGELS, THE BOOK

A little over three months after I filed for divorce, my newly married neighbors, who had been through several divorces each, were trying to get me to go out with them to meet their friends. While I was somewhat acquainted with my neighbors Mona and Mike several doors down, socializing was not an interest. First of all, I wasn't officially divorced and was still, therefore, wearing my wedding ring. And, secondly, I wasn't ready to meet *anyone*. That idea did not interest me at all. I was trying to get out from under a man, not find one, and I wasn't open to making new friends. I didn't think my children needed to even concern themselves with that thought. They had enough adjusting to do. So, I kept telling them no.

And they kept inviting me . . .

I started saying *maybe*.

And then when the time came, I'd say no.

They kept asking . . . telling me that I needed to get out. That it would be good for me.

Finally, they said, "Okay, you can come over to our house for steak and wine, then. Surely, you can do that."

Steak and wine sounded therapeutic as compared to my canned soup and peanut butter and jelly diet. With that fine offer, I accepted. It had been a long time since steak and wine. Boy, they sure knew how to coerce me.

That evening arrived and I really didn't want to go. I had just gone to watch my nephew play football, and Gaye invited me to go with my brother and her to a get-together with some friends of theirs I knew. Tempted to cancel on my neighbor as I much preferred to go with my brother and his family, I almost did. But the guilt of having turned down these neighbors numerous times previously was cause for me to stick with the original plan.

Arriving at their house thinking it was just their family and mine, I was shocked that, without any warming, they had invited a man there for me to meet. Our kids were becoming more familiar with one another, so they had been invited, as well. There we were, all together . . . and then there was this *man*.

Masking my severe disappointment, not wanting to be rude to him, I was very upset. But I ran with it. Two of my kids were there! I didn't know what to do. It just seemed all wrong. My stress level was already unbearable, but unwilling to get into any confrontation, I decided to just roll with it, learn from it, and *never* let it happen again.

While the kids gathered in the home's small living area around the TV, we ate at a beautifully dressed table in their manicured backyard wrought with lovely flowers and a soothing water fountain. It was a break from the constant feeling of barely surviving. These people were actually *living*. Cutting into my steak and sipping a nice cabernet felt good.

After dinner, they suggested we watch a movie. I said that would be fine.

We all lived in these tiny duplexes with one living room. The kids were already watching a movie in the living room. The only other TV was in the master bedroom. Before I knew it, they herded us into the bedroom, threw the pillows off the bed, pulled down the covers, and had the movie going. All four of us were lined against the wall on the bed, fully clothed. And, as if all that wasn't enough, this perfect stranger had his arm around me.

I sat there like a teenaged kid, thinking, *"What am I doing? And how do I get myself out of this?"* when my 16-year-old, Sophia, came through the bedroom door. Mortified, I leapt off that bed, announced, "I am going home," and grabbed Sophia to march her home with me.

All the way home, I apologized to my daughter: "I am so sorry, Sophia! I feel so foolish and can't imagine walking in seeing my mother like that."

Oh, I was so upset with myself, once again.

But this man, Hanz, had hooked me because during dinner, he told me that he could get me divorced on Tuesday. A contempt of court date was scheduled for Tuesday because Seth had not paid child support. He told me not to go down there for that but instead demand a divorce.

Hanz was a successful businessman who had good business sense. He ran his own office design business and had been dragged through a three-year divorce himself. He was simply willing to teach me what he personally, had learned from his own mistakes.

"You have to tell the attorney what you want and what to do," he exhorted me.

Miracle of miracles . . . our beautiful French home had a contract on it from a buyer even though it had gone into foreclosure. All this in 2010, one of the worst real estate markets of all time. Seth was planning on paying the delinquent child support from the money left over from the sale. I knew this because the thoughtful ladies at the title company invited me to their office and sat me down, carefully making me aware of their concern for me as Seth also was trying to finagle every bit of the money from the sale for himself. He was planning to leave me nothing.

Hanz and the couple down the street invited me to a chamber mixer the next evening. Now, those were the people I *did* need to meet. I did need to network with business people in the hope of finding a job. But, most of all, I was intrigued by this man, Hanz, in his confidence in being able to get me divorced. I wanted my divorce and was eager to meet with him again to further discuss it. I decided to go as long as I would drive with the couple and come home with the couple.

Hanz met me at the mixer, grabbed my hand, and quickly whisked me away to a five-star seafood restaurant. Enjoying my favorite meal, sea bass with a glass of Chardonnay, in an elegant environment felt like furlough from war. I did enjoy the evening very much but was still uncomfortable with my whole new life. It just was weird! And I was officially still married, wearing my ring.

Hanz asked me to tell him more about my situation. I filled him in on every detail that had to do with what would need to be dealt with in the divorce. I gave him every bit of my financial situation that I was aware of. He was still convinced he could get me divorced on Tuesday.

We met the next day, which was a Sunday, in the lobby of a hotel centrally located between our respective homes. I showed up in athletic shorts, tennis shoes, and an oversized hooded jacket with my hair in a ponytail. For over four hours, we sat in a little small public living room area writing my divorce on my laptop. He brought a copy of his divorce and, from that, we rewrote it, filling in the blanks with my information.

It was exhausting, and I couldn't believe he was willing to do this for me. Struggling from stress, I wasn't thinking clearly. Mere survival came with such a high degree of stress that to do something like this totally wiped me out emotionally and mentally. He had to do the thinking, simplify the questions, and just let me keep out of his way. He did all the work. He even typed as I writhed on the couch in emotional fear and anguish.

"Why are you doing this for me?" I asked, questioning his motivation.

"I was in a similar situation with my ex-wife," he patiently explained. "By lessons learned through trial and error, I am glad to help others." And with genuine concern, he continued, "Based on my experience, here's how your husband might try to manipulate you and the system."

He went on to explain how his wife sabotaged and manipulated the process, costing him much unnecessary expense, dragging out the divorce over an unnecessary three plus years.

"I've been through something very similar to what you've been through, Susan," he shared. "I have my own story of chaos and craziness in our home. She had a PhD in psychology and was a high school counselor. That's who she was in public, anyway," he went on to say. "At home, she orchestrated an environment of crazy, chaotic mayhem."

"This happened to *you*, a successful businessman?" I asked, astonished, wanting to hear more. "I never dreamed something like this could happen to someone like *you*."

"We will have to discuss me later," he said. "For now, we must focus on getting you divorced Tuesday."

With my divorce professionally written, stored on my computer, and ready to be emailed, Hanz sent me off. I would be calling Carter first thing in the morning.

8

Chapter Eight

Keep your face to the sunshine and you can never see the shadow.
—HELEN KELLER

"Susan! That's impossible!" In strong Texas-twangy language, Governor Ann Richards-style, I heard Carter blare back at me in no uncertain terms, listing all the reasons why my plan to divorce on Tuesday wouldn't work.

"Besides," she added, "I was planning to postpone the court date anyway, because I'm going out of town for knee surgery."

Carter is a no-nonsense attorney who previously served as a state representative and had a Texas-sized reputation for carrying a big stick. I figured if anyone could pull this off, she could. Not backing down an inch, I explained to her every reason why it *would* work, why it *had* to work, and why it had to be done on Tuesday.

"Seth is in this position where he has no options but to sign this divorce that he doesn't want!" I said, submitting what I believed was a convincing case.

"Well, you will have to have Barron represent you then, because I will be out of town," she countered.

Barron! I thought *He's perfect for this job!*

Barron is a towering six-foot-seven no-nonsense *man.* Carter was perfection. But Barron just might get further with my misogynistic husband. Carter had the reputation of a tough commander who could part the courtroom Red Sea, but she wasn't a man. Don't get me wrong: Both of my attorneys were excellent. It seemed necessary and wise bringing in big Barron to face off the high-and-mighty Seth.

Sarcastically laughing upon hearing me declare, "I'm coming Tuesday to get my divorce," Barron responded, "That's impossible!" He listed all the reasons my plan wouldn't work.

"I'm coming to get my divorce Tuesday," I declared, with my heels dug in deep.

Realizing I wasn't backing down, he finally conceded, "I'll look over the information you sent and will see you Tuesday," as though it would be a waste of his time and my money.

Gina drove separately from me but insisted on going with me to visit Barron. We stayed with a friend who lived out in the country. I was still so scared of Seth and didn't want to randomly run into him out in our little town.

Together, Gina and I walked into Barron's office. I greeted the secretary and said, "Good morning! I'm here to get my divorce today."

She chuckled and said, "In my sixteen years working here, I haven't seen any divorce happen that quickly, especially one as complicated as yours."

I assured her that I was getting divorced today, anyway. Shrugging, she quietly left me to myself with a "whatever . . . good luck" kind of *yeah, right* response as she turned her focus back to a stack of papers on her desk.

Gina and I were shown to Barron's office. When he came in, he looked at Gina and explained why legally she should not be in there with me. Not understanding anything he said, Gina replied, "Oh, I have known Susan since we were twelve. There is nothing you'll discuss that I don't already know, I can assure you. We know everything about each other," she added, nodding with the "southern reassuring nod" in her presentation, sitting properly upright, holding her purse close in her lap.

"That's right," I assured him. "She can stay."

He looked at our affirming smiles as if we were Lucy and Ethel. Scratching his head, looking askance, and finally shaking his head, he said, "Never mind," grumbling under his breath.

And . . . Gina stayed.

But he went into another room. Blood rushed from my head when he poked his head back into the office announcing, "I called Seth asking him to come to my office," leaving as abruptly as he came in. These attorneys say as little as possible, but that was a mouthful!

Gina panicked momentarily, only to regain immediate composure, saying with a nod of confidence, "Good, this is what we came for."

Seth had written some pretty ugly things about Barron's mother to me in an email. I was sure to forward those scathing comments to Barron in the hope it would further motivate him. I hoped it would help him see with whom we were dealing.

"He's here," I heard through the closed door as the receptionist whisked by.

Barron soon came back from his first meeting with Seth. He was breathing heavily, and putting his hands behind his head, leaning way back in his chair, he just looked at me for what seemed like several minutes. Gina and I sat still and quiet like statues, waiting and wondering. Barron then broke the long dramatic silence: "I can't imagine the hell you've been living these past twenty-one years," he said. "My God, you can't even boil water!" Then he added, "He speaks of you and your children as though he were training a dog," he said, glancing toward his brown Lab lying on his plaid padded bed. The dog's eyes and ears lifted as if to ask, "Are you referring to me?"

As we turned back to Barron, he said, "Susan, Seth doesn't believe that you really want a divorce. He doesn't believe you are capable of this. That means I will essentially have to be a jerk to him. So I want to be sure you understand this and that you are okay with it," he said, seeking my nod of confirmation.

"I'm fine with anything as long as I get to stay here in your office, away from him," I assured him.

"I will do my best to get you divorced today," he said, whisking his way out the door. We were elated.

The back and forth began. Barron would come in red-faced and mad, slam his hand on a file, grab it, and leave. He'd abruptly return to explain something or ask a question, only to dash away, leaving us for long periods of time in utter suspense. This went on from nine in the morning until noon.

At noon, he returned to inform me that I needed to meet Seth for lunch! In unison, we both looked at him like he was crazy and asked, "What?!"

Absolutely not! I was *not* going to do this!

He then called Carter, saying, "I'm telling Susan she needs to join Seth for lunch," adding an explicative as he explained, "Susan says she doesn't find this agreeable." He put the phone to my ear so I could hear Carter tell me, "Susan, you are going!"

Petrified, I followed my attorneys to the letter from that moment forward. The key to our success was that Barron and Carter understood what I was dealing with in Seth far better than I did. They were experts who knew and understood the man I was divorcing. It was as if they were introducing me for the first time to the man he truly is. I was meeting him with open eyes for the first time while they seemed to have known him for years. *How did I, who had lived with him 20 years, have no idea who he was, yet they, who just met him, seemed to have full knowledge?*

Barron told us where we were to go, for how long, and when to be back. Gina had to leave. Not feeling comfortable with my meeting

Seth alone, Gina thought of a couple friends she met the last time she was there with me for court. Asking for my phone, she called them. Cher answered her call while out in her horse pasture on her riding mower.

"I'll be right there!" Cher said. Immediately leaving her mower out in the field, she made a quick change of clothes and was on her way.

Gina then called Sharon. Gina drove me to Sharon's office, where I was handed over so that Gina could get back on the road home.

Gina, Cher, and Sharon would see me through getting my divorce completed. They all met each other as a result of my divorce and were in this together with me.

* * *

The smell of grilled steak, salmon, and fresh-baked bread greeted us before we even entered the restaurant. This was a small-town popular restaurant where we were sure to run into familiar friends. Nervous, we had to refrain from holding onto one another.

Sharon had already engaged in conversation with another friend when I heard from over the crowd, "Hi, Susan! Good to see you, Hey, I saw your husband over there at the bar."

Wide-eyed, Cher and I stood frozen, in full alert mode. Cutting her conversation short, Sharon joined us as we were shown to our table.

Behind our forced smiles and small-talk, we were finally seated, waiting for Seth to appear. Sharon sat next to me and Cher was diagonally across. We left Seth a space directly across the table from me on the aisle side.

Downing a glass of wine like a shot of whiskey, taking in a deep breath, I marveled at how these two friends would risk themselves for me. Familiar friends were all around us, each completely oblivious to the invisible drama entangling us. Clearly, we looked normal, business as usual. With each of us seated and outwardly composed, our trauma and drama came off unnoticed by the public . . . just as it always had.

Sharon and Cher ordered. I couldn't eat. Seth had eaten in the bar before we got there.

"I see Susan brought bodyguards," Seth observed snidely as he seated himself across from me. *Very telling comment,* I thought. We entered into a little small talk and then Seth began with what was most heavy on his mind.

"I want to maintain rights to disciplining our children," he abruptly demanded. He went into why he felt I was not equipped for that task and rambled on why they needed his discipline and how I was weak and incapable. I just listened, as this, of course, was rote for me. It was nothing new and was mild as compared to his usual tirades. As was my custom, I listened.

Unaccustomed to such rhetoric and treatment, Sharon and Cher grew more and more incensed. Their tweaking posture, wincing eyes, and facial movements indicated they would not stay quiet much longer.

Hunkered down in my quiet submissive posture, I was there to verbally agree, watching the clock for my moment of escape. For me, this was discussion as usual. For them, it was disgusting, and they fought back on my behalf on behalf of our kids.

The conversation was getting heated. They didn't like what he was saying about me or how he wanted to handle disciplining the kids. Furthermore, they were especially upset that of all subjects and issues to discuss, discipline was his only evident concern. Holding back no more, absolutely angered, they erupted, confronting him relentlessly in sync, defending their points and supporting each other's.

Before we left for the restaurant, Barron had laid down the ground rules: "No fighting or arguing. Tears are good. See you back here at two o'clock." So I started to try and calm the girls down. We managed to finish quickly, kept our visit short, and were back at Barron's office on schedule.

"How'd it go?" he asked as he welcomed Cher and me back to his office. After relaying the events, I was bewildered at Barron's delight as he said, "I could not have scripted lunch better."

Turns out that my defending Seth to the girls was even better than what Barron had hoped. Still blinded in the darkness of my cloaked reality, I trusted he knew what he was talking about, but it still remained a blur to me. As Barron navigated Seth swiftly, I could see he knew something I didn't. He knew who Seth truly was. *But . . . how?*

After lunch, Sharon returned to work. Cher insisted on staying with me the rest of the afternoon. Barron moved us to his conference room.

With stress overwhelming me, I took a nap on the Persian rug under the conference table, telling Cher that I would be fine and she was free to go. Completely wiped out and exhausted, the stress was wearing me down. But Cher insisted on staying to the bitter end. I was so glad and relieved she did.

On into the evening, Seth kept texting me, trying to come into the conference room when Barron wasn't there. He wanted to work things out with me, without Barron. I refused by simply ignoring him.

At 7:00 p.m., Carter called to check on everything. Barron looked a haggard mess; with his hair repeatedly wrung by frustrated fingers, it twisted in unnatural wacky directions. He had removed his tie and rolled up his sleeves. He was utterly worn out! From the call, he could hear Carter's voice on the phone. "Susan," she scolded, "you need to close up shop and go home. We will have to finish this another day!"

"This office regularly closes at five o'clock," Barron informed me. "I haven't even called home to tell my wife," he lamented.

Grabbing the phone from me, Barron growled, "Carter! I'm not going home until I'm finished!" slamming the phone down, hanging up on her in mid-sentence. He then apologized to his staff, asking them to stay just a little longer. They, too, were exhausted but agreed to stay.

"Drinks on me tomorrow, ladies," he said to his staff in appreciation.

"All right!" one cheered, as they each let us know what they would like to drink the next night.

"Let me get those!" I offered.

Pulling out a pen and pad of paper, Cher took down the list of requests, making note of what everyone liked. Cher offered to take my payment, create a gift basket with their favorite drinks and snacks, and assured me she would gladly deliver it to them for me so that I could get out of town as soon as possible.

It was now after 8:00 p.m., and Barron felt like they were nearly done.

"What are we doing about custody?" I asked. That was all that really mattered to me. "You're splitting custody," he ordered.

"What? No way, Barron! I can't do that!" I retorted in panic.

"Listen to me, you get passports and you can take your children anywhere, anytime. You have medical guardianship, you basically have custody, but he can get them every other week."

"Every other week is not agreeable!" I argued.

"Susan, your kids reside four hours away, they are in school, they will have activities, and he'll have to drive four hours to get them and four hours to bring them back," he said, listing the challenges. "And look, here," he added, pointing to a line in my divorce decree, "He must show up on Friday at five p.m. No earlier and no later, period," he reassured me. "He can't do it. He'll never be on time."

Barron was precisely correct.

"How do you know him so well?" I asked, dumbfounded at his knowledge of this absolute truth. He was right about him, but how did he know this after spending only a day with him?

"Do you know what a sociopath or narcissist is?" Barron asked.

I told him no.

"Susan, you need to familiarize yourself with those terms. Go home and start studying," he continued, "because that's what you are dealing with."

Seth never *did* come for the kids at the designated time. He danced all around his designated date and time, never even coming close. I, however, became a student of narcissists, sociopaths, psychopaths, and personality disorders; I interviewed children, ex-spouses, and anyone willing to share their traumatic experiences in dealing with one. After familiarizing myself with these people, learning they are a "type" with certain habits and idiosyncrasies, performing similar manners of abuse on a spectrum, I came up with the term Charming Impossibles. It fits. It suits this type of person.

Once I armed myself with knowledge on how these people think and react, I better understood how Barron knew Seth upon meeting him. Once one understands how they operate, the strategy for how to respond becomes much clearer, as they are somewhat predictable. We do have to stretch our minds to make a space for the reality of their existence, however. Kinfolk do not naturally have a capability to understand or comprehend this 5 percent of our population. Like I said before, Kinfolk encompass jerks; idiots; and unlikeable, mean-spirited people. These people may be *bold in your face* jerks. Some of these people may even sometimes behave like a Charming Impossible. That doesn't make them one. It takes concerted effort and study to know the difference. The primary difference in Charming Impossibles is the calculated manipulation of others to achieve certain outcomes while hiding behind the phony façade of kindness they present.

It was late and we were all exhausted. Upon coming up with our final arrangement on which we could all agree, while explaining it to me, Barron finally stopped himself and said, "Susan, don't make me explain this. Just trust me on this, okay?" as he ran his hands through his hair, rolling back his neck.

I *did* trust him. Too exhausted to listen anyway, relieved that all parties had finally agreed, I found Barron's plan to be brilliant, good, and fair. We were done. Just a little after 8:17 p.m., we had a divorce document complete with Seth's special request paragraph stating that he did not want the divorce and did not agree with it.

We were done! I had my divorce!

Cher walked me out into the dark parking lot when Seth unexpectedly emerged from the shadows.

"You cut your hair," he remarked, letting me know of his presence behind us.

Walking even more briskly to Cher's car, eyes remaining straight ahead, I ignored him. He only picked up the pace behind me, adding, "You know I don't like short hair."

"Yes, I know," I said, eyes still on Cher's passenger car door. Just before slamming the door shut, I added, "That's why I cut it."

Just when I thought it was all over, Barron called me on my cell phone asking that I return in the morning for court to get the judge's signature.

"I don't have a change of clothes." I argued.

"I don't care what you wear. Wear that same thing, but be here first thing in the morning," he said.

Wednesday morning, walking a slight pace behind the long-legged Barron, we marched, my two paces to his one, down the city sidewalk into the courthouse corridor. As we opened the double doors to the courtroom, we were met with dark silence. Much to our shock, the courtroom was like a ghost town. The lights were out and everyone had left before we arrived.

"Evidently, court recessed early," said Barron. Adding a few choice words, Barron ordered me to sit as he disappeared through the crowd and around the corner. Returning to a suddenly overcrowded corridor, I could hear Barron's baritone voice echo over the crowd, "Susan! Come follow me!" waving me toward him.

The crowded hallway parted, making room. I nervously scrambled to gather my belongings, making my way to Barron, aware of the feeling that someone who was supposed to be for me actually was. Barron believed in me and was sacrificing to help my children and me. In Barron, I found a dragon slayer working on my behalf. It was humbling and I was truly grateful.

Barron's large framed presence alone was commanding, which translated into protection, for me. Not only having a powerful attorney but having one who truly understood the mind of my husband allowed me to exhale and relax a moment.

When legally fighting a Charming Impossible, choosing an attorney who understands the nature of the beast is paramount. No matter how good they are, how great their reputation, they need to know the mind of their opponent. The court system is like dealing in a foreign land, using a foreign language and a foreign protocol to procure proper procedure and relationships unknown in regular daily life. Our court system is powerful and scary.

Taking three steps to his one long stride, I worked to keep up as I followed Barron.

"I will read lists of questions," Barron instructed. "You are to say yes to each."

"Okay," I concurred, breathing heavily, almost running to keep up.

In a back office, a judge sat behind his desk, waiting. He gestured us to sit in cordovan leather seats, facing him. Before Barron's questioning, the judge read out loud parts of the divorce that involved the custody of our children.

Pausing, the judge suddenly stopped. He looked over his glasses as if to examine me, giving himself time to question what he was about to sign. He was methodical and in no rush.

Barron commented as necessary as the judge read through my divorce.

Barron then read a list of questions to me.

"Yes," I replied robotically to each.

The judge then read aloud the full name of my husband, following along with his finger below Seth's signature.

"He sounds very distinguished," he said, looking up at me. "This must have been really bad," he added, searching Barron's and my eyes for any second-guessing.

Looking back and forth at us, his eyes finally focused back on my divorce document that lay before him on his desk. Slowly, he picked up his pen and signed my divorce. The gavel struck, and it was official as I heard the judge say, "I now pronounce you divorced." I was truly overjoyed much to the surprise of the judge. He looked at me over his glasses and leaned toward me, saying, "This is when you cry."

"Oh no, sir," I said. "I'm very grateful to you, sir. You have just set me free."

With his brow furrowed, he looked at me as if in disbelief. My soulful response of relief evidently was unusual to him.

Driving home alone, quietly, I felt my first taste of peace. Then Seth called, barking out his rhetoric. By pushing the "end" button on my phone and hanging up on him, I enjoyed the most basic glorious freedom of all—controlling my own airwaves. After leaving him, I eventually developed courage enough to reject my habit of fear and replace it with the ability to complete my own thought. This was the simple yet powerful beginning of my psychological liberation from the spiritual and emotional stronghold my husband once wielded over me.

Realizing that I didn't have to listen to his long lectures or sermonettes anymore, that his ideology would no longer interrupt my train of thought, I could think . . . without interruption. I could pick up where I left off . . . listen to myself . . . and gain understanding to discover and rebuild me. It was a simple freedom I hadn't known my whole married life.

I could choose not to read his emails, too. Having been treated like a possession whose purpose was to convert all my wants, desires, and likes to his, a reintroduction to me was required. But uppermost in my mind was to understand how I allowed myself to get here in the first place. *What the hell happened?*

That afternoon, Cher delivered a beautifully wrapped package of beverages and snacks to my attorney's office.

* * *

Finally home, I immediately visited my father to let him know it was final.

"You're officially divorced?" my dad asked.

"Yes," I said, smiling.

My dad then wept like a baby. He absolutely broke down and sobbed, overcome with emotion. While he was greatly relieved, he was also so worried for me.

"It's a tough world out there, Susan."

Retrieving his white handkerchief from his pocket, wiping his eyes, he cried, dabbing his nose. In his pocket, my dad had always carried his handkerchief embellished with the initial of our family name. A gentlemanly habit of his from a bygone era I held dear.

"I don't know how you are going to make it," he said through guttural groaning, releasing his deep inner anguish. My dad knew, too well, that he reared me to be cared for by a man as he had. At 48 years of age, I was starting all over on my own, for the first time in my life, with four teens counting on me to make it. I didn't know either. I just knew that I must. So, somehow, I *would*.

9

Chapter Nine

The important thing is not to stop questioning.
Curiosity has its reason for existing.
—ALBERT EINSTEIN

Weak men do not like strong women.
They don't know what to do with them.
—UNKNOWN

Know thyself.
—SOCRATES

For me, the marriage covenant was a very serious spiritual promise to my husband, between me and my maker. Therefore, marriage, sex, and family were spiritual quests that I believed were important to our creator but were foundational to how I lived out my faith. In essence, faith, marriage, family, and God were one entity; to me, they were all intertwined. So when I failed at providing a good marriage and family life for my children, I not only failed them, I failed God. I failed at living out my faith, and I failed spiritually, leaving me nowhere to go for validation or worth. It was so devastating because the faith I had built had become a crumbled, fallen house of cards. I wasn't sure I could be forgiven.

What are the rules now that I'm divorced? I wondered. *With four children, a failed marriage, and purity no longer a concern, what is my objective moving forward? What do I believe about God?*

Until divorce, the rules were to say no to sex until marriage and never say no to sex, a gain, once married. Quoting Scriptures, women at Christian women conferences actually taught how wives were never to deny husbands sex lest we cause them to stumble. My husband added his own memorized verses suggesting my body was now his so he should have it anytime he wanted. As a divorcee, I felt like a wide open, gaping wound, one that was vulnerable to any bad bacteria that came my way. With no Band-Aid, no protection, no longer sure of what I believed, I walked into my new life curious. I was living a sort of experiment, considering all kinds of options, because while naïve, feeling of so little worth, I sought hope for forgiveness in discovering the answer to creating a healthy, happy marriage. I guess I felt I could redeem myself if I could create a healthy relationship with a man, a relationship God would bless and approve. When, in fact, I actually needed to build a healthy relationship with myself, a healthy thought that would later come to me not through faith.

Remaining divorced felt like remaining broken. To achieve a happy marriage felt like hope for redemption. It is no wonder I felt this way as much of the teaching in churches put a great deal of emphasis on sex and marriage in relation to God.

Upon my return from filing for a divorce, Isiah involved me with the retired professional football players association in Dallas. Like a little sister in a fraternity, I went to meetings, planning events, and wherever else Isiah would randomly go. A day with Isiah was an adventure of not knowing whom you might meet or where you would go.

Some days, I hung out with Isiah as he counseled a depressed former player struggling, wanting to give up on life. On other days we spent the day with celebrity players; still other days we hung out with men from his drug rehab, House of Isaiah; and other times we were deep in planning and coordinating events. No day with him was ever the same. He could hardly go anywhere without someone knowing him, and time seemed of little importance to him, so we were always late. It was a wonderful diversion from my pain, meeting wonderful people with a safe group of guys whom I could question and learn from as they taught me about men.

Broken, I wasn't seeking a relationship, but I was seeking knowledge. What is the key to a happy relationship? What do good men want? Unsure if or how I could regain my worth and value, wondering who would or could validate me, I asked lots of questions. While I learned from them, no one person had come along who could get the "you are worthy" message deep enough to touch that place in my soul where it would plant, root, and grow. Many were speaking it to me, but because I felt so unworthy, I couldn't receive it, a common issue among victims of domestic violence. Shame cuts deep and just doesn't go away.

Brené Brown, author and professor at the University of Houston, teaches the difference between shame and guilt. She says shame focuses on self while guilt focuses on behavior. Shame says, *I am bad,* while guilt says, *I did a bad thing.* Although shame and guilt may seem similar, shame is highly correlated with addiction, depression, aggression, suicide, bullying, eating disorders, and many other forms of abuse. Guilt says, "I'm sorry, I made a mistake," while shame says, "I'm sorry I *am* a mistake." Her findings suggest that shame requires three things to exist: secrecy, silence, and judgment. Shame cannot survive with empathy.[1]

By reading Brené Brown, I learned that having no empathy for myself, serving as my harshest judge, I empowered shame to control and define me. How could I stop this cycle?

"You need to meet with me," Kevin suggested. "I've been single over fifteen years, and it has really changed, especially in the last five years," he added, taking it upon himself to coach me on how to navigate my new single life. Curious, I accepted. I met Kevin during Super Bowl week at a private party for Jim McMahon, the former Bears and Packers quarterback. While working on Super Bowl events with Gina and Isiah, I had the opportunity to meet various players.

Not sure what this celebrity looked like, I noticed a James Bond-like guy with a "thing" in his ear wearing a black suit. *I bet he'll know,* I thought. So I approached him. Turns out he was the bodyguard. When I asked if he could help me find Jim McMahon, he said, "You want me to divulge *classified information*?"

Maybe this wasn't such a good idea.

"Pull out your cell phone," he ordered.

Immediately, I did as he asked.

"Put this number in it," he said, "and push send."

I did.

And Kevin called me the next morning. Smooth.

That's how Kevin and I wound up splitting crab legs at an outdoor beer joint/restaurant in a quaint little town between where he and I lived. It was a start of a long-lasting friendship where he eventually hired my son, Marshall, over a period of several years for certain short-term assignments. Marshall's first paycheck came from Kevin. He framed a copy of it and hung it on his wall. Marshall was proud of his work for Kevin. Kevin was proud of Marshall offering what Marshall craved . . . *approval*, a good man to say to him "Good job!"

In Buzz Lightyear-like cadence, Kevin shared adventurous experiences of guarding presidents on Marine One. He worked with numerous top-ranking political officials and all sorts of celebrities. He was trained in interrogation. He followed kidnappers of wealthy families in Europe and would disappear to the Middle East occasionally without any more explanation than that. He was in the Middle East. Conversation over. His important mission over messy, buttery crab legs was to prepare me for the single world out there.

As Kevin broke the crab shells for me, handing me drawn-butter-dipped pieces of crabmeat across the table, he began his instruction. Over a very fun, messy meal, I thoroughly enjoyed this action figure-like character who seemed to have appeared into my life straight out of the latest *Mr. and Mrs. Smith* movie.

I was interested to hear what he had to say about single life because putting myself out there again caused me to cringe. The more single people I met, the more I began to wonder if this world, so new to me, was the world in which my children actually lived. Had I been this detached from their reality? *Is this what they face every day?* I wondered. I was really trying to understand myself, primarily as to what I wanted out of the rest of my life. What are good men like? What do they want and what are they looking for? I wasn't sure how to navigate my way through this new single life of divorcees. Guys were eager to talk about it: How they perceived women . . . what they thought about women, relationships, and love. Certainly, there were (and are!) many diverse perspectives.

Some saw it in very basic terms, that divorced women carry much more of the family needs than men. Many single men are not even willing to do all that the women will for the kids. Single women are working, caring for kids emotionally and physically, and they have less time than the single men. Women basically drive what the men become. Women no longer want men holding the door for them or even taking time to date. They are more interested in getting the dinner or date over with and moving on. They are busy.

Some men, in turn, have no respect for those women. They feel women drive all the relationships. Women set the tone, the boundaries, and the rules. If women don't have any, men won't either. Why would they? And the whole dating scene becomes animalistic. The whole look of relationships has changed, and it all revolves around self-serving pleasure rather than genuine relationship, so it seemed.

"What about those who do get married? Why does that happen?" I asked.

"Sometimes a guy will want to take a girl off the market," he explained. "A guy doesn't want others to have her anymore and he wants her for himself or, in most cases, it's about timing. They are ready to settle down, and she is the one who is there at that particular time. Keep in mind, too, the competition and what single guys are used to getting," he added, obviously referring to sex with no strings attached.

This bleak report sent me into a cocoon. I was certainly not interested in participating in that lifestyle. Several young people confirmed that this, in fact, was a common approach out there. What was also true, however, is that there are sincere, kind, good-hearted souls seeking genuine relationships and friendships, as well.

I listened to what they had to say. Educating myself on this was certainly entertaining, but what I really wanted to know was what was out there so to avoid another relationship calamity. One significant point they all agreed upon is that women are very powerful. At that point, I felt no power. This phenomenon of powerful women drew me in to learn more.

From the NFL players I had befriended, some had a different take. They said I shouldn't even try to educate myself on what was going on out there because there are those who are looking for "real" and will recognize those doing the same. They said that people looking for real true love will be attracted to those who want to reciprocate. In essence, they trusted it to fate. These men also relied on their faith and in the divine, emphasizing that they didn't want the old life of chasing after something they could never fulfill.

"The flesh always wants more," they said. "It's never satisfied." Many of them said, "Susan, don't try to understand that life. I wish I didn't know it." One went on to say, "What is so exciting to me is that God can take me, who lived one girl to the next with a revolving door full of surface, phony relationships, and can clean me up. Only God can do that."

So, what about me? Here I was broken, divorced, and still so very desperate for answers on how my life turned out the way it did, wondering, *Will I ever feel clean again?*

I was fighting accusatory inner voices that told me I was a failure as a mother, wife, friend, and daughter. So a little affirmation that day was a patch of hope on a little part of my soul. My worth and value wasn't completely destroyed, perhaps.

Perhaps.

Men who chose to draw from their faith to change how they lived out their single life shared with me that by doing so, they then began to attract women who were looking for something real and meaningful . . . and that it worked. They were living a new life and said that it truly was real and a much more fulfilling way to live. And then one of them said to me, "You know, Susan, it's not about the sin being committed but rather the light being rejected. Receive the light." Their explanation sounded similar to the methods I'd used to get me where I landed, in a deep convoluted rhetorical, hyper-spiritual mess.

The term "spiritual abuse" has been referenced a number of times by many professionals. Evidently, this is a more common abuse than is often mentioned, an abuse I hope to bring attention to.

And, to be honest, after sitting back watching some of the men I talked with that day, I wasn't so convinced they really were *living* out that new light of which they spoke, at least, not as portrayed.

But that's okay. I was gathering information.

Common among all the truly successful, independent, confident men with whom I spoke, not one wanted a "submissive" wife. The more confident the man, the stronger he preferred his woman. Only insecure, fear-motivated, controlling men want a submissive wife. Good men want an equal or even more powerful or influential leader.

It's crazy how what's taught in the church actually attracts insecure, control-interested men and women. Of course, many men and women in the church don't live by that verse; instead, they gloss over it or ignore it. Some woman have said they are submissive as their husband loves as Christ loved the church and is submitted to God. In most of those cases, I observed they were equals with mutual respect rather than submission.

Some men shared how their ex-wives used Scripture to control them. It works both ways. I had never considered how the Scripture those women quoted can equally hold a man hostage. Manipulators can masterfully make Scripture pretty much anything they want. I was seeking truth. And if it isn't so, why is all this stuff taught?

Networking while seeking employment, I was also thrust into the world of businessmen, becoming the sole female invited for cocktails after meetings.

"You're kind of like one of us, but you're not," they'd say.

This particular group ranged from the late 20s to retirees in their 60s and beyond. And, in interacting with them, I met a great number of unsatisfied married men with young children.

For them, I was like a "den mother," encouraging them to be patient, shedding light on what their women were facing with young children and what changes they could anticipate once the children grew older. I also met many men who showed up to church with their families every Sunday but prowled around at night, confirming my many suspicions. I learned that many married older women enjoyed side relationships with younger men—there's a big world of swingers, too—but I met a few truly happily committed married men, as well.

As I had no personal interest in these people other than curiosity, knowledge, and friendship, they openly shared. It was a wonderful education in human nature. I felt honored by their honesty and loved listening, learning, and growing, seeing goodness in them all . . . even if they were choosing lifestyles of no interest to me.

Occasionally, they brought in women they worked with. These women shared how they handled flirting, inappropriate comments that could be considered harassment, outright harassment, and the myriad challenges of working in a male-dominated industry. Some of them said they had never experienced harassment.

Soaking in all that knowledge, I enjoyed relationships built outside my children's lives, school, or church. I would eventually discover that all worlds are basically the same, only some don't want to see it or admit it.

My spiritual quest to understand what happened to me, discovering why I allowed myself to fall so deep under another's control, compelled me to continue studying and learning about men. What about me attracted a controlling person rather than a well-balanced person?

That journey led me to a website by Christian Carter.

He wrote about how he was raised by his mother, growing up in a home with his sisters and grandmother. That, he said, gave him a certain understanding of women. He was often in the kitchen listening as they discussed relationships, dating, marriage, and any number of other topics with friends. And they almost always discussed men. That's when he realized how little women understood men. He started helping women see men from different perspective which, he boasts, helped their relationships grow.[2]

I bought his e-book *Catch Him and Keep Him*. The title, in my opinion, did not reflect the content of the material.

Now, it wasn't so much what he said about men, it was more about what he said about *women*. His book helped me see me in a different light. I began to see how unhealthy my choices had been, revealing my severe lack of self-knowledge and self-respect. It wasn't men who I needed to better understand, it was *me* I needed to get to know.

That book became one of the most helpful tools in my recovery. Not only because I hoped to have a good, healthy relationship some day with a good, loving man, but more importantly I wanted to be "healthy" in my own mind, having a good relationship with myself.

With the purchase of Carter's e-book, I also received daily or weekly emails from him. I devoured his wisdom urging his female readers to be true to themselves. I tested what he taught and found him to be absolutely correct. Just as I am attracted to men who know what they want and go after it no matter what I think or feel, I need to do the same. Either the direction we are forging for our own life works and is in sync with another or it is not. We are not to change our direction, our dreams, or our life course to fit someone else, a marital mistake I intended never to repeat. No longer was I to diminish myself for another. I was to make room for myself, whether another liked it or not. After all, not everyone is supposed to be in our life. That's okay. But how we can know is by simply being true to ourselves. Either our direction and course works or it doesn't. That's how you know . . . a simple yet profound truth for me.

At 48 years of age, I was becoming more self-aware, a better steward of me, being true to myself. This common-sense teaching didn't ask what I believed God wanted for me, it asked what was in me, what was in my gut to do and not do. For me, it created a much more simple, fulfilling, positive, and joyful way to live.

In a nutshell, my takeaway from Carter's book is this: Be true to yourself and do not lose yourself in personal quests of any kind. Discover *your* life direction, likes, and dislikes rather than living through someone else's or serving someone else's (for me, this meant including my notion of God). And do not give up what you enjoy simply because a man is in your life. Stay true to you *in* the relationship. The right man will adapt and respect you for it and will enjoy you even more. If one requires you to subdue, change, or give into *his* vision and goals over your own, they are telling you they don't belong. Listen to them.

It comes down to mutual respect. A simple yet profound, truth for one who didn't really know what she wanted, who thought it unimportant to discover because the pleasure and mission of the Christian life, *or so I thought,* came from seeking what God wanted for me and how I could serve others in their quests, especially a husband. I discovered that my old way of thinking was a perfect formula for attracting a narcissist or a control freak. A good, healthy man seeks a woman who has her own mind, desires, and direction; a woman who doesn't lose her goals when she enters into relationship with him.

Remember, a healthy man or woman offers mutual respect rather than requiring another to deny themselves to become "one." And that was a huge difference from the self-denying, deprecating person I had become.

Regaining my sense of self-worth required prioritizing me, something I had discarded as a mother and in my quest in faith. And as I stripped away religion and religious views, I walked a new path with my creator, simplifying it to gratefulness, trust, and getting to know the real *me*.

10

Chapter Ten

The past is where you learned the lesson.
The future is where you apply the lesson.
—UNKNOWN

It's important to learn the right lessons from the past.
—DOUGLAS ALEXANDER

"That's my old boyfriend!" I said, lighting up, pointing to a man's picture in the newspaper.

"Who is?" asked the woman behind the desk at the radio station.

"He is," I replied, turning the paper so she and Gina could see.

"Well, you just parked in his parking lot," the woman said. "And that's his building over there," she added, pointing out the window to a picturesque, beautifully refurbished historical downtown business district favorite.

Gina and I had walked into the radio station for a scheduled meeting. While waiting, we each picked up a local business paper from a stack on the counter. That's when I saw Greg. And what I saw on those pages completely changed the direction the rest of this journey would take me. It was a picture of the man I dated 23 years ago. There he was, featured in an article about the industry in which he excelled.

We had completely lost contact over the years. Twelve or so years prior, a mutual friend had informed me that Greg had gone through a divorce. She also commented on the fact that she heard he was a really great dad. But that was all I knew of him. It was so wonderful seeing his picture. He looked really great. I couldn't believe it!

Nine months since I left Seth, four months since my divorce, I was spun back 23 years for rediscovery on a multitude of levels. Gina had watched me pull myself together that morning, after another melt-down, to help conduct this meeting.

This time, we were meeting with the account executive of a radio station that asked for exclusive sponsorship of the Super Week celebrity softball classic event we were hosting for her foundation. It was an exciting event involving many professional football and baseball players, both current and former. We were also working with media personalities. Coordinating this softball game and working with Gina provided me a more positive purpose. It allowed me flexibility and plenty of down time to contemplate, to deal with the pain and heal. Most importantly, it brought Gina and me together on a daily basis.

Gina stuck closer to me than a sister. She walked every inch of my valley with me and shared a burden that trickled down to her entire family. They were no strangers to valleys and had had friends walk with them through theirs. The foundation we represented was a memorial to their very dear daughter and sister, Tara. She was a very special little girl who prayed fervently for her friends and their entire families. She had a prayer journal and loved her Lord. Tara also played baseball and was the only girl player, not only on her team but also in the entire league. Her final year on this earth, she led her team to the World Series, where she pitched in her final game. The Tara Sawyer

Foundation offers assistance to children and families through various means for sports and education.

The loss of Tara left a dark, empty pit that had no floor to its depth. Creating this foundation was one of the ways the Sawyer family coped with their inexpressible and endless pain and loss. Working on this event was provision for both of us to further confront and heal from pain, but in dramatically different ways.

The celebrity softball game was an event that Gina's family had considered hosting for years. My commitment to partnering with Gina in this gave her the confidence to take on the challenge. It provided me a great opportunity. No other situation would have provided such flexibility to handle and deal with the crises my children and I were encountering. John and Gina were patient, sympathetic, and eager to help. And it provided me an opportunity to give back. Gina and I enjoyed our time together, and every day was such a new adventure! It was exciting and new territory for all involved. Somehow, Gina and John were given the grace to believe in me, and they stood by me even when it cost them dearly.

This particular morning was exceptionally difficult. Gina had wondered if this time I'd be unable to pull myself together to make the meeting. I was at an all-time low. She assured me that she could handle this one without me and encouraged me to just stay in the car. I insisted on joining her, wiping my eyes from yet another meltdown. I put on another forced smile and walked into the radio station beside her. I'm so glad I did.

At the close of the meeting, I told Gina that I would approach Greg for the sponsorship. Checking out his website that afternoon, I discovered that he was indeed philanthropic, and I thought he might truly be interested in our event. But, more importantly, I couldn't help but consider the coincidence was somehow purposeful for me personally, as well. I wondered if he would have insight into what I was going through and what he remembered about my mission trip to Haiti when I was younger. I remembered leaving him with my parents as

I boarded a plane to Haiti. My memory was vague, but I had written about the experience. How did that affect him? I wondered if he ever even thought of me. I wanted to know how he remembered me, what was I like before I married, and why he might think this had all happened. I had no idea how he would respond. But I was so eager to hear from him because he was involved in my life during that great Haiti crisis and upheaval.

Behind Chanel sunglasses, draped in a sleek black sweater dress with black patent cowboy boots, I appeared at his office in true Fort Worth fashion. Upon my arrival, a comedy of errors ensued. Using my maiden name, I asked to see him. He, however, was already headed in my direction, completely unaware that I waiting for him.

Assuming I had been announced, I figured he knew it was me. When he saw me, he just saw sunglasses, with a folder in hand. He not only didn't recognize me but also deduced that I was just another seeker of handouts. He actually attempted an about-face to avoid me. Nonetheless, I smiled and greeted him with a friendly hug.

With that, he invited me to his office. I noticed the bewildered look on his face as he led me up the gorgeous marble winding staircase to his crow's nest office. Assuming he was supposed to know me, since I greeted him with a hug, I was surprised that he kept looking straight ahead, avoiding any eye contact with me. He just wouldn't look at me.

Once in his office, he offered me a seat across from him at a table and began thumbing through my event folder. Still assuming he remembered me, I shrugged off his business-like approach, keeping our conversation event-centered around.

He then asked, "Remind me. How did we first meet?" keeping his eyes on the folder.

"Don't you remember?" I asked. "You worked at the bank and I worked at the Hyatt—"

With that, his countenance completely changed. With his eyes locked on mine, he closed the brochure and pushed it aside slowly. He abruptly slammed both hands on the table and stood to his feet, pulling himself forward closer to me. With deep emotion flooding out of him and looking right through me with those gorgeous steel-blue eyes I so remembered, he said in disbelief, "Oh my God, it's you, Susan!"

From that moment on, it was an intense, intentional conversation of "I've wondered what happened to you . . . what are you doing now? You don't look like you've had four children. You never came back to me . . . why?"

As the "do you remembers" continued, I was stunned at the flood of memories and thoughts that seemed to flow rapidly to the surface. He seemed to hold nothing back.

"Do you remember me taking you hunting at my ranch? I still have the antlers," he said.

They were in his garage after all these years. Ours was the last deer he ever shot. He expressed disappointment and sorrow that he shot it while I was with him.

I said, "Oh no, please don't regret it. That was the only deer hunt I have been on." I continued to tell him how glad I was for that experience.

I couldn't believe he said he still had the horns from that deer in his garage. I was amazed he kept them all these years through all his moves. I asked if I helped him with the deer and what we did with it. He reminded me of what I said and did on that hunt. The memory finally began to come back to me. I remembered helping hoist that huge creature onto his Volvo. We tied him on with a rope. We had gone to visit his parents that weekend in West Texas. On the way, we pulled off the country highway so he could take a picture of me in a cotton field. He took me shopping to buy me a pair of Wrangler jeans. It was all coming back. We talked of great memories and lighter times.

Over two hours of rapid-fire questions and answers between the two of us, I felt the cloud of the dark place, in which I was still, hovering over me, and I wondered what he must see sitting across from him. Desperate for answers and understanding, I was in no position to posture myself or even put my best foot forward. I was simply struggling, trying to cope, and I couldn't imagine how pathetic that might look to someone who seemed as successful and together as he.

I was far from together and didn't even want to try to seem so. I was just desperate for answers and understanding from anyone who could help me make some sense of my crazy life. He seemed so understanding of where I was. He had been there twice, it turned out. His second divorce he referred to as his "mulligan." The marriage lasted only eight months. His willingness to humbly share with me put me more at ease. He understood where I was and assured me that this feeling of crisis would pass.

I asked if he would be interested in reading my book. I had started a book about Haiti and four of the chapters were written about the time he was in my life.

He said, "Really? You're writing a book? That's no easy task."

He glanced over at a stack of books in his office. I looked over to see a pile of books including one he had written: *Getting to Yes with Your Banker.*

"I'm not published," I clarified as I walked over to his stack of books. "May I have a copy?" I asked, reaching for a paperback.

"Sure, grab a hardback," he said.

"Will you sign it?" I asked, handing it to him.

Our conversation kept the pace. Every once in a while, he would look down to write something in my manuscript without taking a break from our talk. I wondered what he was thinking. What would he write in my book? What would he have to say to me? He looked so much the same. A little older, of course, but still very distinguished and very much the handsome guy I remembered. His demeanor was still very cool and calm.

His office was covered in pictures of his two gorgeous children. We discovered both of our daughters were debutantes. We were both very involved in the symphony. We had traveled to many of the same places and shared many of the same interests.

"You gave me my first Bible," he said. "It was blue."

"Yes. I remember," I said, fumbling for words in the emotion of that moment.

"I still have it," he said.

We discussed the footprints poem that I wrote in his Bible, and he told me of a Bible study in which he had been actively participating for many years. "I started it for my son, but stayed in it for me," he said, "I learned about it from you."

In disbelief, I sat in awkward silence. He was beautiful.

As he handed me my copy of his now-autographed book, I opened it to read, *12/30/10: Susan, Great to reconnect. I bet you are the best mom in the world! Greg P.S. Thanks for the book you gave me 20+ years ago, the* Bible!

What a treasure that afternoon turned out to be! And though it was time for me to go, I was amazed at the deep emotion of our meeting. It wasn't a "slap-happy, hey, good to see you" kind of meeting. It was much deeper than that. It was evident that he felt it too. I was grateful and a bit taken aback. It was apparent to me that he felt more deeply for me years ago than I ever realized.

He walked me to the door and invited me to return after hours for a glass of wine so that I could bring him a copy of what I had already written. I accepted with eager anticipation. But first, I had to go back and take a harder look at my past where Greg and I had begun. *What had happened to us so many years ago?*

11

Chapter Eleven

Avoiding danger is no safer in the long run than outright exposure.
The fearful are caught as often as the bold.
—HELEN KELLER

If only abusers would leave their Targets alone once they leave. Following the loss of a Target, Charming Impossibles stalk, harass and, too often, kill. Most domestic violence murders happen *after* a divorce. Charming Impossibles do not give up or let go.

According to the World Health Organization, a partner or spouse is responsible for 38 percent of women's homicides worldwide.[1] In the US, the study suggested that intimate partners carried out more than 40 percent of homicides of women and about 7 percent the homicides of men.[2]

While many therapists urge battered women to leave abusive relationships, the Justice Department says the majority of domestic assaults reported to law enforcement take place after the couple separates.[3] Statistics are that "women in abusive relationships are about

500 times more at risk when they leave," said Gaye Hahoney, executive director of the Mississippi Coalition Against Domestic Violence.[4]

According to the United Nations Office on Drugs and Crime, 79 percent of all homicide victims were male and 21 per cent female, almost four times the global average female rate.[5] While statistically, women suffer abuse from men much more than men from women,[6] (understanding men often do not report), any victim of abuse should be treated the same, with equal acknowledgment, compassion, and a sense of urgency for assistance.

* * *

In the beginning, the choice my children and I made in choosing to remain silent, quietly trying to move on with our lives, irritated many, particularly most of those supporting us. People wanted me to stand up for myself. They saw my stance as one of weakness. While it may have appeared so in the beginning, it actually required considerable strength of character and self-respect to ignore, ignore, *ignore*.

After receiving several slandering emails from Seth, one friend called me and said, "My God, you can't let him bully you like that! You need to put a stop to this! And if you won't, I will!"

Well, he tried.

In short order, he called me right back, "My God! He wouldn't even listen to me. He talked over me, raising his voice!" he said. "We ended up in a shouting match. You're right. He was not willing to even listen to me." He paused, waiting for me to respond in shock and disbelief.

I think it surprised him when I replied calmly, "Yep. Thanks for trying but it's best for us if you ignore him as we have chosen to do." He now understood . . . and agreed.

Another man called: "We are so sick and tired of his emails!" he said. "I'm trying to defend you, but you need to give me something to work with, here, Susan."

"Thank you, but I don't need you to defend me," I replied.

"But I want to!" he responded.

"I don't understand the need to defend myself and children against such ridiculous slander. Who listens to this sort of nonsense?" I replied.

"Just give me *something*, Susan," he insisted.

Now, this was a very well-respected man. He wasn't one to get caught up in drama. The fact that a man like him (a military veteran, a no-nonsense man's man type) was even willing to stand for me was humbling. I was honored by his request to intervene.

"I'll send you the most recent email Seth sent to the kids with no commentary from me," I finally conceded.

From that, I received emails, phone calls, and text messages offering not only support but also expressing gratitude that we were able to "get out of *that*." Some support was immediate, other support trickled in. While it didn't change how we would move forward, we still appreciate those who made an extra effort to defend what was right and true. People are full of wonderful surprises. It's inspiring to experience good men and women standing up for good from a vantage point such as ours. They inspire us to be better and to do more for others . . . as they have done for us.

* * *

Ten plus years have passed, and we have moved on with our lives. Yet Seth's smear campaigns continue. Evidently, as long as people will listen, he'll talk. Targets do move on, but many Charming Impossibles just *don't*. Many of them are forever addicted to creating unexpected chaos, popping in with drama, and exposing to others any encounter with their Target in half-truths. There is a method behind the lies, the false accusations, and the spectacle made of my children who are caught in this disruptive web.

* * *

After reading some of Seth's emails, my attorney recommended I get a restraining order. Due to my new home address, I would need a local attorney. Gina took me to meet her friend who is a judge downtown. His dark-wood trimmed office decorated in beautiful art originals was spacious and intimidating. He reeked of power, and that scared me. *What if he doesn't believe me?* I wondered. *What if he turns on me?* My situation was still so confusing to me; it certainly could be even more so to others.

He advised us on the whole process, what it would look like and what to expect. But the next step, what was required of me, nearly took me down. I was not at all prepared for how deeply hidden I kept the pain that was about to emerge. I had no idea it was even in me because I held it so deep and it came with feelings of gross shame. Upon the judge's instructions, Gina took me to the District Attorney's office. Gina explained to the clerk that I needed to get a restraining order and that we were told to file a report. The clerk handed me a pad of paper and a pen and asked me to write down each physical assault I had experienced and the date or time of year the best I could.

Sitting at a counter in a sterile waiting room crowded with people, with pen and paper in hand, I came face-to-face with all that had happened for the first time in writing. As I wrote the memories down, it all flashed back to me so vividly. I became literally sick with fear that with providing this information to the court system, I was not only handing over control of whom would learn about my shame but also control of how the courts would respond. *Would something happen to Seth? To me? To my children? Would I be judged for what I chose to endure? Would this backfire on me or, even worse, on my children? Will they see me for the stupid fool I've become? Will this stupidity cause me to lose them? Oh my God, if I tell the truth about what has been happening, will my children be taken from me?*

My internal turmoil had physical implications. Turning white and feeling faint, my continual visits to the restroom ground the process to a halt. Struggling at watching me suffer, Gina suggested I finish it another time. Even the clerk came over to express concern. Soon, other people in the waiting room did too.

One was from a women's shelter. She came over to talk to me and reassure me. Unfortunately, in my anguished state of mind, though I saw her moving lips, I heard nothing. I grew increasingly weak from multiple trips back and forth to the restroom. Determined to push through, I told myself I would not leave until I was finished. But the implications were still daunting. I realized that my abuse would not only be public, it would be transcribed in a legal document to be signed by a judge so that I could get a protective order. What a soap opera my life had become. This sort of thing happened to other people. I could not believe this was happening to me. I felt trashy and dirty.

After that painful ordeal, the court ultimately determined that I could not qualify for a restraining order because my physical abuse was too long ago and I was not under any certain current threat.

It's just a piece of paper anyway, I thought, consoling myself. *No piece of paper was going to keep anyone away.*

Temporary restraining orders are usually valid only 10 to 15 days and are granted with great discretion. After a series of Seth's emails, I would later be issued several restraining orders. This eventually lead to being granted a permanent injunction through the district court stating my ex-husband could never, ever come within a mile of my home or place of work *indefinitely*. The court approval for such deep measures speaks for itself. Should he ever violate this, he will go straight to jail. But this entire process brought back all my confusion, guilt, and shame. It resurfaced with a vengeance. Could I ever forgive myself? I had to figure out how I let this happen to myself and my children. There was still some serious soul-searching I had yet to do.

The only other time I ever dealt with such anxiety was right before we left for good. Even though Seth left huge bruises on me before, he held fast that he never had done anything to me he wouldn't do "potty training a puppy," another reference comparing us to dogs.

"If I'm so bad and unworthy, why don't you just divorce me? Let's get a divorce," I suggested numerous times.

"No" was always his refusal. Besides all his biblical assertions, he was holding onto correct my real problem, which was, according to him, the fact that I had never *really* been beaten up.

12

Chapter Twelve

*Never mistake silence for ignorance, calmness
for acceptance, or kindness for weakness.*
—Unknown

Still lingering was a comment Hanz had made while helping to write my divorce. He said his past marriage was much like how I had described mine. My curiosity kept his words alive. *What did he mean by that?* Assuming it impossible that a successful businessman could possibly struggle in his marriage or compare his struggle to anything like mine, I wondered if he could help me understand how I wound up in my marital mess. Perhaps hearing his story might shed light on me to even better understand myself. So I called him.

An urban rustic bar decorated in old-world Texas style—humorous signs on the walls with a Western twist, spurs, and an eclectic mix of cowboy artifacts scattered about—was the backdrop for our meeting at a four-top table nestled in a private corner. Hanz introduced me to his friend Tony, an international attorney. Eager to talk, they called over the server, ordered two orders of bacon-wrapped shrimp, two draft beers, and a Chardonnay so we could get right down to business.

Hanz explained that they both had similar stories to mine. How could this happen to an attorney who looks, talks, and acts like a tough New Yorker? *What will these men have to say to me?* I could not imagine.

Throughout my journey, the fact that men are also victims of domestic violence had been mentioned with increasing frequency. Granted, it was usually an "oh, and men, too . . ." kind of addendum. At the time, I was unaware of any details or true examples of real cases in which men were victimized—both psychologically and physical-ly—at the hands of their wives.

That was about to change.

Hours passed as we poured over their family pictures. Hans and Tony shared how they met their wives, built very successful careers, and parented beautiful children, all while enduring traumatic crises behind beautiful doors. Both men had gorgeous *Architectural Digest*-type homes in North Dallas. And both lived their married lives main-taining phony images of a successful family life while living in chaotic, crazy madness behind closed doors. Judging from their family photos, they had perfect lives. No one would ever guess they were anything but very happy families, which, of course, didn't faze me: the same was true of me.

At one point, Tony began beating his chest, saying, "How did this happen to *me*? I work for a billionaire. I fly all over the world, talking to kings of nations on a monthly basis. I am a powerful person!"

Hanz, a more austere personality, never broke from his gentleman-ly, soft-spoken, kind demeanor, yet both shared their grief, deep pain, and sadness in heartbreaking detail. Both were more concerned about their children and their mental well-being above anything else. Their affection for their children was unmistakably their biggest priority; it was also their reason for staying in their marriages for so long, both waiting to leave until the kids could see what was really going on for themselves. Both were understandably concerned that their wives would turn their kids against them.

There we sat together, each having recently broken away from marriages of 20 plus years, each heartbroken for our children, each wondering if we or our children would ever fully heal, each wondering how this had happened to us.

Shortly after that encounter, I went to a private military event. Arriving early to this beautiful buffet-dinner event on the top floor of one of Dallas's most prestigious private clubs, surrounded by the majestic Dallas skyline showcased through floor to ceiling windows, I was greeted by another early-arriving guest.

"What do you do?" he asked me after introducing himself as the CEO of a large well-respected Dallas business.

Tenuously, I replied, "I'm writing my story about leaving domestic violence and hope to speak out on behalf of powerful, successful C-suite level men who suffer as victims," I heard myself say.

"Interesting," he said. Inquisitively, he leaned in closer to me, adding, "Please, tell me more."

"Well," I said, "I recently have learned of such men realizing they do not have a voice. I mean, men who have never experienced it are likely to haze or ridicule any guy who would admit it. I've encountered people in the domestic violence industry who have trouble believing my experience because of my background and appearance. I can only imagine how much more difficult it is for successful businessmen. I have two precious sons and can now see how young men could easily be targeted and victimized. And I hope to be a voice for *anyone* who suffers such abuse."

"Really?" he asked. "I'm one," he confided, folding his arms and looking askance.

"You, *too*?" I took a deep breath with my eyebrows raised, inviting him to share more.

He went on to tell me he had a military and medical background and was now in business. His first marriage lasted over 20 years. His second marriage of 16 years was to a wonderful woman. He had found true happiness in his new life with her.

"When a 5-foot-2 crazy wife grabs scissors or comes after you with a broken bottle, you have little defense," he added.

"I hope to have a radio talk show someday," I said. "We can protect the guests, change their names, alter their voices, but we'll give them a voice. I believe it will encourage many more to speak out than we can imagine."

Handing me his business card, he agreed. "If you ever get that radio talk show, I'll talk," he said. "I hope to hear from you, Susan. This is important."

Guests began crowding in. We parted ways. But my mind was churning as I tried to digest yet another such man who suffered greatly yet kept it all to himself, muting that part of his life.

The more I spoke out about it in intimate one-on-one settings, the more men came forward. Top surgeons in their fields, business owners, former Marines . . . the list goes on and on. While each had many dramatically different scenarios, they all had certain similarities.

One man who lived in an exclusive area outside of West Palm Beach refuted my findings, saying, "That doesn't happen in my neighborhood."

"Oh, yes it does!" I volleyed right back.

He lived in a prestigious high-rise, one of the most exclusive in the city where world leaders from other countries reside. The very week of our discussion, fire trucks and police converged on the property. I later learned a bloodied man was escorted out by police on a gurney while his tiny, slim wife came down in handcuffs. With no talk, no media coverage, and no known report on the events of that day, it appeared that any record of that episode vanished. Both the man and woman were said to be powerful attorneys.

Some in the law enforcement community have shared with me that they have as many domestic violence calls to the most exclusive neighborhoods as any other but that most go unreported. Those people don't file. Statistics are based on reported offenses. With most domestic violence offenses in upscale neighborhoods going unreported, we truly do not have accurate statistics on certain demographics in the US.

* * *

Some fathers are falsely accused of sexual abuse—not because their wife necessarily wants custody of the children but because she is a Charming Impossible. She enjoys the power in keeping the Target suffering.

To leave a narcissist often requires leaving everything behind, including any hope for maintaining a decent reputation. Leaving can also be far more destructive for children. A mother of two told me that after her divorce, custody of the children was divided evenly, shared every two weeks. Inevitably, after spending two weeks with their Charming Impossible dad, her children came back to her emotionally exhausted and confused. At the end of her two weeks, she would finally detangle the crazy emotional web their father had created only to hand them back for another two weeks, further exacerbating the confusion and turmoil.

Some narcissistic parents try to turn their children against the "good" parent, which is sadly very often the case. Many good parents wind up choosing to give custody of the young children to the narcissistic parent to save their kids from being divided into two emotionally. Their hope is that when their children are grown and can think for themselves, they will see the truth and develop a relationship in later life with the healthy parent. Usually, the children *do* return, but so many years are lost. Sometimes, this strategy works; other times, the grown children remain indoctrinated against the truly loving parent, never to reconnect. It's no wonder the courts are confused and wrong decisions are often legally made.

In an Old Testament story, two women who both claimed to be the mother of an infant come before a judge. The judge says to the two women, "Cut the child in half and each of you can have half" (1 Kings 3:25 NKJV). One of the women agrees, while the other woman says, "No, she may have the baby" (1 Kings 3:26). With this, the judge declared the latter as the true mother (1 Kings 3:27). Many parents partnered with a narcissistic sociopath spouse understand this story very well.

A narcissist would rather destroy a child than lose one. While they claim it is out of love or protection, it is not. They seem to get some sort of sick satisfaction in destroying anyone—be it their partner, their child, or a friend—rather than admit any wrongdoing.

Many are committed to the death, literally.

These are people many of us will never comprehend and struggle to even imagine actually exist in our everyday church, workplace, neighborhood, and children's school lives. They are hiding around us in plain sight. We simply can't see them because they have not singled us out into their web as a Target. Even stranger to me is that they *know* we don't see them. Unless you have specifically been chosen by one and are personally lured into their web, you do not and *cannot* understand how they work. You may watch someone else go through it or see troubling signs and some narcissistic behavior, but you will never fully comprehend it without having experienced it.

After having met too many men to count who shared similar tragic stories, I called Kevin, my Secret Service contact, the one who reads body language and between the lines of what people say. The one trained to serve on Marine One. Kevin was trained in interrogations and is a skilled professional at psychoanalysis. I was curious what he would say about my new discovery.

"Susan, these are 'mean girls' and 'bullies' from the playground who are now grown and married. Toxic, egocentric, insecure, self-loathing, or overly self-loving people, they vary in degrees from mean girls and bullies to narcissists, sociopaths, and psychopaths. They have no conscience, allowing their interest in power and control to preside over truth. They crave power and control, no matter the cost to others or to themselves. Period."

"How did this happen, Kevin?" I asked. "How did this happen to me and how on earth did this happen to such strong, confident, successful men?"

"It's simple, Susan," he responded in a matter-of-fact manner. "You're good people. You don't think like they do. Period."

"That's it?" I was still looking for more.

"That's it. Your elevator doesn't open on their floor. Good people cannot believe that someone so adorable and charming who has professed their love and devotion can possibly be that devoid of emotion and capability to truly love.

"For someone who has a deep capacity to love, like yourself," he continued, "it's almost impossible to imagine their partner is utterly devoid of that emotion. Look at yourself. You were married 21 years and you still haven't accepted this about your ex-husband. They don't feel like you feel, Susan. They can't. What you need to understand is just as you can't comprehend them, they can't comprehend you, but they do know what makes you tick because their elevator does open on your floor . . . and they walk all over it.

"A toxic person is paranoid about ever giving over the upper hand, even to those closest to them. They fear their lover will take advantage of them. That's why they fight. They don't trust. Likewise, the good people, like yourself, still hold fast to hope for love. But it's impossible," he said. "Accept this."

Common among many abusers is a tactic known as "triangulation." This is when one brings in a third person, such as an in an extramarital affair, creating a sort of competition using one or the other for control and manipulation. Other times it's a parent placing one child on a ridiculously high pedestal above the other siblings. Not having earned their "high place" creates insecurity or fear of losing it to the others. A Charming Impossible parent will then treat one better than the others, keeping all of his or her children striving for approval. The "favored" child suffers the deepest insecurity of all due to the fear of falling from "on high." This phony prestige creates defensiveness in its victim. Defending their position, they learn to tear down their competition, those with whom they feel threatened. In fact, this is one way the next Charming Impossible is born. People raised on a phony pedestal have no character but are brilliant at *appearing* good. Unfavored children are actually the lucky ones as they have a better chance at breaking this cycle in their own families.

"Most of society is good," Kevin continued. "The majority of society is confused on this issue and rightfully so. Neither the court system nor the public want to believe it. They keep trusting that there is good in everyone and that there are always two sides to every story. The public maintains an understandable distance, hesitating to get involved in something they can't understand.

"This is the vicious cycle that allows narcissism to grow and destroy our society as we know it," he added. "Getting to the truth where a narcissist is involved is nearly impossible when approached with common sense by a 'normal' person who doesn't have training or experience with this particular personality disorder. That is some deep, murky water to navigate.

"Like a chess player, one must navigate those waters and one can still be checkmated by the narcissist. They are clever, cunning, manipulative, and *very* charming. This leaves true victims at risk for being further accused and judged for that which they are victims. In couples counseling, the victim is often charged with being the problem. This emotional abuse happens to men and women alike. I see it all the time," he said.

"But what would you say to the professional who says that any *man* who is a victim of domestic violence, *by a woman*, needs to grow some balls?" I asked.

"I would say, 'Lucky them. They obviously never had one invade their personal life. Their comment is naïve. It can happen to anyone. No one is beyond this subversion. *No one!*'" Kevin replied.

"Have you ever heard of the honey trap?" Kevin asked. "It's a military term for a century-old means of getting information. The military uses it regularly. It's one of our most effective means of gathering information."

Kevin went on to explain that the honey trap is where a military man or woman seduces an officer for information. They form a romantic relationship with officers who are not only trained, skilled, and aware of the honey trap threat but are professionals in reading people's body language and detecting underlying intentions. When such professionals are informed that they are victims of the honey trap, most do not believe it. Fully trusting that their relationship is real, most need debriefing.

"If this can happen to a skilled, trained officer, Susan," Kevin continued, "why could it not happen to you or a doctor or lawyer?

"Move on, Susan. Keep on the high road. Go embrace your future. Leave your past behind," Kevin said.

"The world awaits you," he added. "The best thing you can do is leave your ex to live with himself, facing himself in the mirror every day. He knows who he is and who he is not, I assure you. That is your best revenge."

13

Chapter Thirteen

Every girl deserves a guy who looks at her every day like it's the first time he saw her.
—UNKNOWN

One cold, early January evening, donning my white mink vest with jeans and my black patent leather cowboy boots, I walked along the dusky, crowd-thinned downtown sidewalk to Greg's office. I had been out of town for the holidays and Greg had gone on a trip, as well. We had emailed each other a little, so we were a bit more familiar with each other's sense of humor more than anything. Greg was an absolute riot years ago and he still maintained his wonderful sense of humor. I remembered loving that about him. He was fun.

From the sidewalk I could see him moving about upstairs in his empty office. A January chill made me shudder as I knocked on his locked door. It had been a couple of weeks since we had seen each other. Greg came down to let me in. As we walked up the marble stairs, Greg shared some of the history of the building and what his part was in renovating it. He pointed out his art collection and gave me a personal tour that ended with him offering me a glass of wine in his crow's nest office.

We visited awhile when I heard a noise downstairs. Obviously, someone had entered. Looking to him for a read, I realized he was not caught off guard as he offered me a reassuring glance. Rapid-paced footsteps made their way up the stairs as he sat expectantly.

It was his daughter. Greg introduced us. She was home from college for the holidays and would be returning to school soon. She was as beautiful in person as she was in the pictures that Greg had displayed all over his office. They exchanged pleasantries and we all visited for a bit before she excused herself and slipped out as quickly as she had come. He soon received a text message from her and turned his phone to me so that I could read, *She's cute.*

Having been a wife for so long, never ever considering another man or that I would one day really be free from my marriage and divorced, it felt as though I were sitting there in someone else's body. Divorced only four months after a 21-year marriage, my new reality had not yet sunk in. I wasn't sure what I wanted for myself anymore. What kind of person was I supposed to even want to become? Being single would require me to become the opposite of what I had aspired to be the past 21 years because I had aspired to be an old-fashioned wife and mother.

Now, I guess I was supposed to aspire to be the modern, independent woman. What was that supposed to look like? And how would that affect my kids? They were my greatest concern.

Obviously, meeting Greg at his office was a new type of adventure for me. Still recovering from my war-torn life, sitting in his office was peaceful, hopeful, and ethereal. A deep sense of purpose surfaced within me in reconnecting with Greg. The depth of that was yet to be discovered, but the role he played in my past and my present was both nostalgic and precious. Comfort gently replaced guilt and shame when I was with him. I just wasn't yet comfortable in being single or in how that reality would manifest in my life. Meeting Greg's daughter, however, took "Wow, this is what my new life looks like" to a new level.

She couldn't have been sweeter or more welcoming. She was obviously used to meeting friends of her father. And that was good. I thought of my children, however. This was all still so new for them. Not only was this life still so new and difficult for me, it was even more so for my children. Our world just had the rug pulled out from under us, leaving everything toppled over and shaken into chaos. I worked at being very sensitive to them in this regard, and that's why I regularly turned down most offers for dinner, dates, and even trips. Most, but not *all*, as I tentatively explored a lifestyle I had never imagined as divorced mother of four. My children were my priority, however, and I wanted to see them heal as quickly and completely as possible. Dragging them through a litany of strange men would not have helped them heal, and I doubt it would have helped me either.

But Greg was different. Our meeting seemed like an appointment from above. At least, it seemed so to me. And it seemed so right and full of hope.

Offering to treat me to dinner, Greg took me to a nearby seafood restaurant where we shared another glass of wine with smoked salmon and a salad over easy, gently familiar, yet still somewhat guarded conversation. How rare it was for me to dine like that. These days, my meals usually came straight out of a can. That I was with him again warmed my heart, soothed me, and awakened an excitement I'd forgotten existed. Walking to my car in his parking lot, I was reminded of my first time there, only a month or so before. Never would I have dreamed he and I would be right where I had parked that day, again, together.

My written story was now in his hands. I felt really vulnerable that a published author was reading my writing. I had been working on it since I knew Greg. Now, he was reading it.

14

Chapter Fourteen

I have so many mixed emotions about this trip. I am anxious.
Today I fought tears every moment of the day.
I don't know what to do about Greg. I love him.
—Journal entry, Monday, January 19, 1987

Do not be ready to listen to anyone who is ready to show you
your past mistakes. Instead, be ready to listen to someone who is
ready to show you the untold lessons from your past mistakes so
that you may be able to skip your future mistakes.
—Ernest Agyemang Yeboah

I was 20 years old and dating Greg when I sat in a church service that changed the course of my life. With an outstretched hand, Eleanor Workman, a missionary from Haiti, said from the pulpit, "If God is calling you, come!" From the back row I saw an aura of light frame her body as though she were eclipsing the sun. All I can say is, I knew from that moment I must go.

Greg rode with my mother, father, and me to the airport. The three of them walked me to the gate with the same look of bewilderment as I had. It was a cold, rainy day, so I wore a coat over my t-shirt dress. Handing my coat to my mother almost felt as though I were handing over to her my whole life as I knew it. It was as though I were saying goodbye to all I was and that God was going to remake me into a complete transformation. I felt as though I were going into some kind of science fiction-like surgical procedure where I would return to them an entirely new creature. That I'd look the same on the outside but would become something completely different on the inside. I was scared but wanted to hide my fear because I knew they had enough concern and worry without knowing all about mine.

I hugged and kissed my parents goodbye and held on to Greg for one last long embrace and kiss. He was the most difficult for me to leave. *What will become of us?* I worried. I hated having to leave him. I thought everything that was happening to me was permanent, that it was going to be a whole new way of life. As we said our farewells, I truly thought it might be three years before I would see my family and Greg again. Greg figured it would be only a couple of months.

It was difficult looking into those three faces of worry and confusion. They did not understand me but were doing their best to support me. I didn't understand it myself. Greg seemed to think it was just some simple thing I had to do, that I needed to go do it and come back so that we could pick up where we left off. I knew it would be more life-changing than that. This was too big a move of God's hand. Perhaps he did have a better understanding of this than even I. They each wanted to understand why I wanted to do this. Explaining that I didn't want to do this but that I felt I had to did not offer them any comfort. I just simply had to go.

I had no sooner boarded the plane, packed my bags in the overhead compartment, and belted myself in my seat when I was summoned to the front over the loud speaker. Excusing myself through the aisle, I made my way to a stewardess who escorted me back out of the plane. This was, of course, before 9/11 back in the 1980s, when we could walk our friends and loved ones all the way to the ramp where passengers would board the plane.

Standing there were my lifelong friends, some going back to the third grade and beyond, including Gina and Nell. Racing to the airport through crazy traffic and rain to see me off, they begged the stewardess to let me deplane so that they could say goodbye to me. I was so full of mixed emotions. Wanting to laugh and cry, we hugged and enjoyed a moment of well wishes before it was time for the plane to depart.

Boarding, again quickly making a way to my seat, I buried my face in my hands and sobbed. I cried almost the whole way to Haiti. Up until then, I had to be so strong facing off all the questions: *What business does a sheltered, blue-eyed blonde have going to a place like Haiti? What good do you think you can do there? Why don't you work in your own country? Don't we have plenty of work for you here? Why are you doing this? Don't you know how dangerous this is?* And the question that hurt the most was *How can you throw this in your parents face after they've sacrificed four years to put you through college?* Having no answers to those questions, I felt isolated and alone. Not one single person was patting me on the back or encouraging me.

And now, it was my turn.

"Why are you taking me to this awful place?" I demanded of God. *"I gave you my life, but why did you have to take it . . . all? I have tried to honor your Word to honor my father and mother. This is not honoring them! Not when the night before I leave, my understandably worried father says to me that I am going without his blessing. Why are you doing this to me? Why are you putting me in the position that I can't even obey your Word to honor my father in this? And what about Greg: why do I feel you want to take him from me too?"*

This wrestling with God would become a very significant lesson of my life. It forced me to experience that it was right to go to Haiti even though it was not "honoring" my father's wishes. This wrestling forced me into a situation that was not black and white. I knew that I knew I was right in going. Anxiety, fear, and trepidation engulfed me as I could not get any clarity on how that was true, yet I was not honoring my father. Knowing I was right in going, I had to shrug off the contradictions along with my personal set of principles. How are both right? This would later become the key lesson and example I relied upon to justify breaking a marriage vow in leaving an abusive marriage.

Never before did I feel so stripped naked. This choice to follow my faith was costing me everything. This cost me the comfort of home, a safe country, and familiar friends and family. Nothing that used to be important to me mattered anymore. I couldn't impress anyone with whom I was friends. It didn't matter what club memberships or what possessions I had acquired. It didn't matter whether or not I looked attractive. In fact, looking attractive was no longer anything I pursued as it could possibly work against me anyway. Nothing, absolutely nothing that I had put value in mattered. It seemed that so much of what I valued was no longer of any significance or importance. And during that flight, I made a quick discovery of how much I valued things that actually have no worth in this life. By the time I reached Haiti, I realized I was a complete empty *zero*!

From the window I spotted the little island in the Caribbean. Strangely, it appeared to be split in two, as if someone had drawn a line right down the middle. One half looked green and lush, like a typical tropical island. The other half looked brown, like a barren, dry land. From my vantage point in the plane, the two sides looked as if they were from completely different parts of the world. *How could one half of an island be so dramatically different from the other?* I wondered.

I was hoping to land on the green side. We headed straight down to the brown.

Haiti was far worse than I had imagined. Seeing poverty on television while eating popcorn is nothing like experiencing it. From the security of your home, you are protected from the oppression felt in just entering a place like Haiti. There was a heaviness that rested on me while I was there and it only lifted when I left. The stench and odor was like nothing I ever smelled. Everything seemed dirty and unsanitary.

I arrived folding my arms in anger. During prayer time, I questioned what kind of God, who is supposedly *good*, allows His people to live in such filth and horrible conditions. That eventually led me to Eleanor in tears questioning why I was even there.

"God has you here for a reason, and you must stay until that is revealed," she reassured me with the tenderness of a mother.

Befriending these beautiful people who suffered hunger, sickness, and desperation led to my eventually growing in awe of them for their overflowing joy, gratitude, and grace. They taught me that God meets His people where they are. They experienced God in a way I never had. God was very real to them.

Experiencing the supernatural appears somewhat dependent upon tenaciously seeking it. Crises often lead us to that place. For many of us, asking of God or truly seeking the supernatural, opening up ourselves to it (however one interprets God, our creator, or a higher power) is often done at the end of our rope or in sudden crisis. In Haiti, most people live in a continual state of crisis. That may explain the heightened supernatural evidence of good and evil I experienced.

At 20 years of age, I sought, craved, and nearly *demanded* experiencing the supernatural. What I learned is that the supernatural is very real; it's powerful, and we don't get to control it. It doesn't necessarily conform to holy writings, interpretations of such writings, or one's opinion of what's possible or not. It's unreasonable and is not subject to our wants or wishes. For me, it became real, too real. It totally overwhelmed my 20-year-old, naïve self.

I returned from Haiti with a new understanding of how little I understood God and myself. Having experienced faith in a way that made me realize how much bigger our creator is and how little I knew Him, I grew, perplexed, confused, and in awe of what I had seen. Having experienced such severe, traumatic living conditions of everyday people who lived with no hope of ever escaping the poverty in which they were born took a much harder toll on me than I realized. That I could escape at any given point, jump on a plane, and leave that hell while they had little or no hope of ever escaping, was unbearable to comprehend.

Having traveled alone, I returned alone, lacking the skills to communicate or even understand all I had experienced. There was no debriefing; I felt no one could understand what I was going through. Feeling alienated in Haiti, I returned feeling equally isolated and alone with everyone at home, too. While this experience in Haiti was life changing, having met children in the orphanage who experienced miraculous healings of incurable skin diseases and other maladies, explaining what I had experienced felt impossible to do. My inability to communicate what I wasn't even sure had changed in me caused me to isolate myself. No matter how hard I tried to be understood, I felt misunderstood. That caused me to feel lonely, vulnerable, and, eventually, depressed.

At home I was given a wonderful, warm greeting. My friends, my church family, Greg, and my family all wanted to hear about my trip. Everyone was excited to see me, placing me back in the mold I had once filled. It helped that I sent home newsletters and updates about what was happening day to day, but no one could possibly grasp what I saw, the treacherous daily life of four children being brought to the orphanage because their young mother fed them their family puppy, only to kill herself from the guilt when she saw their devastation on being told they just ate the puppy they were trying to find. I was changed. And once again, even I couldn't explain it. It felt as though I didn't know how to relate to my friends, family, or Greg . . . let alone, my future.

How I looked at chasing a career, my motivations, and my desires were all under the siege of change due to being sifted through an entirely new filter, one of which I didn't even comprehend or understand myself. Doors were opening for me to speak about my experience. I was invited to speak to students in Teen Challenge, different church groups, and even my grandparents invited me to visit them to share my experience.

All my life, my greatest fear was feeling isolated from others. I didn't mind being alone as long as I was connected emotionally to others. This fear and lack of confidence in what appeared a new direction caused me to grow further emotionally estranged from my world. People I knew and loved weren't relating to me the same. I'm sure it was me not relating to them. Having hopes of writing Eleanor Workman's book about her missionary life in Haiti, which we both believed to be my purpose, yet feeling afraid of losing connection to friends and family, I grew frustrated.

Longing to be just ordinary ole me, wanting to be like I was, I stopped accepting public speaking invitations. Having not grown up with this kind of faith, it was real and beautiful, but it came on too fast and strong for me to process. While I got what I asked for, I lacked the confidence and guidance or mentorship to proceed.

Finally, I asked God to back off, telling Him, *You are too close.* I didn't believe in myself and lacked the confidence to continue in the direction my life seemed to be going, jumping ship, running fast back to my formula faith complete with roles to fill and rules to follow. That, of course, eventually led me to empty promises. Being the gentleman that God is, He allowed me to run, but I never felt His presence leave my side. And while this was a bad move on my part, I was beginning to learn experientially, we can't go so deep that God won't go deeper still.

15

Chapter Fifteen

Dear God, if I were in control, here's what I would
do with me . . . I would like from you a husband . . .
one I could love, serve, and be devoted to, one who would
appreciate my devotion and would reciprocate the same.
—JOURNAL ENTRY, THURSDAY, SEPTEMBER 17, 1987

You don't even have to be remotely religious or spiritual to
understand what the Universe is communicating with you.
—DEEPAK CHOPRA

All I've ever wanted was to be a wife and mother. Since I was a little girl, becoming a wife and mother was what I considered would be my most important and amazing purpose. For me, it had always been why I was here.

Upon my return from Haiti, I was encouraged to attend a women's leadership conference. I didn't have any money and could not imagine asking for more after having just returned from Haiti. I felt it would be irresponsible not to get right back to work and certainly could not see asking someone to pay for me to attend a conference. My pride was too great. I did not see myself in ministry anyway. I didn't really know what was becoming of me.

My lack of confidence and not believing in myself got in the way of vision and purpose. With my dad's folded arms, tapping his foot, ready to see me begin a career, *not* a ministry, in the back of my mind, all I could think was that it was time for me to get right back to work and start making money to support myself. After all, he made my fresh college diploma possible, and I wanted to do something with it to honor him, his generosity, and his sacrifice.

Torn between two worlds, I did consider Eleanor dreaming with me that I could write her book and become her traveling companion, accompanying her at speaking engagements. I could see myself doing this and had even envisioned it my junior year at the University of Texas where I so voraciously read about the many faithful followers. Corrie ten Boom was my favorite. Her story of surviving Nazi concentration camps, her whole family suffering encampment for hiding Jewish people in Nazi-controlled Holland, encouraged my faith. Her later life of supernatural direction in traveling, speaking, and sharing her story was extraordinary. I longed to know such a supernatural life. Standing at the threshold of that dream, considering becoming to Eleanor what Corrie was given—a youthful traveling companion who did eventually marry, upon which time another was provided. Fearing that if I accepted this position, I'd forever be a spinster, doubting I could even write her book, lacking confidence to go against my father's vision for me to get a good job with my fresh college degree for which he so willingly sacrificed to pay, I struggled. Not wanting to let my parents down, I chose not to pursue this ministry opportunity. In reading my journals, I wondered, *Why, if I wanted so badly to get married, why not Greg?* I wondered what my logic was with regard to him. He was gentle and didn't persuade me in anything. Here I was worried that I'd miss the opportunity to marry and someday have a family, yet Greg was there all that while. *Was I so blind? What was I thinking?*

I had to dig deeper, still.

* * *

Growing up, I saw everything in black or white, right or wrong, yes or no, truth or lie. Period. I'd latch onto truth (or my version of it) like a pit bull, my teeth clenched in fervor, defending it until death as if at 21 years of age I knew. I have no idea where that came from. It was not from my parents. This tenaciousness did become my virtue, perhaps, in getting out of an abusive marriage, but it most often backfired as my vice. Because of this, I found myself forced back to my corner with my tail between my legs many times, contemplating how to make right of messes I'd created with dogmatism. How I wish I could show that young me all the gorgeous greens, blues, pinks, and hues between black and white. My stubbornness kept me from learning important life lessons. Regrettably, I would have to learn many life lessons the hard way.

At the University of Texas, I joined a Bible teaching group. Desiring to learn more about the Bible and God, learning about Him and communing with Him are two very different experiences, I discovered. He is personal. He teaches gently in a whisper to the soul, requiring a hushed listening deep inside. Religion, on the other hand, teaches dos, don'ts, rules, roles, and "according tos." My young zealot self could not discern the difference between relationship and religion.

In this group, I joined a group study. There, I learned social rules and mores to follow "according to the Bible." I learned the importance of marrying a man who could lead me because I was to be a "submissive" wife. I learned that I should not become "unequally yoked" and a whole list of other dos and don'ts. This is where I began to develop a "formula" for life. This is where I derailed in life.

Rather than keeping my new God awareness pure and all about love and listening within, I invited my perspective of Bible interpretation and the instruction of others to override the actual relationship. I began setting up lists, standards, and formulas for how to move forward in life. All I had to do was keep myself pure and a man would treasure me so much more than if I had sex with another before marriage. Check. I could do that. What next? If I married, he must be the "leader" and able to lead spiritually. Check. Any man I marry will know the Bible better than me. What next? I already planned on submitting, so I needed someone who knew how to lead. And so on and so on . . .

This is how I moved forward, extremely confident that I would have the best marriage ever, because I was determined to follow these instructions to a tee. Therefore, no matter the love I may have felt from or for various boyfriends, each relationship was put through a new filter. It was through these misconceptions, thinking that once I get A, B, and C in place, D will fall in its place kind of logic, that I lost my way. Eventually, I did meet just the guy to fill my checklist. Turned out, my checklist was filled perfectly by a toxic person.

To illustrate my thinking at the time, here is a poem I wrote about my new faith explaining how I relinquished my rights to myself when I was 17 years old:

I Don't Belong to Me
By: Susan Knaack—1980
(The year I became "born again" at 15 years old.)

I don't belong to me, you see,
I've been born again.
Jesus bought my life—a costly price
And His blood washed away my sin.
His Word says I'm a child of the King of Kings,
That I'm a royal priest.

Life, I'm to live abundantly
In love, joy, and peace.
I no longer decide what's best for me
Not even the "hows," "whens," or "wheres"
God created me with specific reasons in mind
I surrender to Him my cares.
Jesus lives in my heart; From God I'm no longer apart,
Never alone are we.
Jesus is my brother, my lover, my Lord, my friend
When I'm hurt, his healing mends me quickly.
I don't belong to me, you see,
I've been born again.
God has chosen me specifically for His work—a job barely begun.
The Lord loves me with agape love—unconditionally.
I may smite Him, ignore Him, refuse Him, adore Him . . .
Regardless, He loves me continuously.
I like my Lord. He is real to me,
A true personal friend.
I know he is real—not by what I feel
But by changes He's made within
I don't belong to me, you see
I've been born again.
He's the potter, I'm the clay,
and I am remolded every day.
His workmanship I will be to the end,
The process isn't usually fun.
But a perfect product I will be
When my Master is finally done.
God is not finished with me yet,
A sinner, I still be.
God sees me, though, not as I am
But through Jesus eternal Glory!
I'm His righteousness without wrinkle or blemish

A perfect mystery
His Word says I am perfect, sinless and blameless
Through His blood I am forever free.
My God is three persons all in one
The Father, Son, and Holy Spirit.
He's a mystery I can't comprehend
But with faith I receive, believe and hear it.
I believe my Lord—I take Him at His Word
He's never let me down.
Though trials come with a ghastly sting
My eyes stay fixed on His crown
I don't belong to me, you see
I've been born again
The Lord took control of my life and of my soul
To make me completely whole.
My Jesus is coming back for me
To take me home to my Father
Until that day, I travel this earth and pray
That my life be a blessing and not a bother.

This poem sums up why I attracted and was attracted to my ex-husband, a man who was reared and very well versed in the fundamental Christian mind-set I chose to adopt. We were a perfect match, each quoting our Scriptures to support our unhealthy, abusive relationship . . . even to the point that it was disobedient for me to leave.

* * *

Having watched Oprah's *Super Soul Sunday* show, I'm well aware how she allows her audience to view what appears to be her own active faith journey. Her vulnerability in this is courageous and has been very helpful to me. After much soul-searching, interviewing, and contemplation, Oprah says that true success and happiness come from fulfilling the highest, most truthful expression of self.[1]

Based on the life experiences that Oprah, Lady Gaga, Brené Brown, and others have so boldly shared from their personal lives, I've learned that oftentimes, secrets or untold truths can be the root of many great people's demise. By boldly living out our individual authenticity and truth—no matter how outrageous—we defuse the ability for others to use our past against us. We are also able to lead much more fulfilling lives.

But throughout my renewed spiritual quest, the most life-changing quote of all came from Socrates: "Know thyself."[2]

Greg's return into my life seemed serendipitous and purposeful. It deserved my delving deeper for understanding.

But first, I had to learn more about me.

16

Chapter Sixteen

You brought me out of an isolated box where I felt
NO harm yet no longer did I feel joy. Now that I'm alive
with emotion, I still find myself longing to stifle my feelings
back into that old box of a self-protected sanctuary. I don't want people
to know how I feel. Lord, crash that box. Make me transparent.
Teach me how to share myself. Take away my pride.
—JOURNAL ENTRY, THURSDAY, SEPTEMBER 17, 1987
(I WAS 23 YEARS OLD.)

Another couple of weeks went by before Greg read my story. He invited me for dinner at his country club. Sitting in the lobby waiting area, watching him walk toward me, my heart skipped. Wearing a full-length black overcoat with my manuscript in a large envelope tucked under his arm, still in his suit from work, he escorted me into the bar area. Uneasily wondering what he would have to say, yet eager to hear, I greeted him with a hug. I wanted to know what he thought, and I truly desired for him to be honest with me.

Once seated, over a glass of Chardonnay in the bar, we kept the conversation light as he kept my manuscript off to his side. His body language was suggesting that he was putting off discussing my book. I thought he was working hard to let me down easy. And that was okay. I could handle it.

Interrupting my train of thought, he said, "Is that going to be us one day?" with his eyes guiding me to join him in glancing over at an older couple sitting at a table across the room.

"Yes, we'll make ourselves keep doing and going when we get older," I heard myself say without hesitation.

What an unexpected, funny conversation we were having. Was he too wondering what the meaning of all this truly was? Was he suggesting that we might grow old together, and was I actually agreeing? It was all so tender and magical. What was happening seemed so much bigger than either one of us. We intuitively knew it wasn't simply a coincidence, so we couldn't help but wander into future possibilities and dreams.

By now, we had known each other, this time around, only a few months. We had emailed each other and text messaged. Over dinner, my heart sank as Greg pulled out my manuscript. He had read it entirely, had notes in the margins, underlined much of it, and was full of compliments about my writing.

Much to my relief and sheer exuberant joy, he was in tune with my story, which took me by surprise. I was overwhelmed with appreciation that he would take such time, effort, and interest in my story when no one else had. Of course, he was mentioned in it, and I'm sure that his involvement in my life at that time proved to be cause for his personal interest, as well. Perhaps it even answered some unanswered questions about me and why I left like I did back then. But, nevertheless, I was so moved and very touched by this. As a fellow writer, he knew the vulnerability I was experiencing.

Because he chose not to get involved with my fundraiser, I knew he wouldn't say something just to say something. He had already given me his fair share of criticism in other ventures, so I knew he would be honest—boldly so.

He reiterated that very fact when he encouraged and affirmed me. I was elated. This meant so much to me. The effort and time he offered my project meant so much more than did the compliments. It spoke volumes about the man inside this man. He was special. And he was growing very special to me at that very moment.

I had worked on this since I knew Greg years ago. It was so much a part of who I was and what I was trying to understand about life. For him to enter into my world on this level struck a special chord deep inside me.

And then he handed me a copy of the book *The Shack*. He had written a note to me on the inside cover of the book and had underlined passages that were special to him, things he wanted to share with me. This book would soon become instrumental in my digging up rich discoveries from our past.

Greg was planning to leave the next day for another trip and needed to go home to pack. He gave me two options: I could go home from there or follow him to his house so that he could pack.

I followed him home.

17

Chapter Seventeen

I'm not crazy, I was abused.
I'm not shy, I'm protecting myself.
I'm not bitter, I'm speaking the truth.
I'm not hanging onto the past, I'm facing my pain.
I'm not delusional, I lived a nightmare.
I'm not weak, I was trusting.
I'm not giving up, I'm healing.
—RENE SMITH, FREEDOM FROM NARCISSISTIC
AND EMOTIONAL ABUSE

"Mom! I just received an eviction notice!" Audrey said, calling from her dorm room. "I called Dad and he said I had to go get a job, to figure it out that he wasn't supporting my rebellion." As her sobbing intensified, she added, " "And Mom! He's killing Duchess! He said he is putting our dog down."

This led us into a classic case of what is referred to as "financial abuse" and "pet abuse." In some countries, the threat of damaging or killing a pet is outlawed as a result of this common occurrence in domestic violence cases. Many shelters are expanding by providing space for pets, as well. In response to Audrey's call, I did arrange to pick up the dog to bring her safely home with us, but that didn't erase the emotional turmoil Audrey experienced believing her dad had killed her dog.

With regard to financial abuse, as he always said he would, he stopped paying everything, including insurance, car payments, and even our daughter's education and housing. Evidently, this was about the same time my divorce registered with the IRS because I also received six letters from the IRS for the previous six years of unpaid taxes (of which I had no idea). Not only had I never paid taxes before, I had never handled any of the financials in our home, did not have a credit card apart from him, and I would soon discover a line of credit loan (of which I had no knowledge) had my name attached. All this was happening while friends who kept up with Seth texted me photos of Seth on white sand beaches and various other luxury vacations. From his "friends" I learned he and his father were building a multi-level travel business with many in our old hometown who I thought were friends of mine. They were all traveling together, making money with Seth's father, bragging to a few too many people how they set up Seth's travel business in such a way it would not be traceable because his father didn't want Seth's money going toward child support. Friends of Seth sent us photos of him from exotic locales. Seth sent photos of himself in Africa, supposedly on a mission to save sex-trafficked children. Yes, abusers commonly volunteer for organizations that support victims of abuse. Volunteerism is a favorite hiding place for abusers.

Seeking professional counsel, I removed Seth from my credit history and paid off the car loan and taxes. The IRS forgave one year of debt due to the legal Affidavit of Abuse document Carter recommended.

In the beginning, my financial heavy burdens weighed down my father. We were tanking my dad, draining his funds, compromising my dad's financial security. Over the coming years, I did eventually build my way back and beyond to excellent status financially, in part at a deathly cost to my father.

With domestic abuse on the rise, more organizations are raising support for situations like ours. Unfortunately, our situation was not unusual. Seth was self-employed, without regular wages that could be garnished. Besides, he swore to quit working before he'd ever pay us anything. The day of our divorce, Barron warned me of this. "Susan, he will never freely pay you the child support or insurance directed in this divorce decree; therefore, you will need to find a way to make it until all the money is past due," he said.

With foresight, he added, "Once *all* the money due you is *past* due, take him to court *one* time. Otherwise, legal fees will eat up what little you will get."

I did precisely as he said. With the threat of jail and a judge eager to see him there, I eventually received most of the child support he owed without any medical or insurance provisions (just as Barron predicted), but that wouldn't come to pass until several years later. In the meantime, I applied for waitress jobs, secretary jobs, hostess positions, college campus jobs, and career positions. Nothing came of it. My dad sustained us and paid off Audrey's school expenses so she could finish out the year, putting him in serious financial peril. The financial stress felt like a steel jacket, heavy, immoveable, and confining.

As Sophia said, "We were every man for himself."

We were. Not only did my children lose everything at home, they lost the doting, mindful, aware mother that I was. Leaving my marriage spun me into a frenzy of survival and terminal trauma, leaving them to figure out how to cope through their trauma in a way they had never imagined. My plate was full, and for the first time, I had to save me before I could reach back to rescue them. Hoping they'd hang on, I moved as fast I could to get myself afloat. We were drowning . . . and we were going down fast.

Most shelters for the abused offer counseling for the entire family. Looking back, I now realize that while a shelter environment would have been traumatic in many respects and that some would not have accepted us with teenage boys, we still would have received immediate emotional care, which we all desperately needed.

Knowing what I know about shelters today, even though I managed to move on my own, services from a shelter or women's center should have been my immediate *first* call. And anyone helping a friend or loved one going through a similar situation should encourage that as the very first step. These centers offer education, counseling, and financial, legal, and medical aid. Oh, if I had only known then the many benefits a call to a shelter could provide. Anyone thinking about leaving should contact a shelter long before they leave and create an escape plan with professionals equipped to assist them. The beautiful souls at shelters like The Family Place in Dallas or the Women's Center of Tarrant County are Ordinary Angels in waiting. Most cities have organizations such as these. People are available to help.

Once Audrey was financially situated and reinstated into her dorm, I received another call from her.

"You don't even care about me anymore," Audrey cried. "You have moved on with your life and really have no concern about me!"

Audrey called me from her college dorm room to discuss what degree plan she should choose. Expecting me to tell her what to do, I encouraged her to dig deep inside herself for answers. "You will need to answer this for yourself, Audrey. The answer is in you," I said.

Accustomed to dictation, still shackled in self-expectation to comply, my giving her a wide open space to explore rather than a wall in which to comply, she responded in tears, venting her frustration. What she didn't know is I was giving her the freedom and trust my parents afforded me.

Allowing her to complete her venting, I reassured her, "Audrey, there is no one on this earth who loves you more than I. This *is* loving you. I trust you. You are now free to trust yourself and believe in yourself," adding, "You will never have anyone dictate how to live your life ever again."

I went on to share that I was relearning how to truly love and trust myself again, too. "We are no longer shackled to *comply*. We are free. Real love offers freedom. We are no longer in a relationship where you need to fear hitting those places of condemnation, judgment, and fear of failure.

"You are free, honey." I couldn't say it enough. "You are loved, trusted, and free."

I reminded her that I, too, was remembering how to live again.

"I'm passing on this freedom to you," I said. "This freedom is scary for me, too. So embrace it, honey. Trust yourself. I trust you, and I love you so very much." As she struggled with me, I struggled, too.

While this is exactly how my mother and father loved—and parented—me, it may have been buried, but it wasn't lost. Having not known this kind of love in my adult life sapped my emotional development. In some respects, I was the 23-year-old who married into oppression. While 48 in actual years, I had the maturity of a 23-year-old in many regards. With underdeveloped maturity, my children and I were discovering and learning to live and love together all over . . . or perhaps, for the first time.

This brought me to a point of acceptance: Finally accepting me, right where I was and was not. No longer wrestling with what ifs, if onlys, what could have beens, and what should bes, accepting that I could not understand God, I could not anticipate Him, and that I could only rest in the fact that I was not in control.

Surprisingly, it brought me peace. Rather than asking how or why I messed up all our lives, I asked, "What am I supposed to learn from all of this?" I learned that it wasn't all a mistake, after all. "You have four beautiful children who have a purpose and must find their destiny in all this," Greg would often remind me.

Moving forward, no longer shaking my fist in the air at God, quieting myself, I sat still. I realized that life doesn't guarantee me anything. I am not owed anything. As my children healed, I rejoiced gratefully. I realized that they, too, must process through their faith, shattered dreams, disappointments, expectations, and assumptions. They must each find their way of reaching up and out. Through sharing their own stories with their friends, they would discover friends reciprocating in kind, opening up to them. They would realize that we are not the only ones, as many are hurting . . . just like us. We are not alone; together, we are empowered and can overcome. And it was only through the process of sharing that my children began to see other's pain, looking beyond their own. Baby steps. We kept going.

A couple weeks later, Audrey called. "Mom, I have made some decisions," she said with great confidence and clarity. She continued, laying out an amazingly clear vision and plan for herself. It involved finishing up her school year, earning a dual sociology and marketing degree, and moving to be closer to me and her siblings. She was excited and at peace and I could hear such strength in her vision. She felt good about her plan. And the kids and I were looking forward to her returning to be near us.

Periodically, as I felt myself mature or emerge more, I'd say to Gina, "I think I'm back now. Am I me yet?"

"Well, you're closer," she would honestly respond. "You're definitely closer."

One day Winston said to her, "Thank you, Gina, for the change you brought about in our mother." He went on to say, "We don't know this mother, but we sure like this Susan better."

"This is the only Susan we know, Winston." Gina said. "This is your mother."

After a few more years of healing, I said to Gina, "I think I'm back now. Am I me yet?"

For years she'd say, "Almost. You're almost back. Yeah, you are getting there . . ."

Finally, almost five years after I left Seth, I heard her say, "Yes, Susan, you are back." Finally, Gina said, "You are all you again."

18

Chapter Eighteen

Survival mode is supposed to be a phase that helps save your life.
It is not meant to be how you live your life.
—MICHELLE ROSENTHAL

You never need to apologize for how you chose to survive.
—UNKNOWN

While Greg was away, I emailed him saying that he seemed to have been strategically placed in the middle of my two greatest life crises and that I made the greatest mistake in letting him go years ago. I also told him that if it was wrong for me, it was probably wrong for him, too. Apparently, two opposing truths can both be true and right. This lesson keeps circling back at me, and I'm still in the process of absorbing it. While I believed I made a mistake and should have chosen Greg back then, Greg argued that we had to have our children. I believed both were right. How can two conflicting truths be correct? I do not know.

Unsure of what he would think of this, I realized my assertions could have very well run him off. But willing to take the risk, I sent the letter anyway. He called me when he received it and invited me to come see him. When I arrived, he didn't say much about the letter other than that if he didn't like it, I wouldn't be with him right then.

This led to a unique relationship of utter freedom with no expectations, boundaries, or rules. We were both passionate, willing, and wanting. I'm sure this whole thing was against his better judgment, because I was still traumatized and not anywhere near emotionally healed. It just was what it was. So we maintained distance, yet we reeled in at times, too.

I'm sure he didn't know what to do with me and this strange interruption I was becoming in his life. But something special was growing between us, and he helped me work through my many crises. I deeply needed him. My God, I needed him. He was my lifeline to hope. But he remained self-protected. I recognized it. That's how I lived much of my life. But I discovered that hurt comes with self-protecting, as much if not more, than with openly loving. For the first time, I conducted myself without any self-protection, completely vulnerable and open only with him. And at least with loving, one is the richer for it. With both of us having limitations on what we could give and receive, I wanted.

Never had I allowed myself into a relationship where I opened myself completely, with no boundaries or expectations. Letting us organically become one without lines of definition was both invigorating and frightening. Knowing I could not put any expectations on myself, much less him, I explored a new emotional territory of my own soul. Utterly vulnerable, with no self-protection, I moved closer and closer to him, throwing all caution to the wind. I could take the risk because it was *Greg*. He was back in my life. We were no accident. He was supposed to be in my life, and I was excited as to where it might lead. Curious, impatient, and lacking self-discipline, I threw myself into us.

Sex outside of marriage had been the unforgivable, indeed, near blasphemous sin to me in my religious life. In all my Bible instruction, sex was strictly forbidden outside of marriage. As a divorcee, I am damned if I do and damned if don't remarry because according to Matthew 5:32, either way I am an adulteress. "[W]hosoever marry her that is divorced committeth adultery" (KJV). Something was terribly systemically wrong with my former religious life. *So what did I have to lose?*

Embracing my humanness in opening myself to Greg actually brought me closer to my maker because my God did not leave as I had previously thought He would. Not only did God not leave me, I felt Him nestled close, remaining where He had always been. His love never left me because of the so-called sin of divorce or sex outside of marriage. In fact, it was through this experience that I learned more about unconditional love in a new and beautiful way.

In my brokenness, I could never hope to be a healthy partner to a man. I wasn't capable of giving what's necessary in a healthy relationship. Being so needy, having so little to give, my huge needs drained others as I took and endlessly needed. Anyone in my life at that time was reaching out with a life raft at the risk of drowning if they let me hold on too tight. I could have taken anyone down with me. I wasn't healthy, nor did I feel that God required me to be. I felt free to just be. And I felt safe learning to be just me with Greg. He gave me what I needed; God blessed me with Greg.

But why?

Who are you? I wondered to God.

Dear God, How can this be? How can you be holy and bless me with this relationship that is healing me yet seems to contradict all that your Word says is good and right? The Bible says I'm an adulterer. It says I'm an adulterer even if I marry again. Yet you don't treat me as such.

Through discovering myself with Greg, my intimacy with God grew. No longer focused on denying myself, I focused on learning about myself. In learning about me without worry of submission, I grew.

"We were never like this before," Greg said wryly one day. "We only kissed . . . a lot."

Greg was my only intimate experience outside of marriage. I no longer wondered if a clap of thunder was going to sound while lightning struck, bringing angry disapproval from God over our unpardonable sin. It was a paradigm shift in my thinking. Because according to my former belief, we were the epitome of the most "ungodly" relationship . . . yet somehow, we weren't. We were actually a beautiful gift. A treasure of deep healing.

Yet doubts remained.

Sensing that he was already in a relationship before our first encounter in his office, and perhaps even still, I felt as if I had become his secret. *Was I sharing him with someone else?* Never would I have thought I'd be willing to put myself in that situation. But never would I have thought I'd be an abused, pathetic divorcee either. In my brokenness, I was taking and receiving so much, much more than I was giving. Having little or nothing to give, I would not have dared to expect anything more from him than what he chose to offer. Life had taken such an extremely strange turn, and with it, so did I. In all of this mess, I was discovering grace with no defining walls, restrictions, or expectations. Sharing my concerns with him, telling him that I was not at all healed, I asked him why he was investing so much time into our relationship. He told me it was because he knew it was just a phase I was going through, one that he knew all too well. He, too, had gone through this phase.

Entering his life a broken, hurting, half-empty shattered remnant of me, not anywhere near fully healed, I was a walking open wound, desperately craving soothing balm, just what Greg offered me. I could not resist nor did I ever even try very hard to do so. I wanted him. I *needed* him. And because this was Greg, after all, I rationalized that it was okay.

19

Chapter Nineteen

*Little victories lead to bigger victories, that affect
the battles that eventually win wars.*
—UNKNOWN

*Give yourself permission to be excited and celebrate small
victories because they are subtly guiding the way.*
—KRISTIN KOONCE, kristinkoonce.com

"Susan, I would *never* hire you," said my longtime friend Daniel, who was a partner in his own law firm. "How would I explain *that* to my wife?" he continued.

"Explain *what* to your wife?" I demanded.

"Put your hair in a ponytail, wear glasses, and a muumuu," he said, "But don't look too good for interviews."

So this is how it's going to be now that I'm single? I'm a threat to married women now? Seriously?

Single women can suffer a unique alienation from certain women and men. It doesn't matter how conservatively dressed and carefully one carries herself. Simply because she's single and not unattractive, she can be a certain threat. A woman who had been single much longer than I told me how shocking it was for her to find that while married, she could chat and laugh all night long at parties with other women's husbands, never giving it a thought. But as soon as she was divorced, the same women would grab their husband's arm when she engaged them in casual conversation, pulling them away from her. A similar shift occurred for me, as well. While I conducted myself the same with friends and colleagues alike, my intentions seemed to be scrutinized under an invisible magnifying glass.

At first, I tried playing myself down, dressing down, and minimizing myself for some such insecure people. Soon enough, I realized that doing this didn't work for my insecure (now ex) husband, and it wouldn't for any of these people either. Their problem was not mine. And I began to walk tall as I came into being me. Either you will like me, the *real* me, or not. I'm fine either way.

After having played myself down my whole married life, I was *so* ready to be all that I could be. It was exciting becoming the best version of me possible without a care of how it might make others feel. This attracted other confident men and women to me. Confidence attracts confidence.

What I learned in trying to understand men is true in understanding all relationships, be it work, family, or pleasure. Others fall in line when we get right with ourselves by walking as authentically true to ourselves as possible. It's amazing, most relationship complications cease when we prioritize being true to ourselves without worry about how it affects others. No matter who you choose to be, some will love you and some won't like you. By being true to yourself, you will attract the jobs, the family members, the friends, and the romantic relationships right for you.

Today, I'm in great company, befriending and talking openly and freely to many married men and women whom I not only don't threaten but also enjoy true friendship. Our world is full of great people. When we are our best, we attract the best. I'm sure those insecure people are all around me, too, but I don't even see them anymore.

Pursuing employment, I chose the same tactic, exuding the same confidence, looking and being my very best. The local steakhouse said that I needed experience. The firm said they were concerned I'd soon leave a secretary position for something better. Many redirected me to apply online. After numerous online applications, I was feeling terribly discouraged. I wondered, *How do you get experience?*"

I was either overqualified due to education or underqualified due to no experience. Finally, a retired former Dallas Cowboys football player, David Howard, connected me with a lady at Cowboys Stadium. And I finally landed my first job working part time at the concession stands.

"Yes!!" I clapped my hands. *I have a job!*

Jill showed me to the uniform store where I picked out my uniform: a light blue top and navy slacks. Though it was part time, complete with a uniform, name tag, and walkie-talkie, I embraced it with gratitude.

"Hey, what are you, the hall monitor?" asked a football fan as I stood between my two hotdog stands.

"Hey, I'm important," I said, going along with his sense of humor. "Don't you see I have a walkie-talkie *and* a badge?"

This initiated a fun conversation. Little did he know I had previously burned the cheese at a nacho stand in the prestigious clubs and was now sentenced to the "nosebleed" section where he found me supervising two less impressive hotdog stands.

I also had just visited Gina, who was a guest of our mutual friends in their private suite. Several of them had flown to town in their private plane for the game, and all had been enjoying a full day of game-centered festivities when it all came to a screeching halt at my entrance. Jaws dropped and eyes began filling with tears when they saw me in uniform.

Breaking their gasps of "Oh no," I corrected their unspoken angst, saying, "I am so thankful for this job. Please. This is great. I'm happy to be working."

It was a great beginning. In fact, before I burned the cheese at the nacho stand in the club area, I would occasionally see some of the guys like Preston Pearson and Ed "Too Tall" Jones from the retired players association. It was fun. Besides, working at the AT&T Dallas Cowboy Stadium was energizing. It was grand, it was clean, and people took pride in working there. Fans took pride, too. Most fans even cleaned up after themselves, I noticed. They did not leave their trash for someone else to clean the way fans often do at other stadiums. I even worked some concerts, enjoying a peek at the various shows.

Returning to my post, the man who met me up in the top section came back to visit. "Apparently all you do is stand around," he said jokingly. "What do I gotta do to get a job like that?" he asked.

"I am supervising!" I said in jest, placing my hands on my hips. Turns out, he had been guaranteed some of the best 50-yard-line tickets in the stadium by his childhood friend who coached one of the teams. Due to some misunderstanding of too many tickets issued, John gave up his seat, landing him in the nosebleed section near my stands. Our meeting resulted in an invite to the victory party following the game. I enjoyed spending the evening with the team coach, his family, and friends.

The bottom line? I enjoyed many adventures as a result of working at the Cowboys Stadium. My advice? Never despise small beginnings. Embrace opportunities, no matter how small, and make them big . . . or at the very least, fun!

20

Chapter Twenty

*If all else perished, and he remained, I should still continue
to be; and if all else remained, and he were annihilated,
the universe would turn to a mighty stranger.*
—EMILY JANE BRONTÈ

"Susan . . .?"

Oh dear, I thought, as this was Gina's familiar shaken voice on the phone in her "bearing bad news" voice.

"Have you watched the national news today?" she gently inquired.

"No . . ." I hesitantly replied, worried at what I was about to hear.

"I have something to tell you," she continued. "It's all over the news and it involves Winston."

"Oh my God! What is it?" I asked, bracing myself.

She then began to tell me that in over 30 years, this had never happened, but due to the massive amount of rainfall over the past few days, the school parking lot at Winston's school had suddenly flooded, and Winston's Mercedes was floating there along with school buses and vehicles belonging to the entire student body and staff! It turned out that this event became national headline news and was played over and over again on Fox and CNN News that day and night. And it had happened at the very beginning of his new school year.

"A flood?" I exclaimed. "In Arlington, Texas? Seriously?" I erupted into hysterical laughter. "Are you kidding me? But, okay, how is Winston?

"Just please tell him that I am glad he is okay and that we will make it through this," I continued.

"Susan, I can't believe you're laughing," said Gina. "Mothers are crying, students are crying, and *you*? You are *laughing*!

"I've been dreading making this call," she continued. "And I'm amazed at your reaction."

"Gina, I've lost almost every*thing* of value to me short of my children and their scrapbooks," I explained. "It's all just stuff," I added, "and I've learned the hard way I can live very well with or without it."

Unfortunately for Winston, it was Seth's Mercedes. Earlier, Seth had requested that we switch out the Excursion for his car because he needed the truck to haul things. After selling our grand home, he moved back into the river property. The truck was a better vehicle for that location. But in the aftermath of the flood, we learned that Seth had let the insurance lapse, and there was no coverage on the car of any kind. It was a total loss. I had no money, we were down a car, and everything with my kids seemed to be going wrong.

"Mom, that car gave me some independence," Winston said. "It gave me some freedom up here. And I *loved* that car, Mom. I would never have purposefully let anything happen to it, I promise." Like many of his classmates, he struggled with his loss.

"Dad said I should have known better since I had experience with floods," Winston added, essentially beating himself up over something which he had no control. "I told the teacher that I was going to leave the classroom and get my car, but she wouldn't let me leave. I wish I had followed my instinct and just forced my way out."

"Winston, they were concerned about snakes and whatever else might be in that high fast-rising water," I explained. "Letting you out of class would put you and them in potential danger of lawsuits or something even worse."

Enter Seth, who later said, "You should have left anyway, Winston. You knew better. You had experience."

Winston was crushed by that exchange. I told him, "If your dad loved that car so much, he would have kept it insured. What concerns me more is that you were driving that car illegally without any protection for you! Furthermore, your dad didn't protect you, but he faults you for not protecting a *car*? Not one car survived that flood, Winston," I continued. "Not one."

It amazed me that a father could accuse, ridicule, and badger his son about negligence when he wouldn't pay the child support or health insurance he promised and signed for in the divorce decree. I held that fact to myself. Winston didn't need to know about that. It was mine to handle.

"I'm so sorry, Mom."

"Don't be so hard on yourself, Winston," I said. "A couple students tried to rescue their vehicles and almost drowned, requiring a fireman to swim after them, risking his life. This flood came on so suddenly, Winston. No one saw it coming! Just let it go," I continued. "You did the right thing. Had you tried, you would have put yourself and others at risk. Let it *go*!"

Gina encouraged me to call the husband of her friend Laura, whose husband, Pat, was the executive manager of a car dealership in Dallas. I borrowed my dad's car until my dad finally offered to help us buy a car so that he could have his back.

Knowing our situation, Pat was eager to help, resulting in a really nice used Lexus for my kids to drive and a great price on much-needed work to be done on my Jag. Best of all, Pat handed me keys to a brand new convertible Z to drive while my Jag was in the shop. With perfect seasonal spring weather, that car with the roof down and the radio blaring became my oasis. I would drive and dream. Experiencing that car was a source of tangible encouragement and confirmation that we were going to get out of our current contagion of challenges. I just had to hold on and trust. Someday, this was going to turn around. That car helped me believe in a new reality.

Many months later, when the school year was just about over, I drove my Lexus to Winston's school to pick him up. The principal was outside. After telling her the story about how the Lexus replaced the Mercedes, she then told me the backstory of the Mercedes and why it remained in the parking lot almost the entire year. Seth had sued the school over his Mercedes. The school attorney prepared almost a year to present their defense to Seth in court, only to have Seth pull a no-show the day of court. Mortified and utterly embarrassed, I asked what attorney had represented them. How dreadful that we would cost them when they had been so good to us and to Winston.

It was my nephew's girlfriend's father, the principal told me.

Unbeknownst to us, this man quietly represented the school at no cost on behalf of Winston. Winston and my nephew spent many days and enjoyed many meals at that man's family table throughout the entire year completely unaware of that lawsuit. We all gathered in their lovely home for a fabulous pre-prom party and photo ops, still unaware of that lawsuit. Throughout all our interactions with them, that lawsuit remained a secret from Winston, Winston's friends, my brother's family, and me.

Not until the very end of the year, as I stood on the sidewalk with the principal, did I ever understand why Winston's Mercedes was the only vehicle left in the parking lot, rotting and molding, almost the entire school year. Seth would not tow it, nor would he give permission for the school to have it towed. It sat there every day as an embarrassing reminder for Winston to face in front of all his peers and school staff every day. Until this moment, we had no idea the reason was because Winston's dad had that car tied up in a lawsuit.

Some Ordinary Angels work on our behalf and are so far removed, we don't see them. I almost didn't learn about this man and the people around him supporting us while hiding in plain sight. I'm grateful for this example of good church people, good people embracing the Christian faith, living it out discretely and authentically. Directly addressing some Ordinary Angels seems to almost disrupt that fragile whispering flow of God's hand moving. Sometimes, it's best to simply sit still and take in the sweet aroma knowing their reward is far more than any thank you we could personally offer.

21

Chapter Twenty-One

Cherish the friend who tells you a harsh truth
wanting ten times more to tell you a loving lie.
—ROBERT BRAULT

"Be careful what you wish (or ask) for" is commonly quoted and apropos to my teeing up Greg for a glorious fluttery, feel-good compliment that swung back at me more like a blunt-faced club.

"I need you, Greg, to tell me about me," I said as we cuddled in his living room on the brown leather couch, each with a glass of Chardonnay. Looking across his dining room table through his picturesque window overlooking the golf course, I also asked, "What was I like before I got married?"

Greg's full-circle return into my life was cause for contemplation and, looking back to the time we dated, for discovery, as well. Mainly, I wanted to know why we didn't end up together. What happened? And why was he in my life now? Desperate to understand how this mixed-up marriage and life "happened to me," I looked for the right time to ask. From that first glance at his picture in that business magazine, this was the single most important question I had been waiting to ask of him. By now, he knew a little more about my tumultuous past. The right moment had finally arrived.

He answered in one word, without any hesitation. But it pained him to say, "You were a 'thumper.'"

"A thumper . . .?" I asked.

Hesitatingly, he continued, "Yeah, Susan, you were a Bible thumper." Rising from his couch where we were seated, he started pacing the room.

"Your ex wasn't the only one who did this to your children," he went on to say. "You did this, too."

"I did not!" I quickly snapped back at him through a furrowed brow, standing to my feet in his living room, facing him off nose-to-nose.

But it was no contest.

"You did too, Susan." Holding my face tenderly in his hands, he continued in a well-intentioned whisper, "I promise you did. And let me tell you why I know.

"My mother was a Presbyterian and my father, a Methodist. I grew up going to the Methodist church with my father one week and to the Presbyterian Church with my mother the next. I was working through my own spiritual confusion," he said. He continued, but I was listening between the lines.

In that moment, I realized he was right. I *had* been a thumper!

This helped me see that some of what Seth had done to me, I had done to others. It also helped me see the error and damage or hurt I must have caused Greg, my children, and others. But it also helped me see I couldn't blame everything on Seth. I not only willingly walked into this, I was somewhat *like* this.

Though it pained me to do so, I realized I *did* push people away with my dogmatic approach and my claims to such an incredible understanding of God's Word that I desperately wanted to impart on others. I wound up shoving God's Word and my understanding of it down other's gullets. I had to face this and get right with those I had bulldozed over by misusing the "truth" as *I* saw it!

What a gross realization I had to face about *myself.* What irony to hear this at a time when I realize, now, how little I know about what I believe or understand. What once seemed as clear to me as dew on a blade of grass is now as clear to me as looking for that blade of grass from the moon. I've never felt so ignorant of understanding or knowledge.

This helped me appreciate Greg and all my other amazing friends and family who loved me through all those years even more.

Fortunately, many have been quick to forgive.

Gina hesitated to confirm what he said. But she eventually admitted that I had been overly zealous with her and that it did tend to push her from me so many years ago. I was able to get right with and thank people for loving me all those years in spite of me! When I brought it up, I could tell some needed to unload some extra baggage of what I said or the guilt I put on them, most of which occurred before I married or even knew Seth. Yep, it was all me, offending people without the help or blame of anyone else.

"Why, if I was such a thumper, did you like me?" I asked, twirling back to face him from gazing out his window. At this, he only paused and looked at me as if he could see right through me. His expression, I could not read. He never answered with a word and his eyes remained silent.

* * *

I would rather walk with a friend in the dark,
than alone in the light.
—HELEN KELLER

One morning, I awakened to Greg sending a text that read *today would be a good day to read the book.* Inside my copy of *The Shack,*

Greg had written that it would be a great book to read on a snow day. The month of February provided just that. Our whole town was snowed in as ice covered all the roads

The story gripped me as the main character, Mac, asked so many of the questions with which I was struggling. I came to a place where Mac had faced his challenge and was going back to face life with his new perspective. The book was resonating until the main character passed over into a more sound understanding of his crisis and was headed towards healing. I was where Mac had been, but I could not bear to follow him where he was going. Not ready, closing the book, I thought of an old box of journals stashed under my bed. Having been years since dusting them off, curiously compelled, I traded reading *The Shack* for reading journals from my post-college days.

Astounded, I found a three-page prayer for Greg that I had written after returning from Haiti. I wrote about Greg, my own hopes and dreams for him. He was the only guy I ever wrote about other than my husband. I had pages of prayers and thoughts to God and never mentioned another man other than Greg. Devouring my memories, seeking answers, I read the inked pain and hardships of my marriage. It would be days before I could pick up *The Shack* again. Feeling regret, wishing I could go back and do it over, I realized I was exactly where I was again 23 years later after writing that prayer for Greg. It was as though I was being given a second chance. In time warp fashion, I was back facing the same fork in the road with the same man in my life.

Greg was anxious to read my prayer. I couldn't wait to show it to him. After dinner one night, propped up by pillows on his bed, we were settled in together and he asked me to read it to him. I couldn't. I said, "You read it," handing him my pink floral-patterned padded journal with my heart written all over the pages. He read my prayer about him. It was powerful and heartfelt.

"You prayed for my business, my employees, and my future success," he said. "I have become what you prayed for me."

We sat in silence for a long while.

He then asked if he could read the next entry. This entry was where I found myself once again just 23 years later. It detailed my hopes and dreams of someday getting married, what I wanted my marriage to look like, the kind of man I hoped to marry, and the wife I hoped to be. After he read it, he asked, "Do you know on what day this was entered?" pointing to the date I had written. I wasn't quite sure what he was asking me and just looked at him with questioning eyes. He then said, "This is my birthday." I had written my hopes and dreams about marriage to God on Greg's twenty-seventh birthday.

Over a period of months, we would get together. We would prop pillows up on his bed and watch movies. One day, I brought *The Notebook* over for us to watch.

"I know why you had me watch this," he said with a grin after it was over. "It reminds you of us."

Tingling inside with great pleasure and thrilled that he made that connection, I knew we each were communicating something so much deeper than words.

"Yes, it does," I concurred. "It reminds me of us." There—it was spoken.

Everything that needed to be said was spoken in that moment. There was a longing, a yearning, a wondering if and what if going on inside both of us.

Then I asked a question that would send me on the scavenger hunt of my life.

In the movie, after the young couple separates, the man sends love letters every day to the girl of his dreams for a year. She never received them because her mother intercepted them.

Relishing the tender moment, remembering the love letters I sent to Greg from Haiti, I asked, "Do you remember the letters I sent you from Haiti?"

Anger disrupted like a bomb in our precious moment as Greg sat straight up, dropping me to his side, exclaiming, "You never sent me letters from Haiti. I didn't get any letters!"

Anger from years ago surfaced through his raging voice.

"I wrote you three letters!" I said, escalating my voice. "In fact, I remember seeing copies of them in a green folder just a year before I left my marriage. I ran across them while thumbing through some papers in an old desk. I had written 'I love you' across the top of each of them in big, bold letters!

"I remember feeling weird and a little awkward about sending my love letters to you through my mother," I continued. "Mail in Haiti was so unreliable, so all my correspondence was sent in a large envelope for my mother to distribute in the states. That's why I assumed they were copies she kept. They were part of a bundle I sent her. She sent out my letters individually from home."

"I never got those . . ." he confirmed again in a curt manner with a furrowed brow.

I was sick. I could not imagine what happened to the letters. Just like in the movie, did my mother keep them from him? She wouldn't do that! She absolutely adored Greg and was a hopeless romantic. In fact, he won her heart when he gave me a pair of silver earrings. We were standing outside church with my family, waiting to see a Christmas special. Greg kept patting his pocket and looking at me. I looked at him askance, and he just smiled and kept patting his pocket, like something just might be in there. I dug in his pocket, and there were the most beautiful silver teardrop-shaped earrings! My mother loved how he gave those to me. He won her heart at that moment. So I knew that she wouldn't have kept my letters from him. So what happened? I became obsessed with finding out.

My Haiti basket was a hand-woven treasure I bought myself. It held memorabilia from my Haiti excursions. It was in the garage of our river home, along with many other keepsakes and various belongings. I had put off retrieving it to avoid additional confrontations with Seth. This was just the motivation I needed, however.

Kevin discouraged me from going, sensing danger and warning me of consequences of breaking an active legal protective order. But my brother agreed to drive me and off on a four-hour mission to the garage for that Haiti basket we went.

With the truck loaded, I leaped into my seat and began rummaging through the basket. I found a paperback journal. I wrote of my first day and how Greg drove me to the airport with my parents to see me off. I also wrote of my first impressions of Haiti. There were six short entries. All but one mentioned Greg and how I didn't want to let go of him, how I didn't know how to but how I thought I was supposed to. And then, I read, *I wonder if I should have Mom send Greg those letters . . .*

It was me! *I* kept those letters from going to him! Oh, the gravity of this was so heavy and disturbing to me. I was sick! No wonder Greg held me at arm's length! I knew I had hurt him in the past. But now, I knew how, when, and why. I felt so stupid and couldn't imagine what he must have gone through at that time. We had talked of marriage. We had declared our love for each other and then I just disappear?! I know I returned to him because I gave him his Bible after Haiti. My prayer for him in my journal was after Haiti, as well. But things were different between us. Now, I understand why.

Forgiving myself for this didn't come easy. I could only hope that reading my story would give him some sort of understanding of my internal struggle. Trying not to lead him on if I was supposed to let him go, I didn't send the letters. There was a better way to express my thoughts to him, of course. I took my questions to God. *Why? Why, Haiti?! What was the meaning in all that? Why did I leave Greg? Are you bringing us together now? What is this all about?! Are you mad at me? Are you mad I didn't write Eleanor's book? Is that why my life is so messed up? Is this punishment?*

The following months with Greg ushered in a time of rapid healing for me. It wasn't just the passion. Greg was a sounding board for me. I took him opportunities, ideas, and possible plans. He would advise me and let me know what he thought about them.

He was a true friend.

* * *

Friendship marks a life even more deeply than love.
Love risks degenerating into obsession.
Friendship is never anything but sharing."
—ELIE WIESEL

One day Greg called me. "What are you doing?" he asked. I told him it was the first time I could remember since we moved that I was alone in my own home. All the kids were gone and I was enjoying watching a movie all by myself.

"What movie are you watching?"

"*Remember the Titans,*" I told him. It was a favorite of mine as it reminded me of the great relationships I enjoyed in high school that were similar to those portrayed in the movie.

"That is such a typical Susan movie," he responded.

This is what drove him so deep into my heart. He knew me. He remembered what I was like and truly knew me. That he knew it was a typical movie for me meant the world to me. At a time when I felt so buried and far from myself, it provided reassurance and security. After discussing the movie and a little bit of light chatter, Greg invited me to church.

We went to church together that Sunday, dressed in suits like we used to do 23 years ago. Revisiting memories on the drive there, he shared that he was a member of the church we attended with some old friends so many years ago. This particular morning, we would be visiting another church, however. Everyone there was very friendly and welcoming and really seemed to love Greg. In fact, the minister announced from the pulpit how pleased they were to see him visiting. Our presence was easily recognized as we were the only white people there.

This African-American church body started off as clients of Greg's and quickly became friends. They asked Greg to become a deacon, to which Greg didn't initially respond. The pastor made a follow-up call to Greg asking him why. Greg explained that he was already a member of a church where he worshiped with his children and did not see fit to change memberships. Greg also explained that because he was divorced, he could not be a deacon in his church. This pastor said that in *his* church, Jesus could use Greg even if he was divorced, adding that nobody said anything to him about him changing memberships or becoming a member. The pastor went on to say that sometimes they just needed a white man. To this, Greg accepted the position of deacon and had served many years.

The sermon was similar to what I had been journaling. Becoming enlightened to what I had asked for in my journaling, I began to see a pattern. I was like the Israelites who were miraculously freed from slavery and fed as told in the Old Testament. Then they started complaining, asking God for a king because they wanted to be like other nations when, as the story is told, God desired them to be free people to govern themselves. Still wanting a king, God gave them Saul. The name Saul means "asked for" or "Inquired of God." Saul was a bad king.

My journaling revealed that of all that I asked, most everything came my way. This served to heighten my awareness of how careful and mindful we must be when wanting or asking for something.

In her book *The Hiding Place*, Corrie ten Boom wrote of her miraculous survival and release from Ravensbruck concentration camp. A movie was made about her book. In her sequel, *A Tramp for the Lord*, I was inspired by the supernatural life she lived traveling all over the world telling her story about how her faith and how God sustained her.

While at the University of Texas, I read these books, praying to meet someone like Corrie so I could write her book. Corrie had a traveling companion. I even remember thinking how I would love to be a companion for someone like Corrie.

My dreams matched Eleanor's. Eleanor lived a miraculous life similar to Corrie's and had prayed for someone to write her book. She believed I was sent to do so. Corrie would stand in line to buy a train ticket without a dime only to be handed a ticket from the man in front of her before she reached the cashier. Corrie would then hop on the train to the destination of that ticket. She'd disembark to wait while sitting on her suitcase only to find a perfect stranger come for her saying they were waiting for her. I have a shoebox full of Eleanor's interviews on tape telling the same type of extraordinary stories. Desiring that kind of life, I asked for it and was handed it, only to complain and push it away saying, no, I want a husband. And what did I get? A Saul, an "asked for."

Being careful—indeed, mindful—of what we ask for is the lesson of my life. Meeting Greg thrust me into my journals for answers. The answer was becoming clear. Choices and opportunities are what catching a wave is to a surfer. You've got to seize it or miss it. You also have to live with it, even if the best one was right behind. If it's too big for your ability, ride it anyway. Life will stretch and grow us. Learn when to say no. Finding balance is all in the journey. It all requires risk. When you fall, get back up and try again.

Looking at all my missed opportunities, I didn't recognize my apparent self-sabotaging until the final edit of this book. I could choose to continue beating myself up or I could learn from the experience and ride the next wave. But with all those missed opportunities, I wondered why we self-sabotage in the first place.

In her article "Why Do We Self-Sabotage? You may be self-sabotaging without even realizing it," Dr. Ellen Hendriksen, a psychologist, states: "Self-sabotage can interfere with the best-laid plans and goals. Why do we do it? Turns out, there are many reasons why instead of shooting for the moon, we end up aiming right for our foot. Self-sabotage is any action that gets in the way of your intent. . . ."[1]

There are countless ways we sabotage ourselves. So why do we do it? Here are four big reasons:

1. Self-Worth—feeling undeserving of happiness, suffering self-imposed inadequacy.

2. Control—controlling our own failure feels better than being blindsided by the surprise of success and unexpected direction it may bring.

3. Perceived Fraudulence—with promotions to new positions, we feel fear of having further to fall.

4. Familiarity of that which we know is preferable to the unknown.

To summarize it succinctly, Dr. Hendricksen said it all comes down to three words: fear of failure.[2]

* * *

While Greg and I drove around together, riding this wave, determined to ride it all the way to shore, we drove around the city. The city he now calls home is the city where I was reared. We went through the car wash and kissed like two young lovers before we drove to another of his office buildings.

Reading the sign, I asked, "You have two locations?"

"Four, actually," he said, pulling out the keys to the building.

We walked inside the renovated original city post office building where the original maple wood floors had been beautifully refinished. Some of the wood was used as trim throughout the building and was used to frame the original blue prints on the walls, as well. His artful attention to detail and historical preservation was exquisite. The original rooster weather vane, now repaired, was returned to its proper position atop the building.

His other location was more of a formal downtown location with traditional grey, black, and white marble throughout. Gold-trimmed revolving doors and fixtures and large Corinthian columns with tall ceilings adorned his other location. It was the picture of big city elegance.

This location was more of a small-town rustic redo. Both were equally impressive, touting a Texas-proud flair with his personal collection of Western artwork, animal heads, and hides. A darker, more rustic granite was used in the old post office building. It was all so classy, unique, and historically sound.

He walked over to a beautiful black baby grand player piano and keyed in "love songs." The music from the piano resonated with the accompaniment of the sounds of strings and brass. It was our own private symphony.

"I bought this for my daughter," he said as he turned it on. "The piano at my other location is for my son," he continued. "He doesn't even know it yet and could probably care less at this point. But, one day, he might . . ."

I loved so very much the priority he made his children in his life. His love for them was evident, making obvious his position as "Dad" was the most important to him. So often, people give of themselves to others at the expense of their family—especially their children. That was not true of Greg. His children truly *did* come first. I remembered him dreaming with me about having a little girl one day. He dreamed of holding her hand and taking her shopping for dresses. He became that very dad. For me, this was his most attractive trait.

Continuing the tour, he told me about the gorgeous impressionist artwork on the walls. One, a massive Monet-like floral splash of color framed in a Gaudí-like gold frame was particularly breathtaking. His history on the acquisition of the masterpiece and its beauty was accentuated with the romantic music resonating from the exquisite sound system.

In his downstairs conference room, we admired more interesting original restored features. I loved seeing him in his world, sharing what was most important to him. Returning back upstairs, he took my hand, twirled me around, and we danced beside that baby grand. Then he pulled me to him, pulling to himself a little more of my heart. I fought falling for him, but he was becoming more and more irresistible. I had forgotten what a great dancer he was. Oh, the memories; and oh, the regret and thoughts of what could have been. But what a magical ending to a magical day.

When we arrived back at my home, I invited him in to meet my children. It was the first time I had brought anyone home for them to meet. Having enough upheaval to deal with, my kids needed me . . . but they needed a "happy" me. I did talk to my children about Greg and was eager for them to meet him.

My friend who was divorced and remarried told me he thinks that having Greg there for me probably carved off two years of my healing process. I had others say the same thing. The emotional safety Greg provided allowed self-discovery completely free of condemnation, fear of rejection, disapproval, or disappointment. On a thin string, like a flittering kite, I could feel myself tug on him occasionally. Sometimes, he'd let out more string; other times, he'd reel me in. With no expectations, I allowed myself to feel sometimes like a wild animal inside, crazed and angry as my regret dug deeper. How would I overcome this mistake 23 years ago? A piercing reality of choosing to marry Seth rather than holding fast to Greg seemed unforgiveable. Why didn't God stop me when, after all, God was whom I was trying to please.

Or was He?

That Greg wanted me began validating my self-worth. Perhaps I had not fully destroyed myself. Evidently, he saw something of value in me which gave me hope that I, evidently, still had value. The value I was beginning to believe in hung on a thin shredded thread to him. Could it hold me through the coming storm?

22

Chapter Twenty-Two

All God's angels come to us disguised.
—JAMES RUSSELL LOWELL

Every setback has a comeback.
—TIM STOREY

""Mrs. Foster, I'm sorry to call so late, but Audrey is in the emergency room. She's had two grand mal seizures," Audrey's boyfriend called to inform me from the Denver County Hospital lobby. I had never known Audrey to have seizures. My slow groggy awakening quickly turned to hysterical inner panic.

My God, my baby is in Colorado. I'm in Texas, and I can't get to her. The stark reality of the situation thrust me back in time, remembering the day she left with her boyfriend several months prior.

"I will always love you, Audrey. There is nothing you can do that will change that, and you are always welcome to come home. Always."

But in my last words spoken face-to-face to my daughter that day, I told her: "I do not support you in this and I will not financially assist you. If you go, you are on your own."

As I sat next to Audrey in our duplex on our worn out loveseat that was once a feature designer piece accenting our beautiful French home, we cried out our goodbye. Given that our duplex was crowded with two too many dogs and what felt like a mass of humanity where we each desperately tried to carve out a corner of a room for personal space, I couldn't blame her for wanting to move. But from Texas to Denver? My efforts to make this place feel like a home had obviously fallen way short. We didn't even really *feel* like family.

"You keep trying to act like we are a family, Mom. Stop it!" she exclaimed. "We are no longer a family."

Her words blew a hole in my heart.

Sitting beside each other in what felt like a foreign land, in a foreign home with foreign family members squished and squeezed in a small place pretending life was going to get better when it just seemed to keep getting worse, who could really blame her for wanting to leave? Seeing no other viable alternative, I reluctantly accepted her choice.

In all honesty, I didn't blame her. I didn't blame her at all. How I longed to be able to give her more. How I longed to give her something to hold on to, a reason to want to stay. Our past seemed a desolate fake, phony façade that made hoping for a future even more bleak. What do we believe for? What do we hope for? That the next time I go to the grocery store, I'm reduced to choosing between milk and bread because we don't have enough money for both? I obviously didn't inspire her to dream or hope for a better future. No wonder she wanted to leave.

We each faced the door with tears streaming down our cheeks. Audrey had returned from the University of Hawaii to more affordably continue her education in Texas only to quit school and move to Colorado with a new boyfriend. She was packed. We were waiting for him to come for her.

And come for her, he did.

As they backed out of my driveway, my daughter eyes locked on mine. Tears streamed down our cheeks, filling in the empty spaces that words could never fill. And as her boyfriend backed away, he also backed out over my very soul, squishing it beneath his tires and dragging it behind him all the way to Denver. He tore out a core of me that left a deep, dark chasm. He stole one of the four pillars in my heart, causing it to cave in and nearly suffocate me. Just like that, I had to let her go. My beautiful, talented, first-born love of my life. I had four loves. My soul ached at this loss. She was the oldest. She was who the others looked up to. She was always their second mother, their role model, their leader, the one who held the standard and whose successes developed belief for the others following her with anticipation. Her leaving, her *quitting*, took me to my knees. It appeared that one by one, we each were going down. I wondered if any of us were going to survive.

I only had so much of what was left of me to give. We were five links in a circular chain. If one went down, we all surely would. As they instruct in airplanes that we give ourselves oxygen before assisting our children, I had to breathe in hope if I ever could offer my children some. Did they have enough breath left in them for me to find a life raft strong enough to hold me so I could eventually reach back to assist them? Could they hold on long enough? I wasn't sure. As shattered as they were, I had to focus on me. "It was each man for himself," Sophia would come to say of this time.

In the best of times, they always had me to lean on. Now, in the very worst, I offered them very little more than trying to keep myself afloat. I was near empty, forcing them to dig deep within themselves, finding their own true grit determination to survive. Or not. Each day grew more perilous. So before it was too late, I had to figure something out for me. With one seemingly sinking, it seemed so wrong not to reach out to her with the oxygen mask. Against my motherly instinct, I decided to trust it was best that I let her go, focusing on saving myself. What option did I have, anyway? She was 21 years old and could decide for herself. I would focus on the three still in my home.

Applying every night online for secretary jobs and any job of interest resulted in nothing, I called businesses, going by in person, still nothing. I was told to go online and apply. Nothing. I updated my resume; I even had professionals look at it and work on it. I networked and met anyone who would meet me and went anywhere I was invited, always looking for work. Nothing. I volunteered, trying to create a resume of experience. I had to look strong, professional, and perform as though I was not this broken, helpless, fearful shattered hull of a person. Over the years, I had learned to do that well. I was a master. It helped me survive.

Audrey called from Colorado. She couldn't find work. She applied at numerous places. Nothing. She started giving plasma for money to eat. We were quickly being reduced to hopeless and desperate. Sending Marshall to McDonalds to apply for a job, then to the movie theater, I took him to men's clothing stores and to other fast food operations. Nothing. No job. I even went with him to meet the manager, to introduce myself and him. Still no job. If not for my dad sharing what little was left of my mother and grandmother's life savings, we would have already drowned. Instead, we were dying a slow, torturous death, potentially taking him down with us. His savings were not enough for all of us. It was intended for him. *Could it get any worse?* I wondered.

* * *

After calling every medical professional I knew, researching everything about seizures, taking copious notes, and finally being convinced that she wasn't well enough to fly home, I realized that it was best I not fly to her but rather find her a neurologist near me to see her even though I had no job, no money, and no insurance. When I did reach out and ask for help, I was lectured on how my ex should be assisting with this as should his dad . . . as if that was my reasonable solution.

They didn't understand that we were rebellious, disobedient prodigals awaiting enlightenment so that we could return to the good prodigal father for a promised feast and a beautiful coat. According to Seth and his father, we deserved this struggle and had this coming. It was their righteous duty to sit back and let us struggle. It was our just reward. We were the prodigal son eating with the swine. A message Seth and his dad believed and sent to us and to many others.

Their refusal to assist us was so righteous, it was above the law. Therefore, they felt justified in not paying child support. This was their truth of us and one of which they spread (complete with Bible verses) to many in their regular email blasts. To force child support requires money for court costs. Money I didn't have or want to waste. But it also required energy I could not spare. Besides, my attorney said it would only be worth it to take him to court once, when all the child support was past due, as legally we couldn't require him to pay money due in the future. So we had to make it on our own until then. Even then, it wouldn't be much . . . but it would be something.

After exhausting everything I could possibly do, think of, or try and still coming up with nothing, I walked. I walked the neighborhood streets up and down. I walked and I prayed and thought. Then I walked some more. I couldn't eat nor could I sit still. And there was nothing left that I could do. I wondered what God said to Job. I read it and it only aggravated me more. God talked about the gazelles and the ways of the lions. He spoke pages and pages about Himself, His creation, and His greatness. He asked Job who caused the ocean to stop at the shore and who hung the stars in the sky.

"Really?" I asked God. *"How is* this *supposed to help me?"*

It made me mad.

I looked up into the brightly lit blue sky littered with puffy clouds until it turned navy blue with a crescent moon and twinkling little flickers of starlight. I looked at the leaves on the trees, and I watched tiny ants carry leaves five times their size past me. Little specks of dirt stuck in the concrete driveway suddenly seemed magnified as if seen through a special looking glass, revealing significance simply because they *were*. Those specks of dirt were a part of all this. And then I looked at my four children and me in relation to all of this. And I realized everything was much more than I could handle. It was too big for me. I had nothing to offer my children or my daughter, so many miles away. I had nothing to offer even myself. I had no choice but to trust God—whoever He was, wherever He was. I had to believe He would somehow get us through. My children and I were but a speck of sand in this big universe with no answers, no ideas, and no realizations other than we were small but not insignificant. We were part of a huge universe that was going on with or without us.

Then I began to think about what I could be thankful for at that very moment. Lying on the hot driveway in the blazing summer sun, I turned my head. There, among the blades of grass, I saw the miracle of weeds. They grow. They grow in spite of all efforts to destroy them. In fact, weeds continue to grow when sprayed with poison, picked by gardeners, or eaten by grub worms and locusts. Nothing stops weeds. They are survivors. Against all odds, weeds live, grow, and thrive. They grow faster than most wanted plant life. They get mowed down, driven over, and dug up, yet they still multiply and spread. Weeds are valiant survivors of all sorts of human abuse.

"Thank you for weeds!" I cried out to the universe. "If you can hear me," I said, "Thank you for weeds." Too sad to cry, I lay there. "Thank you for ants, too!" I cried out, scooping one ant up on a leaf. And though I removed him from his place in line, he never stopped, he never gave up. Carrying him down the street, I moved him from his home as far as Colorado was from Texas in his world. He kept going. He didn't quit. It didn't kill him. He had shelter, he knew how to find food, he didn't need clothes. He was okay. Laying my head back down on my hot driveway, still dry-eyed, a fly landed on my forehead.

"Thank you for annoying flies! Do you hear me?" I cried out from my hot driveway. "I said, 'Thank you for flies.'"

Laughing and crying at myself, I wondered how many horsetails, snapping dogs, and newspapers had swatted at that fly that day alone. I couldn't imagine how many times a day some force of nature tried to destroy the fly my hands were swatting. The more I swatted, the faster it returned to me. It was still part of this universe. Here this fly was, taunting me, sharing the universe of my driveway. I realized that both of us were noble survivors in our own right. Our individual existence carried no more—or less—weight. We simply were part of creation— the weeds, the ants, the flies, and me. Nothing more, nothing less at that moment, we—the weeds, ants, flies, and me—were okay sitting under the vast galaxies above. Below us, beneath my driveway, lay the earth's surface with another galaxy all its own deep below. At that very moment, we were in this third galaxy of life in between the galaxy of outer space and the galaxy deep under the earth. Us. Together. Okay.

Remaining in the moment, I thought how I did have shelter, we were not hungry, we were clothed, and today, at this moment . . . we were okay. That was as far ahead as I could handle considering. Any further ahead than the present was overwhelming. Survival required me to live and be only in the present. In the moment, I remained . . . finding fragile calm. One thought of five minutes beyond the moment created panic. No thinking beyond the very now.

After a full day of discovery, I went inside my little duplex with a new sense of fragile, frail calm, surviving moment by moment. My life had become a revolving door of crises. Audrey's health issues warrant- ed my having a conversation with Seth. As her father, I felt he should be informed and perhaps he would help. Seth returned my call leaving a message that he had an idea to share. Feeling somewhat hopeful, I called him.

I should have known better.

He wanted to meet with me and Audrey to offer her an opportunity to apologize to him for her rebellion of leaving the head of her home, our royal priest as according to Scripture, believing her apology would provide the necessary foundation to her and our family for healing. Then, and only then, would he offer an apology but only if she apologized first. But financial assistance of any sort was out of the question.

This problem, he explained, was all spiritual in nature, of course, as she was out from under his authority and, thus, in rebellion, had suffered physical calamity. This rebellion was at the "root" of all his explanations for *any* grievance under which we came. That was the last time I ever communicated with him. No longer would I feel obligated to inform him of any situation involving our children. From that point forward, if there was to be any communication with him, it would be through them by their own choosing, not me.

I was finished with him, forever.

The next morning, Gina called suggesting I consider going to the Women's Center of Tarrant County. *The Women's Center,* I thought. *Have I really become that desperate? These sound like more of the same kind of people who recently rejected me and don't believe me.*

"Seriously, Gina? Have I fallen this far?"

"Well . . . I just thought . . ." She was trying to be so gentle with me.

"I don't know anything about them," she said, "but they might be able to help."

She encouraged me to give the industry for abused women another chance. So I called, immediately asking them what services they offered. They provided me a list of things, none of which would help with Audrey. But it was something. So I said, "Sure, sign me up for counseling. Yes, I would like to sign my children up, too."

Then the woman I was talking with said something about a class.

"Class?" I asked. "You have a class? What *kind* of class?"

I was immediately transferred to the teacher of the class. And when I asked her the same question, she replied, "We have employment training classes."

My pride, not yet completely annihilated, reared up within me. I probably sounded a little haughty as I replied, "Ma'am, I have a college degree."

"Yes," she responded, "but do you have a *job*?"

So much for what pride I had left. Like a tennis racket whacking at a ball, her words knocked me across the room and off the wall, ricocheting my pride to its final standstill. I would attend her class on Monday.

23

Chapter Twenty-Three

Sometimes, I guess there just aren't enough rocks.
—FORREST GUMP

Victim blaming comes in various forms. Charming Impossibles know just how to twist the dagger they leave in the heart of a victim. They know just the button to push and how to blame the victim for a situation they actually caused. Consider the following text that Audrey received from her grandfather:

Audrey, I told the 3 other children what I want to now share with you. It is all about me, but I am so thankful to honestly share with you that I have forgiven you for the way you have treated me since the family disaster. Further I ask you to forgive me for the judgmental thoughts I have had until I was finally able to make my peace with you in absentia. No response necessary, just wanted you to know I am free now and will always love you, my first granddaughter . . . the one that named me Bomma! Love, in Christ, Bomma"

Appropriate words had she written them to *him*.

This is classic victim abuse, a favorite Charming Impossible tactic to drive their abuse even deeper. This is what experts refer to as "blame shifting" or "casting their own guilt upon another."

Another form of victim blaming casts skepticism and doubt on the victim. And it comes from people who don't even know the situation.

In casual conversation one day with a church friend, Gina experienced it on my behalf.

"I don't believe your friend Susan," the woman said to Gina. "Something about her just doesn't add up."

"You have been in my Bible study for over ten years. You know me really well," Gina replied. "I have known Susan since we were twelve years old and you are telling me you don't believe her?"

"I do not believe her," she reiterated.

This is the harsh risk for anyone who chooses to speak out about abuse. Not only is it painful to finally speak out about what has been kept hidden, it's also often just as painful enduring the scrutiny, doubt, and disbelief of those who are nearest and dearest. For them, the truth doesn't seem possible or it's too much to believe. And believing the truth may require an action or decision of which the "hearer" is not ready or willing to take. Gina's friend was a board member of a local woman's shelter. Therefore, her judgment—inaccurate as it was—hurt. It hurt deeply.

With full knowledge of her doubts about me, I attended, as Gina's guest, this woman's fundraising dinner for the women's shelter where a woman from a foreign country was giving testimony of her abuse.

Gina turned to her friend and said, "You believe this lady who will be sharing her testimony at your dinner. You do not personally know her, nor do you know anyone who has personally known her for any extended period of time. Yet you are giving her a microphone and podium to share her story before all your friends and family."

Gina continued, "I've known Susan almost forty years. Her mother and my mother were close friends. You have known me over ten years, yet you remain willing to believe this stranger and not my friend?"

"I'll have to think about this," Gina's friend responded. And that's all she ever said.

* * *

While counseling at the pregnancy center years ago, I met a mother who didn't believe her daughter. In fact, the daughter was punished for lying and making up a story about her uncle. The girl wound up in my office because she had become sexually promiscuous, suicidal, and worried about getting pregnant. Her greatest regret was that she wished she had never spoken out. She wished she had just kept the truth hidden.

Sadly, in many respects, it's just easier that way, which is one reason so much abuse goes unreported and untold. When the statistics indicate one in four girls are molested by their teen years and many of those assaults go unreported, what a devastating reflection on the actual condition of our society. Many reports suggest one in four boys are molested before their teens. It is startling and is something we, as a society and church, do not really know how best yet to face. Therefore, many choose to live with it hidden deep inside. I have several close personal friends who never told their mothers or other family members their truth of having been sexually abused in their youth, most of whom were abused by their fathers.

On the flip side of this horrible equation, you hear of mothers filling their young children's minds with ideas so that they wind up convincing them of a manufactured lie: falsely accusing the father of sexual abuse in order to secure full custody. Unfortunately, a big truth in our society is that innocent men have been accused by manipulative, lying women. Men have lied about women and children have lied about parents to the point no one knows what to believe. It's so crazy out there in the world of accusations and lies that it is simply easiest and safest for the truly abused victim to stay quiet and deal with it in secret. And that's why many do.

One common perpetrator that is widely overlooked is children abusing children. Several have opened up to me about childhood experiences they never discussed until talking to me. It's a trauma adults don't know how to talk about because while it seems minor, for many, the trauma has lasting effects. Knowing this challenge is very common, I am choosing to address it with Mary's heartbreaking story of child on child sexual abuse.

* * *

Mary's Story:

Our first experience of sexual abuse involved me walking in on a kindergartener molesting my first-grade daughter. She was my neighbor's daughter, a friend of my daughter. By my taking the kindergartner to her mother and explaining what had happened, that family uncovered an ugly truth about a grandfather who was molesting two of their children. His wife, the children's grandmother, stood by him, lying to the children, saying their mother was aware of this and was okay with it when the older child threatened to tell on them.

Because of the circles I happen to run in, all the situations I personally share involve dedicated church people. In this case, as highly irregular and unusual as it was, the grandparents abused the children in front of each other. There were witnesses to the abuse. This resulted in the family successfully pressing charges, sending the grandfather to jail.

That particular grandfather was a deacon in the local Baptist church.

* * *

Another woman, a teacher at a local school, told me she recalls childhood abuse from an uncle. However, she is not able to recall one certain memory involving that uncle instructing a young cousin on what to do to her. She says that memory is blacked out. Years following the incident, she and her cousin talk about it, but she still does not have any recollection of this particular memory.

Mental health experts refer to these blackouts as "dissociative amnesia," linking it to overwhelming stress—which might be the result of traumatic events—such as war, abuse, accidents, or disasters. A survivor of an airplane crash, for example, was on video when she was told her parents were killed in an accident. Even after watching the video of herself being told, she has no memory of that moment. Blackouts are common where trauma is concerned. Some have abuse memories return with no face. Experts say having no face is an indicator the abuser is a person who shares a close relationship with the victim.

Other symptoms of abuse and trauma include fainting, panic attacks involving sharp chest pain, nightmares, and even seizures. The medical world is awakening to how trauma is often the root.

While sexual abuse at the hands of adolescents is finally beginning to receive attention, the existence of child perpetrators is largely dismissed and denied, according to the National Library of Medicine and National Institute of Health.[1] Of 47 boys between the ages of 4 and 13 described as having molested children younger than themselves, coercion was involved.[2] According to the Children's Institute International in Los Angeles, 49 percent of these child perpetrators had been sexually abused and 19 percent physically abused by adults they knew.[3] The male child perpetrators all knew the children they molested. In 47 percent of the cases, the sexual abuse involved a sibling.[4]

Of the other half of child perpetrators who did not admit former abuse, I have my suspicions. Because most were abused by people they knew, their abusers quite possibly knew the child would be taken to a center where their story is recorded and statistically preserved. Half the children admitted their wrongdoing, saying they, themselves, had never been abused. This is classic behavior. No one and nothing could have convinced many adult women who were molested as children to talk of their abuse. Once an abuser knows a child or adult is going in for questioning, they create havoc and fallout that is far worse than choosing to speak that truth.

While many more are speaking their painful truth today, we have a long way to go. Hopefully, society will understand the need to allow these stories to surface in order to heal or we will see even more drastic emotional societal challenges ahead. We need healing. To heal, the truth must first come out. There's so much stuffed pain we prefer stays stuffed and quiet. As crazy shootings and other forms of tragic abuse grow at rapid rates, we better learn how to effectively listen and allow people to heal. And we must learn how to better respond to abusers.

Here's where statistics are helpful but fall severely short. When a child speaks out about abuse, they're in perilous danger of suffering more harm, even if the person to whom they turn believes and defends them. The disgusting, evil monsters, low enough to sexually violate an innocent child, are manipulative beyond imagination. Some have even been known to publicly expose and accuse their own child, further victimizing, abusing, and shaming their child in effort to build a case to protect themselves from the consequences of their heinous actions.

Remember, it's only when a Charming Impossible fears the consequences of a situation that they speak out about it first. This is so they can spin it to their advantage. Any parent willing to exploit an innocent child like this is most likely exposing their own guilt.

If a child turns to you about an adult sexually abusing them, the most dangerous thing you can do is confront the accused adult. That only puts the child at even more risk. We need much more education and training on these issues.

The Olympic gymnasts who were abused by their physician are prime examples. Many spoke out long before it was disclosed publicly and suffered more for it, with their abuser protected in plain sight. The same is true about some professional female journalists. What courage and class those women exude in exposing this societal epidemic.

We must come up with a better strategy in the professional world, in schools, socially, and beyond on how to approach this issue. And while I do not yet know the answer, I hope to influence positive change.

Up until very recently, child-on-child sexual offenses have been dismissed as "kids will be kids." Statistics on the subject are difficult to find as it has not been extensively researched. In my own findings based on 15 women who opened up to me about having been molested as a child, only one abuser was a perfect stranger; another abuser was a boy at school with whom she had not developed a friendship; and the rest were close adult men . . . family members . . . usually the victim's father. Of the 15, 3 of them reported to a parent and 1 to police. The other 12 keep it a family secret to this day. Of those 12, each woman says she feels she has a close relationship with her mother but would never tell her in order to protect her. And among these 12 "faithful" church-attending abusers is a prominent doctor, a lawyer, a man in ministry, and an educator.

Discussing with these women how young children often act out what has been done to them, some admitted doing just that. When asked had they been caught, would they tell what had happened to them or just accept full blame, they all said they'd accept the blame before telling on their abusers.

A surgeon married to a Charming Impossible shared with me that his wife and her younger sisters were all abused by their father as young children. While she admits it was traumatizing, he claims that she not only has not dealt with it, but says it's a sick freak show every time these grown adult women with families of their own go to visit their father. He says, "They all put on their best party dresses with their makeup and hair just so to parade in front of him when they visit him in his home." He went on to say they even still sit on that "sick father's" lap.

With these complications, the lack of research in this arena is understandable. My hope in writing this chapter is to shed light on the prevalence of this subject and the need for better strategy in assisting innocent victims. I hope to expose how child predators who suffered abuse from another are silenced, choosing rather to accept unwarranted blame for their victimization. I share these shocking stories because until we are no longer shocked by this, we won't accept its prevalence and serious need for action. If we remain naïve and shocked, we as a society will remain stuck, gasping in air, doing nothing about it. At some point, churches, legal systems, schools, and corporations must all realize this is happing in their world. The bubble must be broken!

There is risk in telling stories like these. It takes courage to speak out and can come at a great cost. But I must hold fast to the hope that in time, the truth will eventually set us free. The Tarrant County Women's Center is making great progress on these issues. I'm grateful to have been directed to this organization for help as they have been a support to us through multiple avenues of service.

* * *

Arriving early to my Monday morning class, sick with worry about Audrey, I was warmly welcomed by the others in the class, women and men from all walks of life. *This place might actually accept me*, I reluctantly thought. Desperately seeking something—*anything*—that I could do for Audrey was something seemingly denied by the universe. But there was something offered for me here. So I went to class with Audrey heavy on my heart.

Taking diligent notes, I studied and absorbed. I soon learned that my approach to finding a job was outdated and all wrong. This class was going to give me the edge I needed. Meeting highly educated and wonderful women who were not in crisis but there to improve their already successful lives motivated me to trust and believe this was a good, safe place for me.

But what about my Audrey?

That's all I could think about.

During a break, I told a volunteer there about my crisis with Audrey. She encouraged me to go the John Peter Smith County Hospital.

"Ask to meet the director," she said, handing me a piece of paper with the director's name. "After hearing your story, she might be able to help."

Only months before when Marshall broke his arm horsing around with friends, I was rejected by several doctor's offices due to not having insurance. Even doctor friends of friends would not see Marshall. I had to drive him all the way back down to our former hometown friend to put on his cast, so imagining a hospital willing to assist my daughter's more serious need seemed an impossibility.

After class, I went directly to the hospital, chose from a cluster of numerous buildings, and by random chance, walked in. I was cordially greeted by a doctor standing at the elevator.

"Can I help you?" he asked.

"I'm looking for Ms. Sanders," I said, reading from my note.

"Well, can I help you?" he asked again.

"Yes, can you help me find her?" I asked again.

"But can *I* help you?" he reiterated, seeming insistent.

Exasperated, anticipating the coming rejection, I explained that I had come from the Women's Center, had no insurance, no money, and no job, adding a little about Audrey's situation and how she needed to see a neurologist.

To my surprise, he said, "Follow me. I am going to help you, and we will get your daughter a neurologist." He turned in circles with his hands out as if he were groping for bearings on this sudden change of direction. And then I saw his face light up with that *Oh, yes, this is what we should do* look, and down the hall he went, me following close behind.

As we entered a nondescript office, he introduced me to a lady who, upon his request, immediately sat down with me to begin processing the necessary paperwork.

"Are you his friend?" she asked, a bit awestruck at the prospect. "I guess I am now," I said. "Do you know who he is?" she asked.

Everything had happened so fast, I had not taken time to look at his card. He was the senior vice president and medical director of the hospital, Dr. Jay Haynes. "Well, because of him, you just bypassed about a month's worth of waiting. Who *are* you?" she asked.

I told her a little about my situation and how I turned to God throughout this journey. She gave me a list of documents to bring to her the following day so we could finish up then.

In the meantime, Dr. Haynes asked me to have Audrey's records sent to him. Upon reviewing her records from the Denver Hospital, Dr. Haynes realized he knew her doctor. The two doctors discussed Audrey's case, agreeing upon diagnoses and treatment, ultimately concluding that it was safe for her to fly. With a doctor's appointment in sight, I needed to get Audrey home. My sister-in-law came to our rescue once again, offering to use her flight mileage, and arrangements were made.

Having a brother and sister-in-law for support was essential to our success in leaving. That some people are in my position without family for support is alarming to me. I can only hope to one day be in a position to help others as I have been helped. This is not something I could have done without the support of so many.

The next day, after my class, I returned to the hospital with my stack of requested documentation. The lady was so excited to see me. Fighting tears, explaining that I had inspired her, she said that my life was so exciting and that after having met me she realized she wanted more out of life.

Exciting? I couldn't believe my ears. Here I was in such a desperate place but am somehow inspiring and exciting? When I left the meeting with her, I checked my phone. Dr. Haynes had called, leaving me a message to visit him at his office. As I filled him in on our history, the events that led up to meeting him in the first place, he said, "You are not only going to be okay but you will be stronger for having gone through this."

After telling him my story, I thought he'd think of me as "trashy" or "lesser" for having gone through all this, which was a growing fear I had in meeting anyone new. Feeling safe with people who have known me, I avoided the risk of being judged by getting to know new people because, naturally, they wondered what the other side of the story might be.

"What about you and your other children?" he asked, offering to help them, too.

"That is very generous of you to offer my family medical assistance," I said, thanking him. "I cannot accept it, however. For you to help my Audrey is more than I can ask. Please just help my daughter."

His gentle persistence seemed genuine. Appreciative that he would ask about the rest of my children, I already felt I imposed such a burden on friends, family, and society. I didn't want to add to my list of burdens and indebtedness. Humbled and overwhelmed with how much a "taker" I had become, I increasingly felt as though I had absolutely nothing to give. I just took, took, took.

"When did you last have a checkup?" he asked.

I couldn't recall.

He continued, "Do you want me to be your doctor?"

"Yes, I would be so grateful for you to be my doctor," I said. Thinking about all my recent stress, I thought it might be smart to be under a doctor's care.

Dr. Haynes saw my daughters and me that Friday. Audrey left with a health and vitamin plan, and we were all under a doctor's care.

A perfect stranger cared for us, gave to us knowing we were not capable of giving back, saw our ugly reality, and not only didn't judge us or push us away but rather embraced us, and best of all, called us friend.

We left Dr. Haynes with renewed hope.

24

Chapter Twenty-Four

Those who lead give sight to those who follow.
Those who follow give vision to those who lead.
—GREG

Insecure people do stupid things. This character trait of others once drove me nuts. I had no patience for them and couldn't understand why they don't just "act" normal even if they didn't feel it. *Why are they so weird?* I have always wondered.

That is . . . until I became one of them.

"Susan, you need more time . . . much more time . . . to heal," I'd often hear.

Frustrated by the fact that everyone else seemed to know where I was in the healing process better than I even knew myself, ready to be healed, longing to be all better, I escalated the real problem: *me*. Growing more annoyed I couldn't shake the insecurity, aware of it but unable to avoid acting and behaving in a meek manner, I was an embarrassment to myself, a pathetic soul. I had become the very woman I used to criticize. Women who behaved as I was were annoyances that created chauvinistic challenges. I would say of women who behaved as I was, "Of course, men think so little of such weak-minded foolish little girls who can't control themselves."

Problem was, I had become one of *them*.

And what's really disturbing is I knew it and couldn't stop myself. That's what I always found so weird about them. I'd think of them, *Get ahold of yourself!*

Now, I understood. I wouldn't and couldn't either, because when you're in this state, you just can't get ahold of yourself. It has a hold on you and wags you to and fro like a tail of a dog.

Experiencing severe insecurity and shame eventually became a beautiful life lesson for me of which I am now grateful. Much of the compassion my mother prayed for came to me through that experience. When we feel unworthy, it shows. There is no faking it till you make it when pain is *that* deeply rooted. It makes its ugliness available for the whole world to see.

Having a completely new awareness of what that feels like, I only mention it to offer hope to anyone still stuck in it. It takes time and effort to know and to understand yourself. We are all worthy. We all are here for a purpose. We all have something to offer and must be patient as we go through various seasons of life, training and learning, even though we sometimes still do and say stupid things. Never have I felt more equipped to help others but for this time of self-devaluation.

While still in search of me, I tried out all kinds of new personas with Greg. One day, I tried the sleazy approach, the way some of the guys I met suggested. Another day, I became an emotional mess, mad at something trivial and stupid. That wasn't really me either. I tried out a little temper tantrum on him. Another day, I kept changing my mind on him. But, mostly, I tried to be stable and "normal," the way the old me was. Trouble was, none of those personas were *me*.

This part of my journey was when I needed Greg most. Not even a year since my divorce with my financial circumstances still dire, unsure of myself, yet regaining a smile as my kids were smiling a little more, I hung and clung to Greg, indulging myself in him any chance I could.

It was quite selfish, really. My life was all about *me*. I would apologize to him for not really being there for him. And how I hated that! How does one know one is being selfish, express their knowledge of it, and continue to do it anyway? That wasn't me; oh, but it *was*. It was *me* . . . the only me that could emerge from that rubble. I didn't know *how* to be there for him. I only knew how to be with him for me. Words couldn't express my state of shock at how self-centered I'd become.

Yet as he helped me grow in a multitude of ways, a new problem emerged.

Growing stronger, I grew more disgusted with myself and the drama still surrounding us with Seth. Embarrassed that Greg was *watching* the ridiculous process we continued to endure with Seth, wanting him to see the strong person I knew I would be one day, wanting to be all better, I spun Greg's little pinstriped, conservative, controlled environment into utter confusion and chaos.

He did finally text me, *You so confuse me,* at which point I determined to put both him and me out of our misery. I met with him, explained that I had fallen deeply in love with him even though I knew better, could not control my emotions, was not able to keep myself at his pace, and was about to face the final challenge with my ex that was going to spin me into an even bigger emotional mess, so I needed to pull away until I got "to the other side."

That actually was one of the most sensible decisions I made, and he appreciated it. During this time, I went back into my memory of experiences. Back in high school, I began to recall that I decided I wasn't meant to be truly loved by a man. This was an unfounded old record that had evidently played in the back of my mind, dictating my choices and decisions. Finally, I was learning the root of all my problems. I realized I was fighting myself through my own misconceptions.

While we are young, we wrap a story or explanation around everything that happens to us. Due to a teacher's comment, we wrongly judge our intelligence; due to a physical violation, we conclude we deserve it, and so on and so on. In our adult lives, we must go back to every event, separate our story from what happened, and allow the event to stand alone without explanation because the truth is, we really don't know why things happen. The only healthy response to trauma in our youth is to remove our interpretation, accept what we can't change, and choose how to best move forward while ultimately leaving the incident and the interpretation separate and behind. That requires facing pain, hurting all over again, but only for a while. We must be willing to remove a scab of trauma, clean out infection of shame, and apply the ointment of acceptance for what we can't change to fully heal. It may leave scars. Scars are but a memory without the feeling and shame attached. Scars remind us we learned something and had the courage to move on. Our scars are what we use to encourage others.

Embrace them.

25

Chapter Twenty-Five

We can't solve problems by using the same kind
of thinking we used to create them.
—ALBERT EINSTEIN

It was my second Christmas as a divorcee and I had been contemplating that old gnawing question, *What if hope, love, and prayer don't work. What then?*

It had been four months since I had spoken with Greg.

A little over a week after we had our blow up, I did send him a handwritten letter letting him know that no "blow" of ours would ever overshadow what he did for me and was to me. I let him know that I loved him and wished him happiness and joy. Then, I let it be. I was no longer, "Greg, Greg, Greg, Greg, Greg . . . Oh, and did I mention Greg?"

I could tell my friends were relieved that I was no longer so preoccupied with him. Finally, they could be around me without having to hash through my thoughts, feelings, and questions about Greg. My manic obsession with the guy had subsided.

When I finally could think about him without crying, I started hearing his voice repeatedly suggesting the book *Eat Pray Love*. "You should read that book, Susan," I kept hearing him say, "You write so much like her."

I devoured every word.

In *Eat Pray Love*, Elizabeth Gilbert writes with heartbreakingly vulnerable truth about her process of healing from divorce. She shares about her "Greg." While they did not share a similar history or relationship with ours, our utter similarity was in how she and I obsessed over our guys.

Throughout her book, she fought many similar emotions and challenges as she worked her way through the aftermath of a painful divorce. Most of the time, I felt like I was reading writings from my twin. What was most intriguing to me was her seeking reconciliation with herself over this man with whom she was no longer in relationship but still deeply loved. She pined, whined, ached, and struggled over him in much the same way I did Greg, with all the same questions, misgivings, and challenges. And then she explains to Richard from Texas (who I refer to as one of her Ordinary Angels) our dilemma:

"[T]he reason I think it is so hard for me to get over this guy is because I seriously believed David was my soul mate."[1]

Me, too! I thought, nodding my head in vigorous agreement. *So, yes, what were we supposed to do with our soul mates?*

Richard from Texas suggested our "Gregs" were probably our soul mates,[2] meaning that true soul mates are mirrors who show us everything that is holding us back. Soul mates are people who make it abundantly clear we need to make some drastic changes in our life. A true soul mate may be the most important person we ever meet, because they tear down walls and smack us awake. But to live with a soul mate forever is too painful. Soul mates come into our life just to reveal another layer of us; then, they leave. Our problem was in letting our soul mates go.

When it's over, we *must* let them go.

A soul mate's purpose is to shake us out of a pattern, relationship, or career rut, tear at our ego a bit, reveal blind spots or addictive behaviors, and break our hearts wide open. Soul mates dive deep into our soul, leaving a hole for another to fill. That's their job. It's what they do. In *Eat Pray Love*, Richard from Texas says that they have a "short shelf life."[3] In other words, we can love them . . . we can miss them . . . but then we have to let them go.

Let go of Greg? Seriously?

That's where my tears began. And as I sobbed, I pondered what I had learned. Gathering myself together enough to read on, I discovered that oftentimes, we don't want to let go out of fear of being alone. Problem was, all my life I had been absolutely *terrified* of being all alone.

Even if Greg was not actively in my life, I clung to the hope of returning to him and giving it one more try or just carrying his past support around with me as if it were an active part of my life. But to truly emotionally cut myself off from him? Fearful of even the thought, I wondered how I would cope. I hardly knew what it was to be divorced without him. He had been there almost the whole time. He was all I knew. I wasn't sure I could let go of his hand. I wanted to hold on tight to him . . . if only emotionally. Not knowing who I would be without him, how could I continue on in this life? And though I was hardly able to bear the thought, I learned that by holding onto people who have completed their purpose in our lives, we place barriers in the doorway of our next opportunity.

As I laid the book aside, snuffling, still emotional, I began to see more clearly the direction I needed to go. It would take time, but I began to prepare myself to let go of Greg and begin my journey to move forward without him, alone.

26

Chapter Twenty-Six

Men loved her but she was the woman, all women loved to hate.
—ANNETTE J DUNLEA

Encouragement is the oxygen of the soul.
—GEORGE M ADAMS

"So, *you* were *my* competition when I was single." This was the very first thing a co-worker, Lizzy, said to me on my first day of work as she sashayed over to "greet" me from two desks away. I was the new sales hire, completing, along with Lizzy, our team of four.

"Excuse me?" I asked, perplexed as she broke my concentration of celebrating my first real professional desk, phone, and file-cabinet-of-real-clients job. In my mind, I had finally arrived and was actually going to do this. Inside, I was celebrating my huge victory for my children and me. We were going to make it! We would have insurance, a decent income, and hope for our future. My kids would be able to relax—*finally*—and rely on me. I could actually provide for us.

"Men like blondes, they don't like redheads," she continued.

Seeing a wedding band on her finger, I had some relief that perhaps she wouldn't find my natural blonde hair color in competition with her bottle dyed-red any longer.

"Who hired you?" she rudely inquired. "What process did you go through? Who do you know here?" she asked, the questions coming in like a hail of bullets. The onslaught continued as she began to probe my personal life, asking was I single, did I date, how did I come by this job, did I date our boss, and a host of other inappropriate questions that were none of her business and completely uncalled for.

Defusing her litany of questions, I said, "It's nice to meet you but I better get busy," turning my attention to the contents of my file cabinet.

"Hey, Susan . . . ." I heard a whisper from behind me. "Welcome, my name's Emily. You're going to need to be real careful here. The other two salespeople are very jealous of the clients you've been given. Same thing happened to me when I was hired. It's a timing thing. You and I both were hired after a really big salesperson left. Even though they tried to divvy out the clients evenly, the other two feel you were given the best ones, and they don't think it's fair."

"Thanks for telling me."

"No problem. I'm here to help anytime."

My new boss called me into his office. "A salesperson on your team will take you out with them. You can shadow them and learn by observation. Lizzy has volunteered. You'll begin tomorrow. Glad you are here. I'll take you on office visits, as well. Be patient with yourself. It takes a while to catch on, but you'll be great. We are all really excited to have you on our team."

"Thank you! I'm excited to be here. I'll see you tomorrow."

Lizzy, the redhead? It felt as though that with me, she was keeping the enemy close. Why am *I* her enemy? *What's behind all this?* I wondered. The last thing I need is more drama in my life. I just want to work, work hard, and keep my children emotionally and financially afloat. *Now, this?* The vibe from Lizzy was dark and cunning and one I hoped to avoid.

My desk was between two other salespeople's desks in an open-forum style office. No partitions, no privacy, we were all in one wide open space with a sea of desks and a cacophony of phone chatter. When not on the phone, we spent much of the day shuffling papers, contained by the walls of dry-erase boards and corkboards that surrounded us. But to me, it was prestigious: it was a career, not a job. It was provision for my children. I did it! At 48 years of age, I had finally embarked on my first real career. Caressing my desk as if it were the finest wood, running my hands over the outdated black phone that sat atop my desk, and opening the file cabinet beside me, I was elated with renewed faith. My kids were encouraged. "Maybe she can do this," they realized. We were moving forward. It was really actually happening. I could hardly believe this goodness.

My boss sent flowers to the lady at the chamber who had recommended me. She later said in all her 17 plus years of working there and recommending people to companies, never had she received a gift . . . and this arrangement was gorgeous!

While walking with Lizzy downtown on our second day of sales calls, a cat-call whistle could be heard over the sounds of screeching car tires, honking, and the multiple conversations of passersby. Quickly snapping her head my direction, she said in disgust, "He was whistling at you." Her disdain for me was shocking. That whistle could have been toward any number of others and probably was. I usually could win people over, but not this one. She had it out for me the moment I sat down at my new desk.

Ignoring her, I focused on learning my trade, training with my boss as much as possible, and spending as little time around her as possible. I told him she asked if I dated him. He said he was dating a blonde woman and that Lizzy had recently mentioned something to him suggesting he liked blondes. I thought it strange that she was doing this to him, too.

By the third month, I was leading in sales and had sold one of the highest commission items ever sold for a particular event. We were required to put our daily sales on the dry erase board for all to see. I begged my boss not to. I didn't want to draw any more negative attention from the redhead. But he insisted I put my sales on the board. That's when she pulled me into a conference room, shut the door, and began to chew me out, accusing me of all sorts of nonsense including stealing her clients. That's when I had had enough and told her she had gone too far. I also told her I would talk to our boss about this. He said he had seen what I was putting up with and that he was so impressed with how I continually took the high road.

I was surprised at how aware he was of what she was doing. He said he had two teenaged girls who didn't deal the degree of cattiness I was. Relieved that he recognized and understood what I was going through, I felt confident until a hush was put on my complaint, sales meetings were discontinued, and salespeople were instructed not to talk to each other as an investigation was underway.

Suddenly, we were all being individually questioned, and the air was getting thick around the office. She had been whispering in the ear of others, things about me. I knew this because Emily had clued me in. Emily didn't trust the redhead's motivations and expressed concern for me as she resigned from the job, choosing a new career. Just like that, my one advocate was gone.

That week we had a business mixer to which I had invited more local business leaders than any of my coworkers. The owner of the company was in town from out of state for the mixer, and I was looking forward to meeting him. Not only were my sales the highest, I had more guests confirmed to attend our business mixer. Walking right past our board of accomplishments, he addressed the entire office, immediately singling out our redhead in a personal manner that had nothing to do with work or job performance. Obviously craving his attention, she shimmied, straightening her posture, smiling big. These two apparently knew each other quite well. Spreading praise around to some others, he barely acknowledged me, his new top producer. Offering me little welcome, saying nothing about my accomplishments, he swiftly circled back around with more accolades for the redhead. Afterward, I went to introduce myself to him. But the redhead briskly interrupted, grabbing his arm, eagerly moving him away from me. Interesting that man's wife is the one who actually interviewed and hired me. Strange, I thought. *But, whatever.*

Later that evening at the mixer, I noticed the redhead never left the side of the owner. Nor was he comfortable getting near me. To confirm my notion, I attempted to properly greet him to which he properly responded until the redhead sauntered directly over, placing herself between us.

I had invited Greg to the mixer, and as we left, he said, "She sure is a tall glass of water." She was tall, indeed.

Then came what I refer to as "Black Monday."

My boss called me into his office. All the salespeople were gone. I was the only one left in the office.

He informed me that I was being terminated, that he did not agree with it, and would not do it, so I was to go out to my desk and someone else would terminate me. Calling me back into the office after my termination, my boss just sat there, looking so sad, almost heartbroken. I asked for an explanation. I wasn't given one. I *demanded* one. Still didn't get one. But I was offered assistance in clearing out my desk. In one devastating instant, my new career was over just like that.

Devastated, I called Gina.

"Call Greg," she advised as soon as she heard my voice. "Susan, I've never heard you like this. You're scaring me. Call Greg," she repeated.

Racing from his office, Greg was there to embrace me as I walked across his threshold more broken than ever, wearing a scarlet letter of "Fired" across my chest. This failure was tipping me over the edge. As I stood there, more shattered than ever, struggling to even take a breath, I decided that Greg's response would determine my fate. His attitude toward me would be mine. At that very moment my life hung in the balance on his every word, attitude, and approach. It was a moment of destiny. Would he offer me hope or respond in accusation? The latter would have done me in.

Walking toward me he asked, "What is it?"

In anguish and disbelief, still dressed for a day at work, I said, "I got fired."

"That's okay. That's okay," he said as he hugged me.

Pulling away, I raged, "Did you not hear me? I said I got *fired!*"

"I know. I heard you. That's okay. I've been fired before," he said calmly.

"No you haven't, Greg! People don't get *fired!* How could I get fired? I got fired! I am ruined, destroyed! How can I ever recover from this? Who would ever hire me now? Oh my God, Greg! What will I do now?"

He told me how he once was required to fire a bunch of good people, and when he was finished, they laid him off.

"You were laid off," I said, "I was fired! That's different."

"Not really," he said. "But sit down, tell me about it."

I told him about the redhead. He remembered her from the business mixer he had attended. I told him all the details. When I was finished, he stood to his feet in anger, yelling, "Screw ABC company [calling it by name]. F . . . *them!*"

He was mad at them. Not me! He was *defending* me.

Since he somehow still believes in me, maybe I will make it past this, I thought. Up until that very moment, I was sure this would be my demise. This would totally take me down and break me. I was finished. It was just a matter of time.

Shocking me out of my self-annihilating sure ruin, he salvaged just enough hope to hope.

"You will be fine," he said.

Those words went through my heart and into my soul. *I will be fine. He said that I will be fine. So maybe I will.*

That was a defining moment. All Greg's purpose could be wrapped up right there. If this very moment was the entire purpose for Greg being in my life, it wouldn't surprise me. Had he not been there with open arms to support me in that instant, I don't know that I could have ever stood again. So devastating was this blow, it could have wiped me off the planet. Holding fast to his words, I could barely breathe. As if underwater, my nose and mouth bobbled to and from the surface. Underneath the dark waters and back again, I barely remained afloat in my own ocean of destruction and ruin. But for him, I bobbled at the surface and didn't sink to my end. He was my lifesaving raft that I clung to like a drowning cat in a madly rushing river.

"It will take time to heal," he warned. "But you will heal from this," he assured me. "And you will grow angry."

"I will *not* grow angry," I fired back. "Anger is not an option for me."

I was not about to give any control over to anyone who would do me wrong. If I opened so much as a crack into that emotion of anger, it could potentially flood me, taking over my total being. Too much was at stake. I would walk away alive but not in anger. This I *knew*.

The devastation took me back to really believing a scarlet letter was evidently plastered all over me. All my failures from every area of life came flooding back . . . one failure leading to another with one closed door leading to another to eventual recovery, just as Greg had said.

Two years after I had been fired, I discovered the shocking hidden purpose behind it all when answering an unknown call. A panicked woman said, "Susan, I'm calling you as a friend, because I don't know who else to turn to."

It was the powerful wife of that business owner who fired me. "I'm leaving my husband and wondered if you could help. I couldn't think of anyone else to turn to," she continued. The familiar panic of her voice was such a paradox to the powerful woman I knew her to be. The wife of the former company owner who fired me was calling *me* for help.

In what little time we previously shared through the hiring process, she learned a little about my flight from my husband. Never would I have imagined she was in a similar situation and would turn to *me* for help. But this underscored something else I've come to understand: Purpose resides in all our trials. My purpose was expanding outside of my four children and myself to help others.

We met at a local restaurant for a three-hour visit. "I don't know what to do," she said, channeling the image of me wilting beside Gina when Seth walked by in the courtroom.

"Yes, you *do*," I reassured her, hoping to strengthen her as Gina had me.

After three hours of asking pointed questions and discussing her answers, she sat strong, erect, vibrant, and confident. Her posture began to speak *I've got this*!

"By the way," I couldn't resist asking as we stood to leave, "does your husband have a preference in other women?" Unprovoked, she volunteered, "Oh, yes, he loves tall redheads."

Just as I suspected.

"Have a seat," I said, "I have one more story to share."

What if I had quit and given up? I thought. *I would have missed being strength and support for this woman. And if I could be all this for her, how many others might I be able to help?*

With that encounter, we both were liberated through truth. It also launched me into coaching others who struggle with Charming Impossibles. Through the wisdom gleaned from others' experience along with my own, I have passed on insight and wisdom that has helped so many . . . including myself. Her call and our encounter gave me the springboard to a coming future career.

27

Chapter Twenty-Seven

A lie can travel half way around the world while
Truth is putting on its shoes.
—CHARLES SPURGEON

"Mom! I'm so embarrassed! We had school shut down today because of *my dad*!" Sophia stormed into the house, crying. "Police were at all the entrances and exits. We couldn't leave and everyone knew it was because of *my dad* . . . Oh my God!" she exclaimed, running past me to throw herself on her bed.

Crying into her pillow, she sobbed, "Why doesn't he just leave us alone?"

The night before, Seth had appeared at 5:00 p.m. in front of the school secretary's desk demanding to see his daughter. To which the secretary reminded him of the time and fact that students are released at 3:00 p.m.

"No one is here, sir. The students left two hours ago," she said to Seth. "In fact, I'm packing up to leave, myself," she added, grabbing her purse and belongings.

Just then, the secretary's daughter texted Sophia a video of her agitated, strangely behaving father standing by the girl's mom spouting accusations against me and his kids, bemoaning his unfair treatment. As his litany of complaints escalated, he threatened that he could hardly take any more, that he wasn't sure what he might do, and that he was at a breaking point.

"I want to see the pastor," he demanded, evidently refusing to believe she was the only one left.

"Sir, he has gone for the day," she reaffirmed.

Watching on Sophia's phone, we saw this drama play out. It was understandable that the school insisted on a police shutdown that following morning. Not an unreasonable response to a crazy, irrational man but another traumatic hurdle for Sophia and us all.

Just as Barron had predicted, Seth would never come around on the designated day or time.

"Seth will not be able to comply with the rules," I remember Barron stating. "He will not be dictated to, not even by law. Don't worry about it."

Charming Impossibles specialize in creating chaos and drama. They feed on pulling strings, in this case moving police and school staff to take drastic measures. They despise seeing their Targets happy and content, moving on without them. As Seth had no true intention of finding his daughter at school at five o'clock in the evening, he accomplished exactly his intent, to create chaos. That, for him, translated into control.

Seth had been texting, emailing, and leaving voice messages demanding that the kids "get in *his* car and go with him," refusing their offer to meet him anywhere. His insistence grew, requiring them to "pack [their] bags" and "get in the car with him." Not surprisingly, they declined to meet with him more often than not. Not seeking peace nor relationship, he again brought his theatrics to the stage with no regard for his children's well-being.

A narcissist will often seek to create drama and chaos for his or her family even after they leave the dysfunction, another reason leaving is not always an easy, obvious solution. To a narcissist, that equates control . . . which is all they want. Coming up to where we were trying to build a new life for ourselves, he tried to poison public opinion there, too. It was ultimately to no avail, in large part because this was also the home where he and his father had also lived most their lives, leaving us sufficiently safe among all their broken relationships, financially ruined former business partnerships, and all the support of my family and friends who tried to keep me from marrying him in the first place.

His accusations that I was denying him his rights, was guilty of kidnapping, and any other nonsense fell on deaf ears in this town. His public spectacle only further confirmed what people already knew of him. But was his escalating behavior *crazy* dangerous? That was yet to be determined.

In the beginning, at the designated time, the kids waited for him on the front lawn or at an agreed upon Denny's restaurant down the street. He would be a no-show, leaving a skateboard in our backyard instead, sending a text indicating that he had been outside our home praying all night.

One day Sophia came home from school telling me that I needed to go with her to see the principal. Now, *this* is a girl who is *never* in trouble. In fact, Sophia volunteered in a second-grade class, loving and enjoying assisting the kids who returned her kindness with affection and appreciation. She would come home lit up about how much she enjoyed those kids. Sophia brilliantly found ways to self-preserve as she worked through her trauma.

In the beginning, Sophia was one of the most well-liked girls in the school. Teachers marveled how quickly she made friends, and everyone embraced her. "It's unusual," they would say, as with most it took a while for kids to "fit in." It was high school, after all. Grateful for this new beginning, Sophia enjoyed a fresh start.

The year-end award ceremony also fueled Sophia. She loved an academic competition and was a studying beast. Ribbons, trophies, and medals were handed out at a nice dinner attended by students and their parents. Everyone clapped and congratulated the recipient, which motivated Sophia to commit to a strong regimen of academic study leading her to achieving valedictorian her senior year.

Throughout her high school years, Sophia spent every weekend studying as she socially became more estranged. Engaging in counseling to work through past pain, she became more emotionally distant and moody. With no experience with boys or dating, home every night and every weekend unless she was joining in family activities with her siblings and me, she asked for a dog.

"Absolutely not!" I would tell her. Duchess, our old Great Dane, was suffering with tumors, so the poor dog could no longer hold her bladder. And with family of four kids refusing to agree upon putting Duchess to sleep, I was *not* going to allow a new puppy in this chaotic, crazy mix of our lives. One day, Sophia called me from the pound.

"Mom! she said, "I'm so excited! I'm at the pound and it's Senior Citizen's Two-for-One Day. This lady has been nice enough to give me her second dog *free*! Please, oh please, Mom! It's FREE! And this lady agreed to pay for shots and spaying!

"This puppy is so cute, Mom!" she said, ramping up the intensity in order to close the deal. "The lady really wanted this one and so did I! But the dog picked me! She jumped in my lap and wouldn't go to the lady. So this nice lady said she would let me have it if you agree to this. Please Mom, pleasssseee . . ."

It is not clear who saved whom the day Sophia and Sapphire discovered each other at the pound. But it was *love at first sight*. Sophia had been begging me for a dog since the first week we moved away and our adorable little Papillon, Napoleon, ran out the backdoor of my brother's home. In a flash, our family dog, our source of joy, our dear little family pet was gone! We made flyers, posted posters, went door-to-door, and begged God to please bring him back. I could not bear to endure any more heartache. Then all my kids begged me to bring our beloved Great Dane, Duchess, with us as their dad had threatened to put her to sleep!

But "Mom, *please . . .*" remained Sophia's cry.

And so . . . we added potty-training mishaps; chewed-up shoes, furniture, underwear, and my favorite shorts; crises of "Oh my God, the dog got out please help me find her"; and hyper and ridiculously overexcited, annoyingly rambunctious bouncing on furniture in celebration of our arrival home to our mix of sheer chaos. And best of all, a new smile on Sophia's face . . . one that I had not seen in a long time. I believe it's safe to say that Sapphire saved my daughter that day.

Sapphire . . . coupled with Lynn, that is.

Lynn, Sophia's counselor from The Family Place in Dallas, was the destination of a weekly drive we made for two years. Lynn and Sapphire combined gave Sophia the support she needed to face the demons of her past so that she could look forward with hope to a good future.

Sophia went through a number of counselors, struggling to find one she could feel confident in. Lynn was one of Sophia's Ordinary Angels. She had developed the program for The Family Place of Dallas, a non-profit organization for families of abuse. Lynn had 18 plus years of experience with a stellar reputation among judges and other legal dignitaries within the local legal system. Lynn was held in such high regard that local judges would accept her testimony in lieu of forcing a child to endure the likely emotional trauma of testifying in open court. Sophia liked the thought of avoiding all the emotional trauma should it ever come to that and she liked that those who held such positions trusted her. For Sophia, trust was a big issue, as her trust had been violated by her most important authority. If these high ranking officials could trust Lynn, Sophia thought she could too.

Each week, while I waited in the parking lot, Sophia confronted all that haunted her. And I admire to this day Sophia's grit determination, this hard, hard work that had to be done, work that added to her mood swings en route to healing. She bravely pushed through the difficult process of rebuilding trust and hope through counseling as she faced the darkness from her past. Aware the process made her moody, she nonetheless pressed on toward healing.

As her junior year drew to a close, the competition for valedictorian grew stiff. It was down to four, and they each were fighting hard for the title. Sophia hunkered down and really studied hard. She was so determined to be valedictorian. I wanted it for her so badly. Liz even told her that if she was valedictorian, she would attend the ceremony.

"Just one 'win' for this child!" I would pray to God. Sophia was so close. Right behind her was the associate pastor's daughter and, behind her, the secretary's daughter, the volleyball coach's niece. Parents were involved in this competition because winning translated to money, a one-year scholarship to any state college or university. So the stakes were high and the staff watched this competition closely. Sophia took the lead and was holding it when she came home to tell me that the principal wanted to see me.

"What is this about?" I asked Sophia. She then began to tell me a nightmarish drama that seemed straight out of the adult film industry. Just when I thought it could not possibly get darker . . . just when I thought the sun might begin to shine . . . just when I was beginning to feel a twinge of hope for something good, this dark curtain fell, shutting out all the light. She told me that a boy on the football team was telling all the boys in the locker room a trashy rumor about her. The boys told the football coach; the football coach went to Sophia's volleyball coach. The coaches then went to the principal.

Those in authority at her school knew that Sophia had been a victim of abuse. Abusers all work the same. They understand grooming a child. Therefore, any child known to have been victimized is much more vulnerable to other abusers because the pre-work is already done. Victims of abuse are groomed for more. This explains why victims of abuse are often revictimized: they are the easiest targets. These abusers assumed Sophia would easily cave to them. They underestimated her grit . . . and her strength.

Caught completely off guard, Sophia was called into a room with the three adults and her accuser for questioning after they had all been discussing the issue for several days. When blindsided with the claim, answering that she had no knowledge of what they were talking about, her accuser interrupted, "C'mon, Sophia. Just admit it. You know what you did, admit it. You know why you are here."

The lie grew into the three adult staff members telling her they saw a video of her alleged transgression and that she was to 'fess up.'

For two days, administrators pulled Sophia from class seeking a confession while denying her request to call me, but she bravely never caved. Finally, she came home asking me to meet with them.

"Did you do it?" I asked.

"They say they saw me on video," she said, "I do not believe I did this, but they say they saw it. How could that be?" she asked.

"They have it on video? Have you seen it?" I asked.

"No. But they all say it's on video."

Baffled, not imagining they'd all lie, I wondered, *Was she drugged?*

The next day, Sophia, the principal, the two coaches, and I were seated in a conference room. The principal led the meeting and wasted no time seeking Sophia's confession.

"Let me see the video," I demanded.

That's when I knew this whole thing was a lie.

Like little kindergarteners, they actually thought they could get away with this. Shifting in their seats, their eyes looking anywhere but at me, they were caught. The coaches quickly scattered, and Sophia was directed back to class as the principal scampered to her office, leaving me roaming the hall.

Hidden by a wall in the hallway, I overheard the football coach take a phone call from the pastor. The coach updated the pastor about my request to see the video.

The pastor's involved in this too? What is this?

I went to the principal's office, demanding to see the video.

Closing the door behind us, the principal told me she couldn't find the video because she threw it away.

"Why throw away hard, factual evidence of an accusation that is being denied?" I asked.

"I was trying to protect *you* because I would not want to see such an awful video of *my* daughter," she replied.

"*You* are trying to protect *me*?" I said in disbelief.

This sure is some stupid woman to think I would buy that idiotic notion!

But what have they been doing to my daughter?

I had to dig deeper.

That the pastor of this church and school was related, by marriage, to a minister of a very large, well-known, and respected worldwide ministry was regrettably cause for me to give him unearned respect and trust due to association, as did many other parents, I would later learn. Just as when you see one roach, you know many more are hidden nearby. So we can safely assume that when one act of abuse is uncovered, so much more is yet to be revealed. Many tough lessons of similar suffering occurred in that church and school. But I would only learn about it years later. Although what happened to my daughter is a story that is tempting to simply keep quiet about, I eventually told. That's how I learned of many others who also suffered similar manipulation and lies. I knew of no one else talking until I started talking. Sharing exposed more truth that led to healing. More importantly, we discovered that had we started talking sooner, our revelations could have led to prevention.

Refusing to back down, I asked for a second meeting, this time including the pastor and my sister-in-law, Gaye, who was at the time an active member and leader in the church. At the mention of a video, Gaye protested, "Wait a minute, this building has never had capability to record video and the whole live video system is currently down, isn't it?"

There they sat, caught in their hideous lie. They all lied directly to the three of us about the video. Four staff members in a Christian school lying about an innocent student, and for what?

Three years after this incident, I called the volleyball coach, hoping for some answers. Admitting the staff all knew from the beginning there was no video, she told me that the principal had always had it out for Sophia, that during Sophia's sophomore year, her class overwhelmingly voted her their top choice for homecoming court. When the coach turned in the list of the top four names to that principal, she scratched out Sophia's name and instructed the coach to replace it with the second-place name in her stead. That honor would have changed Sophia's school and, probably, her life experience. As the lie unfolded, I learned the football player was a kid who was brought to this school because he had gotten involved with a bad crowd in Los Angeles. He grew up in an economically disadvantaged rough area of LA. He came to this church school for a better environment and a second chance.

Though I encouraged Sophia to leave this school, she refused. More determined than ever, she would go on to become valedictorian of her class.

Lynn, Sophia's counselor, explained that what they did to Sophia was what police often do while interrogating a suspected criminal. She said that the police get false confessions regularly using these tactics and that many states have outlawed this practice as it leads to too many false confessions. I had no idea that had been going on until after Sophia had decided to stay and fight for valedictorian. "Many people would cave under what they did to Sophia," Lynn said.

The volleyball coach also revealed that historically, the church and school had a long trail of lies and deception that started from the top and trickled down, reaching far beyond Sophia. Her knowledge of lies, deception, cover-ups, and scandals ran very wide and deep. She added that the video lie was characteristic of the pastor and his ways and that I was one of numerous such callers seeking answers and understanding for unanswered pain, betrayal, and hurt from that church and school leadership.

While the principal was fired at the end of that school year and the boy wasn't allowed to return, the lie they all spread will never disappear. The ramifications of that experience are still very painful for Sophia.

We were all so proud of Sophia earning the award of valedictorian. This award represented so much more than academic achievement. Sophia was discovering her own strength and power. She didn't cower to bullies. She learned to trust *herself*. She had become a force.

Only one other student was named valedictorian after Sophia, because the school and church were shut down due to bankruptcy the following year.

A few years after Sophia's graduation, I read an article about two young students suffering the same type of interrogation by several teachers and a principal at a nearby school. I couldn't help but wonder if that same principal at Sophia's former school had moved there and was behind it all. Those parents were pressing charges. I'm not sure what I should have done back then, but I definitely should have done more.

We must stop this code of silence where victims are expected to ignore and move on from abuse and bullying quietly. This is not healthy for society. We must take actions of consequence against abusers. They must suffer for their actions to the point of effecting change; otherwise, we are guilty of enabling them to victimize another innocent. I will forever wonder if my inaction allowed those two students to suffer the same pain as Sophia.

While the actions and involvement of Sophia's volleyball coach are unconscionable, as she apologized, sharing her own dilemma of keeping a job under the influence of her twisted Bible-quoting boss, I was reminded of my own unconscionable acts performed under much the same-spirited husband. I am humbled and grateful that many have forgiven me and I, likewise, forgive her and thank her for her honesty.

28

Chapter Twenty-Eight

Greater love hath no man than this,
that a man lay down his life for his friends.
—John 15:13 KJV

I'm on my way to your house with the police. You better be ready, Seth texted the kids. Racing for the door, the kids fled with Winston driving. According to our neighbors, they came and waited outside almost an hour. Another time the police came, Seth saw my dad sitting outside his garage down the street. Escorted by the police, Seth went down to ask my dad where I was. To which my dad fired back that if he knew, he would never tell *him*.

For my dad to watch my life be reduced to this was more than he could handle. His grief grew to new depths after that. He was so sad for me. And he worried that his finances could not continue to sustain him and us.

Soon after the police encounter, I went down to visit my dad. Cutting my visit very short, I rushed to call my brother. "Arthur, you need to come see Dad," I said. "He doesn't look good, not at all."

My brother called an ambulance to come get our father. The doctor in the emergency room said my dad's body was shutting down. Dad was moved to a room, given morphine, and the family was called to say our final goodbyes. And just that quickly, he was gone.

In his home, his will and family business information was neatly laid out on his desk, awaiting our arrival. My dad knew. He knew this was the day and he had prepared for it. We believe he laid himself on his sword for my kids and me. Money was running out and he was tired. He was sad watching my drama grow in such a ridiculous fashion. It broke his heart. He had had enough. He quit taking his medicine and went to join our mother in their heavenly home.

In retrospect, I realize that my dad allowed us to see what giving up and giving in looked like. He broke over betrayal in a business deal while Arthur and I were in high school. While he numbed his pain with beer, he maintained his sweetness, always pouring himself out for his family. While allowing beer to quietly numb his pain, he walked out of this life the greatest champion in our eyes, having given the ultimate gift for us. He gave his life so that we could hope a little longer and live a little more comfortably. While he may have lived some of his final years defeated, my dad died a courageous hero.

That's when I broke the silence with Greg. I called him to tell him that my dad had passed away. He said he'd be in town that evening and invited me to get together. How I looked forward to being with him again. My God, I missed him.

In my favorite dress, sitting to apply makeup in anticipation of seeing Greg again, I see a group text on my phone: "I'm on my way with the police!" "Arthur! Please come!" I begged in my immediate call to my brother. "Seth's on the way with police . . . *again!*"

Busting in the door, my brother rounded up the kids. Winston had no sooner walked in the door from a family ski trip with his girlfriend, announcing his return, dropping his snowboard and suitcase, when I scrambled from my back bedroom with Arthur booming out orders to get in his truck quickly to flee from our home, their dad, and the police. Dressed, but with my hair still soaking wet, tossing makeup in a bag, grabbing my stilettos, I locked up and dashed out the door behind them.

They peeled out toward Arthur's house, and I was off to Greg's. Like a frenzied cat chased by a dog with saliva dripping from jagged molars, I drove in zigzagging directions, taking wrong turns, forgetting how to go where I had been too many times to count. Emotionally crazed, I couldn't find my way to his office. I got lost. I didn't know where I was. I was driving, lost, scared, and in utter panic. Life was visibly taking its toll on me, and I wasn't sure how much more I could take. Finally, making my way to his office, I ran up the stairs and into his arms. I clung to him like a frenzied chased cat climbing a tree to safety.

Holding him tightly, I said, "I'm afraid I'm putting you at risk. You may be an accomplice to my crime because I was fleeing the law. We may both go to jail."

Yep, I fell right back into my 23-year-old needy immaturity. But, my God, I was scared. And my dad just died.

And oh my God, my kids . . .

"I'm not going to jail, Susan," he calmly replied. "But you might," he added with a smile.

"What? I can't go to jail!" I said, spinning deeper into frenzy.

"Don't worry, I'll bail you out if you do," he joked. Unfortunately, it was no joking matter to me.

Ripped and torn in so many directions emotionally, I can only imagine the madwoman he saw in me. Wet hair; no makeup; and a frazzled, disoriented, crazed, mixed-up me was the very reason I broke things off to begin with. I didn't want him to see me that way. And there I was again, breaking that silence, and inviting Greg right back into a gusty, nasty whirlwind of a storm.

Unfazed, he asked me out for a date.

"How would you like to go with me to the art museum tonight? They have a new Mayan art exhibit to preview and a wine and cheese reception."

"No, I don't think so," I said.

"C'mon, it'll do you good." He was right. It was good. So was the wine and getting away from my crazy.

My Dad's Service

Arthur and Gaye planned a small funeral service for my father.

Seth texted that he would come to the service and demanded the kids go with him following the service. My brother called Seth, insisting he not come. I feared that it would only encourage him more to do so. Greg made arrangements for me to see his attorney, Troy.

The morning of the service, I rushed to Greg's attorney's office to collect a temporary restraining order. I showed up to his office dressed in my black dress, my hair wet, wearing no makeup. My emotions were all over the place, from grief to fear to frenzy. Troy began to explain that as a former state representative, he wrote much of the current civil law for the state of Texas. Regaining some of my composure, I asked if he knew Carter. This led to an immediate phone call with Carter on speaker phone. Following our quick greetings, Carter cut in, "Troy, Seth is as bad as ole Max—" she began.

"No . . ." Troy calmly replied, "he can't possibly be as bad as ole Max."

"Like *hell* he isn't," Carter interjected, "He damn sure is. He's worse!"

While I didn't know who ole Max was, I was impressed Troy had a hard time believing Seth was as bad as Carter was saying.

Thanking Troy for the legal protection, I dashed off to meet the rest of our family at the church.

The service was nice . . . and thankfully, uneventful. Gaye's dad officiated the service. Isiah Robertson, Larry and Byron, Gina, Nell, Jeff, and some other close friends came. My dad was finally at rest with my mom. They were at peace.

A New Home

With both of our former houses sold and the money my father left us, I finally had money in the bank. As the kids and I were no longer savages struggling to survive, Greg decided to drop a bomb on me.

"You should pay cash for a house, Susan," he said.

"What? Are you kidding me?"

I couldn't believe he said that. We finally had cash. We had money to live on, and he was instructing me to pour almost all of it into a home?

Greg was a financial genius. His book *Getting to Yes with a Banker* is full of financial wisdom. I knew he knew what he was talking about. But it sounded insane and would throw me back in that desperate place of trying to make ends meet with hand-to-mouth feeding again.

"Your kids will suck it right out from under you, and you will have nothing to show for it in a year," he said. "But they will always need a roof over their heads."

I knew he knew what he was talking about. So I decided to follow his advice rather than that of many others who told me he was crazy and that he wasn't giving me the sound advice I needed. In a nutshell, I looked at the financial situations of those people and then I looked at Greg's. That's all I needed to know.

Gina's mother, Frances, had a darling three-bedroom home she had just fixed up to sell.

And I bought it.

Frances and I went to a title company where I handed over a cashier's check for the whole amount, and just like that I became the proud owner of my first home. It was darling, situated in a really nice neighborhood that had large oak trees and lots of people strolling the streets, walking their dogs. I felt my parents above were smiling down. They would have loved to see this. I was in Frances' home that she had loved and nurtured Gina's four children in for 14 years. This was where Gina brought her children to visit their "MeMaw" all their young lives. Now it was mine. It was a gift.

Marshall walked into the living room. He stretched out his arms and turned himself around, looking up at the vaulted ceilings, so excited to have a real home, plenty of space, and his own room. Our furniture looked so nice in it. I hung pictures and we began to feel a little more "normal." I was also able to pay cash for a truck for Marshall. Sophia drove my dad's Oldsmobile and I had my beautiful Lexus. The older two were off at college.

All our belongings were paid for in full. It was a miracle. We were making it. Greg was right about the house. It was the best decision I ever made. Granted, it was hard. But many, many times I was so thankful I didn't have rent or payments to worry about. My house was security for us. No matter what else was falling apart, we had our home. I am forever grateful for his advice on that.

But I still needed to find work.

* * *

With a fresh start, hope for all of was slowly being restored. I was barely making ends meet, but I was doing it. The only bit of unfinished business with Seth was that he owed child support. I let him off the hook on his obligation for insurance and medical costs. We absorbed those and kept moving. But with all the kids graduated from high school, it was time for him to pay his overdue child support.

29

Chapter Twenty-Nine

The biggest risk is not taking any risk.
—RICHARD BRANSON

Life is inherently risky. There is only one big risk you should avoid at all costs, and that is the risk of doing nothing.
—DENNIS WAITLEY

After the sale of our two properties, I received a letter from the IRS. It said that I owed $125,000 in taxes. I was to respond by a certain date, or. . . .

Right there, at mid-sentence, is where I put down the letter. I never read what would happen if I didn't pay because it was so huge and impossible that it might as well read I owed $2 million. I knew ignoring it wouldn't make it go away. But it was too big, too awful, and I just simply didn't know how to handle it. Nor did I know what to do when another final reminder came. I just pushed it aside.

One day, at a business networking event, I was making small talk with several business people as usual when one man mentioned that years ago he received a letter from the IRS that he continually ignored. I told him I could not believe he was telling me this as I had one of those letters sitting on my dresser at home. He asked what the deadline date was. I said, "Tomorrow."

Deeply disturbed and concerned for me, he urged me to do something about it that evening as it would lead to a crisis if I did not. I let him know that I had no money, no job, and that I didn't know what to do. And with that, he offered to help.

This nice man named Paul came over and helped me. I gave him complete access to all my files, and he spent hours on my computer scanning information into it. He created a file for me on a flash drive, called his tax man in Dallas, and arranged for me to meet him first thing in the morning, instructing me to hand him this file of my information he had organized and prepared.

That morning, IRS deadline day for me, I met his tax man, saving me from I do not know what as I never could bear to read that letter.

I have been told that I am crazy for letting a perfect stranger in my home, for giving him unfettered access to my computer and all my files. While it was risky, I refuse to build walls around me, choosing to not trust that good people, with good intentions, are out there willing to help when we need it. I suppose I retain what some may call a naïve belief in the goodness of most of mankind. For those who have taken advantage of another's trust, their day will come. It will. Good will win over evil in the end. Good will have the final word. I believe this. I am thankful for all the good people in my life who keep proving there are plenty of reasons to believe in good, to do good for others, and to hope that good does, in fact, still win.

Paul sold me his reliable Volvo for $1,000 so that Winston could drive it during the summer for an internship. At summer's end, I asked if he knew someone interested in it, as I needed to sell it. A true Ordinary Angel, he bought it back for what I paid and sold it to another woman in need. Paul is a great example of quietly doing his part in his corner of the world. He's doing what he can. Offering his car as he did allowed Winston to work that summer. May Paul's generosity be an encouragement to us all to do our part with what we have—or with the knowledge and experience we possess—to help others.

30

Chapter Thirty

The most valuable player is the one who makes
the most players valuable.
—*Peyton Manning*

Today I will do what others won't, so tomorrow
I can accomplish what others can't.
—*Jerry Rice*

No matter the circumstances you may
be going through, just push through it.
—*Ray Lewis*

While at a nail salon having my nails done, I was watching a football game on TV when my young manicurist mumbled out, "I hate NFL football players," dipping her brush in the bottle of clear gel.

"What?" I asked, "Why do you hate football players? I've never heard that from anyone."

"They are all abusers," she said scathingly, stroking my nails with polish.

And that's when I began sharing my story:

Each time a process server tried to serve Seth papers, Seth would run and hide, doing anything in his power to avoid being served. And when they did manage to serve him, it predictably ended in outbursts of anger. As I finally put the legal wheels in motion for Seth's years of unpaid child support, I anticipated his outrageous behavior would be *legendary.*

Here's how the process works: Once a court date is set, it expires if the person is not served and the whole process starts all over again. That means more fees for the court and the server. On the last day Seth could be served before we would have to start anew, Marshall received a text from his dad asking if he'd like to meet.

"Oh my gosh, yes!" I told Marshall.

Seth suggested Papadeaux's, Marshall agreed, and a meeting was set. My attorney scrambled to find a server, getting the papers ready. Familiar nauseating terror built up inside again as I considered how Seth would handle himself after being served papers while meeting his son for dinner. The kids agreed that we all should go. It could not be just Marshall meeting with him alone, and we certainly could not stand him up, fearing what wrath would come from such a setup.

Typically, certain NFL buddies would call to check in periodically seeing how we were all doing. One such call came from Larry just before we were to meet Seth. After sharing my fear of our coming meeting at the restaurant where the papers would be served, Larry, a former NFL association president, said, "Sounds like we need to host a leadership meeting tonight. What time did you say?"

"We are meeting Seth at six," I said.

"And at which location, again, shall we have this leadership meeting?" he asked.

"Papadeaux's on I-30," I said.

"We'll be there for you, Susan," Larry assured me.

"Larry, will you meet me outside and walk us in?"

"I sure will. I'll be there. Don't you worry. You will all be all right."

Isiah, Larry, and Byron, all former presidents of the association, were there waiting for us. The server waiting for Seth in the parking lot called me while I was on the way asking Seth's description, only to abruptly hang up. Within a minute, he called back to tell me that the papers had been served and that Seth had thrown them down to the ground, angry, spewing expletives.

"I told him I didn't care what he did with the papers," the server told me, "he is still held accountable for the content." And with that, the server hung up.

Larry came to escort us in. I went one direction inside the restaurant, showing the kids where we'd be waiting for them, while the kids went over to Seth. They sat down at a table together.

Emotions quickly flared at Seth's table with him shoving Sophia, causing the guests at adjacent tables to get very uncomfortable. The waitress stood helplessly by Seth and the children as if to guard the kids. Seth eventually made his way over to me, shoving me.

Shocked, Isiah exclaimed, "He just shoved you . . . in public!"

It was another pathetic, embarrassing public display of Seth's true nature. After a little back and forth, the kids were ready to leave. Larry walked us out while Isiah and Byron talked with Seth.

They kept the situation from escalating into a really big problem that day.

After spending an hour with Seth, Larry called me.

"He's crazy!" Larry said. "Susan, I'm concerned for your safety."

"Larry, there is nothing I can do. My temporary restraining orders have expired, and I can't renew without a current, direct threat from him." I explained. "It's just a piece of paper anyway."

I truly believe Isiah, Larry, and Byron stood between us and true disaster that day. Without them being there, I believe we would have had a very different outcome. That they dropped everything and showed up for us that day saved us from almost certain tragedy.

With their help, Seth was served the papers, would be forced to show up for court, and would finally pay the child support he owed.

Shortly after that incident people began suggesting that I needed to meet Pat Smith, Emmitt Smith's wife. Hearing this repetitively, I grew curious. Then an acquaintance handed me a ticket to one of Pat's events. "Please go in my place . . . you need to meet her," Cynthia said.

Pat was hosting a small, intimate group at a style-show event at Neiman Marcus in Dallas. Before the event began, she stood introducing herself. She said she felt compelled to share a little about her history. She then relayed her story of backing a white Jaguar with tan leather interior filled with all her earthly goods down a driveway, her daughter at her side, leaving an abusive marriage and a beautiful home and lifestyle for the unknown.

We even left in the same car, I thought. *Wow, I did need to meet her.*

Following her event, I read her book *Second Chances,* her story of becoming a former first-runner-up to Miss USA and leaving domestic violence. Attending a couple of other conferences she hosted to mentor young women, I watched how she would lead, gleaning knowledge and understanding from each opportunity. And watching how her current husband, former Dallas Cowboy Emmitt Smith, supports her, I grew increasingly inspired about my second chance at life and living.

The day of court came. Seth and his dad stood before the judge requesting that Seth not have to pay child support as they explained their religious views condemning us. The judge was furious and wanted to throw Seth in jail immediately, but my attorney, Troy, encouraged me to accept partial payment in a cashier's check with instruction of how he would pay in full later. I explained that we would have to go through this all over again. Troy did not believe he would push such limits with a district court.

This is why additional training should be required for attorneys and judges. Troy is one of the finest and most qualified in his field. His understanding of how a Charming Impossible operates was not even close to that of Carter and Barron's.

Against my better judgment, I agreed to my attorney's advice.

As with any Charming Impossible, Seth truly believed he was the highest authority. He was wrong. With another court fee and server fee, we did finally get our child support paid in full, and I received a permanent legal injunction stating that Seth was never to come within a mile of my home and work, indefinitely. Finally, I had permanent legal protection: Should he come near me, he would be arrested.

It was finally over, at least with the legal dealings, anyway.

We could finally move on.

Or so we thought.

31

Chapter Thirty-One

*Crocodiles are easy. They try to kill and eat you. People are harder.
Sometimes they pretend to be your friend first.*
—STEVE IRWIN

*When we lose an animal species to extinction,
we lose part of our family.*
—UNKNOWN

Running low on funds, I asked Greg if I could borrow some money.
He lent me $10,000, holding the car titles and my life insurance policy
as collateral.

He asked when I was going to get a job.

I said, "I'm trying!"

To which he said, "No, you're not!"

I asked, "What do you mean?"

"Trying is waking up every morning, putting on a suit, and going
door-to-door to businesses until you come home with a job!" he replied.

I responded, "They just send me home and tell me to apply online!"

"Then you get up the next day and do it again," he said. "And you keep doing it till you get a job!"

I didn't know that. I really thought I was putting in the requisite effort networking, passing out my resume, and meeting people who knew people.

So, the next day, I put on my suit and went door-to-door until I met a manager at a men's clothing store. We hit it off and he gave me an application. The next day, I received an email from my friend Sharon, asking for my resume to send to a board member for the organization where she worked. He asked her for a recommendation. She recommended *me*.

Soon, I found myself interviewing for *two* jobs.

That's about the time Sophia called me one morning.

"Mom, I had a wreck!"

"Are you okay?"

"I'm fine, but I don't know about the car."

She had rear-ended a parked car right there in our neighborhood! Our insurance paid to repair their car. My dad's old Oldsmobile was totaled. Sophia started driving my Lexus when she had somewhere to go. Or she carpooled with her cousin to school.

Within a week, I received a phone call from her again. This time she was on the highway in a five car pile-up involving a hit and run. My Lexus was totaled. My insurance provided us a temporary rental car.

Before the month was complete, while driving Sophia to Dallas for counseling in my rental car, Marshall called.

"Mom, I'm so sorry. I'm so sorry. I'm so sorry."

Oh, my . . .

"What is it?" I asked.

"Mom, I'm okay, but I had a wreck. I'm so sorry."

While showing off for a friend performing a 360, Marshall totaled his truck.

In a month, we went from three cars to one rental car and all the insurance money obligated to pay off collateral for a loan.

We were broke, without a car, without a job, with the rental due back in a week.

Embarrassed, defensive, and devastated, I took both Greg and me to a breaking point. Greg called me a "deadbeat," and I listed a host of offensives against him in retaliation. We were finished. This was final.

With barely enough insurance money, I paid off my debt to Greg, leaving me no car and hardly any money to eat.

"What are you going to do about a car?" he asked.

Having absolutely no idea, I said, "That's not your problem. It's mine."

With the rental car due back in a week, I had no idea what I would next. Gathering all my kids in our living room, I explained our predicament.

"I see no way out of this situation," I said, alerting them to the consequences we all were suffering due to their actions. "This will not kill us," I reassured them. "While I do not know how we will make it out of this, I trust we will. And when we *do* make it to the other side of this, I want you all to know . . . it will be because of God."

With no father, no Greg, and a totally worn out Arthur and Gaye, we had nowhere to turn but up to the heavens. So I did. I thought about Eleanor and Corrie, my two heroes of faith. I looked back at all the miracles we experienced; our supportive friends from our old hometowns; Gina and all our friends in our new life; Lynn and Theresa at The Family Place; the Women's Center volunteers; Dr. Haynes; Paul helping me out with the IRS; all the people at the good school (and some good people at the *bad* school); Gina, Isiah, Larry, and Byron; Greg; and so many more. While our journey had been tough, we had so many extraordinarily loving, giving Ordinary Angels step in with miraculous timing to help us. These people were not asked for, they simply appeared.

This whole journey, I had stepped away from the Bible, the church, and theology, stripping my faith down to God and gratefulness, even if weeds were all I could think for which to be thankful. I certainly wasn't living according to what I believed was biblical, yet God remained close, real, and helpful. So did my faith and what I believe even matter? God worked continually in my life regardless, so it seemed.

Then I thought about each person who had stepped in to help along the way. Every one of them were believers in the Bible and the Christian faith. Perhaps they were listening to Him, hearing Him, and being His hands as they gave to us regardless of my doubts and my wavering faith. Without asking for anything of God, I acknowledged what and who had been in our lives that saw us through. Inspired and encouraged by our historical journey, knowing this wasn't going to kill us, I calmly anticipated watching how this all would play out.

That's when I received a phone call asking me to meet with Sharon's board member, Jack, and one of his partners, Craig, of a wildlife reserve for endangered species. We planned to meet at a restaurant in Dallas for lunch.

Driving up with no money in my purse and none in my bank account, I valet parked, where a $12 fee was posted. Without even a dollar in my purse, empty of any funds, and nowhere to turn, I handed over my cluster of rental car keys and walked in to meet Jack and Craig.

Over lunch, Jack and Craig explained they wanted me for the position but that I would have to be patient because this organization moved slowly on decisions like these. I explained that I wanted the job but needed something now and would, therefore, take the other position I was offered at the men's store. No, they said, they wanted me to come aboard, adding that they would try to encourage the wildlife park to hire me.

After lunch, much to my relief, without any suggestion from me, Craig walked me out to my car and paid the parking.

Jack and Craig arranged for me to come in for interviews with the staff on Monday, totally unaware that my rental car was due back Tuesday. Monday, with just enough gas in my car, I arrived and was ushered into a board room with 12 visibly unhappy directors of varied departments. Clearly feeling forced by the board to take the interview, they questioned me. Aware that I was being shoved down their throats, desperate for the job, I stood strong.

One asked, "Why, if you are interested in working here, why haven't you come to tour and experience the park yourself?" It was a great question. I do not remember how I answered it, but the truth was that I did not have enough gas or money for the $25 ticket. The staff broke up into two groups and toured me through the park. My very soul swelled with joy, encountering the wildlife, having them eat delectable treats from my hands. I was spellbound with each encounter of these incredible creatures under attack for survival to exist. It felt as though I were one with them.

And then I heard, "That, over there, is a gazelle."

"A gazelle!" I exclaimed. That was a creature I remembered God mentioning to Job. This took me back to my lowest moment, that moment lying on my driveway, wrestling with things of God and nature while my daughter was in the emergency room miles away.

Oh my goodness, I thought. *These are the remnants of God's creation. They are struggling for their very existence like me, the fly, the ant, and the weeds. Against all odds, we are all still here. God cares about these animals, this work, and their preservation as He cares about mine.*

That's when I knew this job was mine. A power higher than Jack and Craig brought me there. And whether or not these directors wanted me there, I belonged there. I was *sent* there. And I understood the plight of this endangered wildlife in a way they could never imagine.

Soaking up the experience of feeding the giraffe, getting near the cheetah, and seeing the black and white rhinos up close, looking so much like survivors of the dinosaur age, I relaxed and owned it. I was on an African safari in Texas, with God's creation teaching me life lessons connecting with my soul.

Each creature that came near me filled me with inspiration. The people around me faded into the background as the life within each animal imparted an unspoken message of hope and persistence to the core of my soul. While silent, they shouted hope and healing into my broken parts that only they could reach. We were communicating, and I was *hearing* them. This was what God was trying to tell me that day I struggled on my driveway over Audrey.

Aware that I needed to buy a new car on Monday, Craig coached me like a father, guiding the resistant executive director to write a letter of intent for salary since I did not have pay slips or decent credit. Gina's friend at the Nissan dealership greeted me, assisting me, as Craig coached me by phone.

With only a letter of intent, decimated credit, and no cash, I bought my brand new Nissan Monday evening, turning in my rental the evening before it was due. In preparation of my new career as director of development for a wonderful wildlife center, I drove home in my new car with a salary that would cover our needs. We were finally on our way to recovery.

During my time at the wildlife center, I collaborated with organizations, individuals, and various supporters who are instrumental in projects that help sustain endangered species. With significant partnerships in place, I felt confident that further growth and development would continue without me. In due time, my life took on other directions, but I will forever be grateful for the lessons I learned from those animals fighting to survive and their Ordinary Angels working to help them.

32

Chapter Thirty-Two

A friend is one that knows you as you are,
understands where you have been, accepts what
you have become and still gently allows you to grow.
—WILLIAM SHAKESPEARE

When someone else's happiness is your happiness, that is love.
—LANA DEL REY

On my own two feet for the first time since being 23 felt good. Audrey expressed her pride in me for standing on my own two feet. She had returned to school, graduating from college with honors on the dean's list. I had a good paying job with benefits. My kids were going to the dentist for the first time since they were in braces. They could get regular check-ups and cleanings.

While my success created new confidence, it would remain shallow due to the shaky foundation of my need for more understanding about our emotional abuse and its effects. I was finally bringing stability into my kid's lives that they had never known; yet, simultaneously, we had never been more unstable, broken, and shattered. Empowered by breaking away from divorce and years of mind games, we still grappled with years of manipulation that influenced how we processed and thought through issues. It kept us all stuck in confusion and self-doubt.

Eventually, I would learn and study the tactics and strategies used by abusers. Understanding, healing, and self-forgiveness came in the discovery of that knowledge. Unfortunately, the knowledge was scattered, not centralized, nor was it easy to find. Therefore, healing came in layers of discovery through people, research, reading, and meditation . . . which led to this book.

With two in college and one entering the next year, we still lived hand-to-mouth. Finances continued to be a worrisome burden while deep, self-degrading forces still caused me to struggle with unworthiness. Owning a home outright is empowering and comforting. For that, I will forever be grateful to Greg. It was the most financially stabilizing choice I have ever made. I'm grateful I listened to him rather than the many other voices contradicting his wisdom. Anyone can make it on peanut butter and jelly sandwiches. But we, as humans, need a roof over our heads. We need a home. We checked off one big looming concern of where we would live. Greg was right, and his wisdom blessed us emotionally and financially. It was a fantastic investment.

Greg had recommended an insurance agent, Linda, to insure my home. Linda came out, looked it over, and offered to meet me at a wine bar to sign the contracts as her office was a long way away.

With Linda to my right by an outdoor fire pit at the bar, a gentleman sat to my left. Since he didn't seem very conversational, I stepped around him to greet a man I knew, Paul, who sat just beyond him. Paul and I visited with a mutual friend briefly and then I said my goodbye to Linda.

On my way home from the wine bar, Linda called me, saying, "You need to meet the man who sat next to you."

"What?" I asked. "He had nothing to say and seemed completely disinterested."

"I got his card. I talked to him," she continued. "If he agrees, will you meet with him?"

Still recovering from Greg, reveling in my newly single, self-sufficient life, I reluctantly agreed. The three of us returned to the wine bar the following weekend. This time, he was engaging, interesting, and clearly interested. My expectation of his interest lasting was short-lived, knowing my hidden, dark past. After all, any good, decent man would run from me once learning what I had been through, what I had enabled and drug my children through. But once we were engaged in conversation, Linda left us to ourselves. Before closing down the wine bar that evening, JR lined up our next date for the following weekend. That began a consistent, ongoing cycle of his lining up a following date from that day forward.

At first it was one night a week, then two. It grew into how much time I was willing to spend with him. It was as if we were checking off every fine dining experience in Dallas. He'd pick me up in a suit and tie, sometimes with flowers, other times with chocolates or gourmet cookies. Late at night, he'd return me to my front door and give me a kiss on the cheek.

Every date was opportunity to unload more of who I was and why he could not possibly be interested me.

"This will be our last date," I'd tell Gina on speakerphone while combing through my closet seeking a not yet worn *with him* dress for our final date, explaining to her the next layer of my disgusting past I'd elect to divulge that evening.

"Why are you doing this?" she'd ask, trying to discourage me. "You don't have to tell him *everything*."

"He thinks he's interested in a *relationship*," I'd tell her. "Once he knows how trashy my life is, he'll flee."

"Well, you're probably right," she'd agree. "If you share *that*, this will probably be your last date."

This continued week after week after week into month after month. At first, I would only accept one weekend evening as I had other suitors and two high school kids at home. His interest irritated me because he wasn't responding as I'd expected. Finally, four months into this, around two in the morning on the Dallas Ritz Carlton back outdoor patio over an empty glass of Chardonnay, I told him, "I'm done." Feeling deeply confused that he was still sitting there, I added, "I've told you everything."

"You're finished?" he asked, obviously seeking confirmation.

"Yes," I said, feeling completely emptied of any hidden, dark secrets. "You have heard it all."

"Good," he said. "So can you put that behind you?"

"Can *I* put this behind *me*" I retaliated, "is not the question. The question here is can *you*?"

"Why, sure," he so calmly replied. "It isn't any big deal, Susan," he continued in his Texas good-ole-boy kind of way, "we all have troubles in life."

"*Troubles?*" I exclaimed. "Have you not been listening? This is not some ordinary kind of troubles. This is messed up, crazy shit! This is trauma, drama they can't write in the movies ... and I've allowed it all to happen! I've allowed my children to suffer. I brought them into this. I've hurt my parents, my friends, and all those I love most, and *you* say *you* can put this behind *you*?"

"Why, sure," he says, tossing up his arms and relaxing them in his lap with a silent smile.

Hmm. I had to think about that, as this was not what I expected from a self-made, highly successful man who seemingly had no notable trauma in his life. Yes, he lost his wife to a tragic and sudden, unexpected death, but he didn't even have the failure of divorce, so how could he possibly forgive or understand *me*? It didn't make sense to me because the old me, the judgmental me before marriage, before any true trauma, would have not been willing or interested in someone who had been through all I had. So why was he interested when the old me could have never accepted *me. How could he?*

We started spending more time together in awkward, strained silence because I no longer had much to say and JR rarely ever did. The silence cumulatively frustrated me, angered me, and then calmed me.

I reflected on the counselor who answered my question as to why was I attracted to certain men. He answered me with a question, asking, "Who does that person remind you of?"

JR was just like my dad, who expressed little or no emotion. JR was steady, reliable, and *safe*. My counselor went on to say that we often think of the familiar as love. Because we are drawn to the familiar explains why we keep certain relationship cycles going.

Actually being beside someone with whom I was able to complete a thought and think without another fogging my airwaves, knowing I could rely upon how he'd react to anything, I was *safe*. Safe was key. No longer was someone interrupting my thoughts with words meant to distract, control, or cause intended pain. With no fear of him, concerns of unmet expectations, or fear of triggering an emotional outburst from him, I could relax and peacefully reconnect with myself. I could just be.

Now, I'll admit, in the beginning, I'd occasional pop off at him to see if he'd retaliate. I'd cry, feel sad, or be happy, forcing my roller-coaster madness of emotions upon him just to be sure he would be steady should a real emotion emerge. He remained steady and, eventually, I grew more emotionally stable.

JR was a steady source of affirmation, approval, respect, admiration, and little, if any, varied emotion. JR became an immovably reliable constant in my ever-changing life. As I grew back my confidence, my self-worth began to emerge. I studied and read about emotional abusers and how their victims suffer long after the relationship ends. Knowledge created growth and understanding. When I'd go too deep into analysis, JR would center me with good-ole Texas common sense like, "Susan, it's never as good or bad as it seems."

Along with stability, JR also brought "lifestyle" into my world. With him, I lived the life of the rich and famous while actually just barely making it financially. With JR, I returned to the life of shopping, travel, and fabulous dining. Eventually, we did discuss our relationship, the potential of marriage, and what we each saw in our future.

"I want you any way I can have you," he said one day. "If you would like to get married, we can get married."

I asked, "How do you feel about creating our own relationship, building our own parameters?"

He liked that idea. We created an agreeable relationship of mutual respect and love that suits us well.

33

Chapter Thirty-Three

Save one life, you're a hero, save thousands of lives,
you are a doctor or nurse in the ER.
—UNKNOWN

Superheroes don't wear capes, they wear scrubs.
—UNKNOWN

While away in Colorado, I received a call from Marshall.

"Mom, I'm okay, but I had a motorcycle accident and I'm about to go in for surgery," he said, his words echoing into my soul trying to awaken comprehension and gravity.

"Marshall, is there a nurse around?"

"Hello?" answered a harried, intense female voice.

"Ma'am, is this a matter of life and death?" I asked, dread gripping my soul.

"Um, Marshall . . ." she said in a shaky, high-pitched voice, "do you have any final words for your mother?"

"Mom, I appreciate you. I love you."

"I love you, too, Mar—" Click.

Looking out the sliding glass door to the Beaver Creek snowcapped mountain miles and miles away from JPS Hospital in Fort Worth where my 20-year-old son was headed to surgery all alone, I stood grasping for thoughts and emotions. I felt nothing. Empty. Frozen. My mind traversed to exactly a month prior sitting with the family at the dinner table for Marshall's twentieth birthday dinner party, waiting on him because he was uncharacteristically late. He was late because he came on his new Ninja "crotch rocket" as he affectionately referred to it. It was an all-black motorcycle he had just purchased that very afternoon.

"Don't judge me if I don't stop my life to take care of you!" I announced before the whole family at Marshall's birthday celebration dinner.

So this is how he's going to try to end his life? was my first thought knowing Marshall struggled with not wanting to live. Something we all struggled with at times, but his had become deeply concerning.

My second thought was, *No, God won't let him die like this. He just wouldn't. But I fear the condition in which He may allow Marshall to live. Please, not somehow permanently impaired, oh God, no, please: that would be even greater hell on earth for him!* How do I allow myself to even think such things?

"Don't judge me if I don't stop my life to care for you one day," I told him over birthday cake when he told us about his new motorcycle.

"Mom!" "Stop!" "I can't believe you just said that!" was the unanimous response from my other children.

"I'm sorry," I said quieting myself.

But I wasn't. I knew the immature, inexperienced, crazy, reckless boy driver he was. I also knew the angry, frustrated, hanging-on-by-a-thin-thread, wonderful, tender, sensitive, hurting son that he was. None of which was a healthy mentality to be riding a powerful Kawasaki "crotch rocket."

We all went out to see the beauty, his pride and joy. And beautiful, it was! It really was very nice.

Looking brand new, Marshall fought back a huge grin as he was proud of himself, as he so should have been. Having saved his money over the past couple years, he bought it in full with cash, put himself through a riding class, and secured a motorcycle driver's license and insurance without telling any of us. His twentieth birthday gift to himself was our surprise.

We all oohed and awwed over it. It was impressive.

At the close of the evening, Aunt Gaye asked that he spend the night.

"It's dark now, Marshall. Will you please stay the night and leave in the morning?" He agreed.

"Marshall, I really am very proud of you," I later told him. "I've always taught you to dream big and that you can accomplish anything you put your mind to. You have dreamed of having this since you were a little boy."

"It's all I've ever wanted, Mom," he responded. "I did it myself!"

"You did, indeed. And I'm very proud and happy for you."

His calls became more positive. "Mom, I'm making new friends with other guys who have bikes, the kind of friends I've been wanting to get to know. This bike is really turning things around for me, Mom. It's good. Really good," he said. "Things are looking up," he added, in an effort to reassure me.

"I'm happy for you, son," I reiterated. "I am very pleased. It's nice to hear you so happy."

One month later, almost to the exact date of his birthday dinner party, while in Colorado, I received that life-altering call. His call to me left me in silence. I stood in absolute silence. It was as if time stopped. I then group texted his siblings to inform them of what little I knew.

They all gathered in the emergency waiting room, waiting for any news. I waited from afar. Finally, the silence breaks. Marshall is in the ICU. He is stable. He can't see visitors. The children stay in the waiting room. Uncle Arthur and Aunt Gaye go to join them. I wait. Sound stopped again. Silence overwhelmed me. I didn't dare to think. Scolding myself, how dare I not think.

I didn't know *what* to think.

My two very best friends had sent their daughters on to heaven. *One at 10 years of age, the other at 15. Was I to send mine at 20? Stop thinking like that! He will be fine. He will be fine.*

I called Dr. Haynes. He let me know that with HIPPA laws, it could take a while to learn about Marshall's case but that he would inquire and get back to me as soon as possible.

Gina calls. She says, "Come home. Your son needs you."

Still no sound. Only every other word from voices and only the directives from the words. Otherwise, like a character in a silent black and white movie, I function.

On a packed 5:00 a.m. shuttle to Denver International Airport, my phone rings. It's Dr. Haynes.

"You are on your way home, right?" he says.

My heart beating through my chest, I realize that he's talking to me like a doctor, not a friend. *Oh God, no,* I think to myself. His tone is unusually professional. I don't like the implication of that.

"It's a miracle, Susan!" he says, "It's a miracle your son is alive. I am amazed at and so proud of our staff. Dr. Gandhi saved Marshall's life. Do you hear me?"

Yes, I heard . . . rapid speed, no other vehicle involved, internal bleeding, ruptured spleen. Rated from 1 to 5, he now is a 4. He is stable. Broken bones and appendages, but not worried, at least right now. Many die monthly from this in our hospital. Friend's young daughter hit a tree skiing and died on way to hospital due to ruptured spleen. Minutes from his life passing. But he's here. Must stabilize before concerning ourselves with other injuries, no brain or spinal injury. It's a miracle.

Finally arriving back in Texas, I make my way to the hospital. I see smiling faces. Peace. Calm. All the family is there. Gina is there.

Marshall is out of ICU and in a private room. He looks wrapped like a mummy on one side, with machines and patches attached all over his chest. He's barely clad in a thin hospital gown with a white sheet disheveled and crumpled by his feet. He's smiling and says, "I thought you weren't going to change your life for me."

We grin.

My young adults have been taking care of one another for days before I arrive. They have a system and it's working great. Nurses seem more like aunts and uncles, they know my kids so well. A wonderful system is in place. Taking comfort in the confidence my young adult children exude, I rest and watch.

It was good. Very good.

Audrey and I spent nights there together with him in his room. With Audrey returning to work, I stayed nights myself. One day while Marshall was at the end of his recovery at the hospital, I realized he was becoming his old self again. I said to Nurse Lisa, "I'm going home tonight and leaving him with you."

"Good," she said, "I got this."

I knew she did.

"Please make sure he *never* comes in here like this again," I implored.

"I sure will," she said, adding, "This is *nice* Nurse Lisa. I can be mean. And he certainly doesn't want to come back to *mean* Nurse Lisa!"

Perfect. I went home leaving my son behind with not only peace but anticipation of so much more goodness happening in my son's heart and soul for his much-improved general well-being. A miracle took place that they all saw, were so very proud of, and came to his bedside to see. But there was another miracle equally monumental taking place in him that they *couldn't* see. It could only be seen from a mother's vantage point. With that said, any mother understands what I mean. It was good. It was so very *good*. Marshall was beginning to see that there was a purpose in his life being spared. Much of the staff who came to see him would tell him so.

Toward the end of Marshall's recovery, the police officer who tended to Marshall the day of his accident called me to see how Marshall was doing.

"You were part of a miracle," I said, adding how Marshall's life was miraculously spared.

"There's more to that miracle," the officer replied. He explained that the 911 callers who stopped beside the road at the scene of Marshall's accident directed emergency crews to the wrong highway. "They guided first responders to Business 187 just as I drove past the described scene on Hwy 187. Had I not been right where I was at the time of the call, I would have missed it, and help would have arrived 30 minutes or more later.

"It was a miracle I was there," he said.

A few orthopedic surgeries later, Marshall was put back together for an expected full 100 percent recovery, finally released, able to return to his apartment. He could go home, but it would be several months before he could return to work. The Marshall I took to his apartment after several weeks of surgeries and recovery was an even stronger and more confident young man than the Marshall who entered that hospital one month after his birthday. He exuded personal growth in uniquely crucial ways. He had been sincerely nurtured by the staff.

Due to the miraculous nature of Marshall's recovery involving JPS and the community Trauma 1 emergency system, he was asked to speak about his experience before the Texas State Legislature in Austin.

On July 13, 2016, the House Appropriations Committee's Subcommittee on Article II and the House Public Health Committee held a joint hearing regarding the interim charge to study the Texas Trauma System. Over the course of four hours, testimony was given by the Department of State Health Services, emergency care providers, physicians, and allied healthcare providers on the Texas Trauma System. Marshall gave testimony before the joint committee hearing on his own personal experience with the Texas Trauma System. He told his story of what had happened to him just a few months earlier, expressing thankfulness that he was taken to a major trauma center where life-saving interventions and specially trained medical personnel were readily available to care for him. He answered questions the committee asked, was passionate in sharing his story, and eager to have a positive impact on the legislative session and the decisions that would be made regarding his state's Trauma System.

Marshall was recognized by many of the top medical and legislative professionals for presenting one of the most articulate and impactful testimonies they'd ever heard. They credited him for their decision to provide funding that was at risk.

The Marshall I had brought here only six years prior could not look anyone in the eye and was almost mute, hardly able to talk, he was so emotionally collapsed. Marshall had come a long way. JPS played a significant role in his emotional development.

As I celebrated joy for each of my kids and their courageous rebuilding of themselves, another dark cloud hovered in the distance.

Ever since Marshall was 12, he struggled with life, the meaning of life, questioning if he wanted to live. Since leaving, we all faced those challenges. Life was heavy, dark, and kept beating at us with ferocious force. While Marshall recovered at home alone, he spent considerable time feeding his addiction to video games. He began sinking back into depression. He told the mother of one of his friends that he felt like a failure for having wrecked his motorcycle. He told her he felt like a loser, a comment from long ago that kept circulating in his mind.

After an accident of that magnitude, it is common for the most mentally healthy person to suffer depression. It's a common response, one to monitor no matter the mental health of an individual. But the pileup of issues began weighting Marshall down.

"I don't belong here. I don't want to be here," he would more frequently say. "I would never want to bring children into this hell. If I go now, I hurt fewer people," he'd say, trying to convince me. "Mom, please . . . you are the only reason I'm still here . . . I need you to be okay with this."

"No," I'd say, "No, never, Marshall. Stop this. Please."

One day he informed me he was on a 21-day water fast. I was not quite sure what he hoped to accomplish from this. It involved careful juicing and trying natural, healthy specific foods before reintroducing regular meals back into his system. While I didn't understand his purpose, the interest and care for his health seemed positive to me. He was trying . . . trying *something*.

"Mom, I need you to be okay with this, please," he'd more frequently beg me. "I'm done, Mom, let me go."

"No! Never! You can't do this, Marshall!" I'd insist. "We'll find you help," I'd say.

Counselors, programs, self-discovery training, new career training . . . he tried it all, only to say, "Mom, are you finished yet? Are you done?"

"Go see the movie *The Shack* with me," I asked, grasping for new strategy.

"Oh my God, Mom! I don't *feel* like going to see a movie.

"The least you can do is go to a movie with your mother if you're telling me you're leaving me!"

"Oh-my-God-Mom!" That was one word to Marshall. I heard it plenty. To really drive home his point, he'd break it down, "Oh . . . my . . . God . . . Mom!"

"So what did you think about the movie?" I asked on our way home from *The Shack*.

"It'd be nice if it were true," he answered. "I just don't know what is true, and I *want* to know."

Marshall would call every week or two to hash out his questions about life, death, God, faith, truth, friends, masturbation, jobs, drug use, sex, girls, how shy he is, his dreams, broken dreams, and why his breath stinks.

There really wasn't much I didn't know about him.

His friends would tell me stories they thought I had surely not heard. Most, I had. He talked to me about everything. On one hand, he wore me out. On the other hand, I love how he trusted me with some of his deepest thoughts, questions, and insecurities. It was unusually intimate, precious, and very sacred because he was extremely private and rarely trusted anyone.

With him, everyone was guilty, fake, and a liar until proven honest and trustworthy. Everyone would be put through a rigorous study and few, if any, were so entrusted as was I. But I knew that one wrong move, one statement spoken as truth that couldn't be verified, one white lie revealed, and he'd never trust me again. I had to be *very* careful and thoughtful in how I responded to his questions.

Thankfully, he kept coming back. The pressure of his burden to know and understand concepts even Socrates didn't know left him disgruntled. And it kept me up at night, pacing the floors. He was a beautiful 20-year-old son calling his mother weekly for deep hour or hour-and-a-half discussions seeking truth, what is real about God and why we are here. He was my son. He reminded me of the young me seeking a supernatural experience with God, with that same tenacious spirit insisting on receiving knowledge in an *I have to know* determination lacking the same maturity and understanding as I. He was a "mini me" but with an *or else* attached. An *or else I'll go and find out my own way* kind of attachment.

"You expect too much of yourself," I'd tell Marshall. "You are twenty-one going on seventeen. You are immature partly due to having been through so much. Give yourself a break. Some of these questions are not meant to be known on this side of life. Accept your humanity and its limitations. We don't know what we don't know."

"I gotta know the truth," Marshall would retort.

"Well, good luck with that!" I once said in exasperation. "There are how many religions in this world? How many factions within each religion? Within each faction, you could ask people on the same pew what they believe is true, and you'll hear them dissect the same passages to support both sides of an argument. We don't know. It's a personal process. You must come to your own truth that you can accept. That requires living, experiencing life, time, and developing your own true life experience with God, your creator!"

Silence.

I hoped he heard me.

"Come stay with me," I suggested. "Get out of your apartment and spend a week with me. We'll exercise, get outside and walk, breath in fresh air, and work on you."

Finally, he agreed. Finally, I had hope. I talked with Gina and others about activities and things we could do. But the day he was to come, he called.

"I'm not coming."

There was no talking him into it.

Then he stopped answering my texts. I'd call Winston to text him. "Please make sure he's alive. I need to know he's alive."

"Mom, he isn't going to do anything. We're all miserable, but we'll push through. We always do. He won't really do it," Winston would reassure me.

He's fine, Winston would later text to confirm.

My heart would calm, at least enough for a decent night's sleep.

There is a vulnerability we expose ourselves to when we chase after our own dreams. The fear of failing at our own dream is greater than any other failure. Because what do we do when we feel we have failed at achieving our dream? What else is there to live for? Especially when you suffer from seeing things in stark black and white, as Marshall and I do. Learning to see hues and other beautiful colors takes time with people like us. Would he give himself time?

In reading about the many people who have achieved their dreams, we learn most fail many times and in multiple ways on the road to success. While at the cusp of breaking through to the next level in our lives, we always must anticipate a great battle. They seem to come right before every breakthrough. That's when we must fight the temptation to quit. In his book *The Dream Giver,* Bruce Wilkinson calls these challenges "Border Bullies."[1] They fight us at the precipice of every new breakthrough.

Marshall was in what I call the "breakers" of life. It's kind of like the waves in the ocean that crash one after another after another. He was fighting feelings of failure having literally wrecked his dream, but he was also engaged in the often unknown psychological battles that come with traumatic accidents and a foundation of childhood trauma.

In this moment of emotional instability, still suffering from inability to concentrate and focus and other childhood trauma-related issues, he decided to initiate a complete career change. That can mentally challenge even the healthiest of minds.

"Mom, I can't do this job another day," he said one day. "It's stressing me out. I can't remember what to do. I can't focus, I can't do it anymore."

Looking back, Marshall had been showing signs of PTSD even before his accident.

Marshall was an installer for AT&T. After several months on leave recovering, his return to work stressed him severely. Derailed emotionally, he could no longer handle the technical job. The pileup of childhood circumstances, divorce, and strained relations with his father and grandfather threatened his sense of worth. Probable injury to his brain no one had yet considered along with emotional trauma that often accompanies serious life-threatening collisions was likely another obstacle to his well-being. These factors combined with his lack of concentration and ability to focus caused him to start shutting down.

Marshall's return to work was on a feeble foundation. Even more challenging was his determination to quit his job, forcing himself into starting a new career path (a heavy load even for a healthy soul). He was slowly becoming buried under the weight of it all plus the pileup of debt from his leave and medical bills. I helped him financially with what I could. He met with Maryanne from JPS, who was able to assist him in creating an affordable payment plan. Because that stressed him, he shoved aside the plan and paid off every medical bill in full. Paying those bills was very important to him. Paying that debt devastated him financially. He was spiraling down . . . and fast.

"Marshall, you are creative and enjoy working with your hands," I'd tell him when discussing other options for him to consider.

"I'd like welding, I think," he said numerous times.

Then came the call for help: "Mom, I quit my job today. I'm done." *Oh my God! He is in real crisis, now.*

It threw both of us into deep turmoil. Marshall prided himself on making a good salary, his independence, sense of responsibility, and taking good care of his finances and belongings. He needed a plan and fast!

When I was in crisis, the Women's Center of Tarrant County offered me excellent professional instruction, training, and direction. Remembering that men were also in my class, I called to ask about their current services. The woman I spoke with read me a list of their services and education programs. She mentioned a work-training program where grant money had been donated to help people learn certain skills. Local businesses collaborated with the Women's Center students to provide them jobs upon successful completion of their training.

"Please list the areas in skill training," I said. "Computer, medical, welding—" she read from a list. "Welding?! Did you say welding?" I interrupted.

They provided welding training! I couldn't believe it! The application deadline was the next day. If accepted, Marshall would be required to pay $150. The other expenses were covered through generous donations and grants.

"Marshall, have I great news for you!" I said when I called with the news.

"Mom, there must be a catch because I know how much it costs for welding training. It's $20,000, minimum," he protested.

"Marshall, generous people donate and corporations assist to help people like you."

"No one cares about *me*," he volleyed back. "Who would do that, anyway?" he continued. "Who would give that much money to help someone they don't even know?" His stubborn immaturity fought on.

"Marshall, there are a lot of caring, generous people out there who want to help you and people just like you," I said. "It's humbling to need their help. But sometimes, we need a helping hand," I continued. "One day, when you are on your feet, you can help others as you've been helped," I reassured him.

"Mom, I'm tired of leaning on other people," he mumbled. "It's embarrassing. Besides, that program can't be any good if it's only $150," he added.

"Give it a try, Marshall," I urged. "You have to be there by eight, and you can't be late!"

What he didn't know is I had gone there, met with the woman who would register him, shared with her that he would enter looking like he had it all together, but warning her of the thin thread holding him to this life.

A mother herself, she felt my panic, reassuring me she'd take good care of him. She did.

The next day, Marshall enrolled.

It was a two-month training program. That meant two more months with now, little income. A friend helped him land a part-time job with a cabinet company. He worked during the day and went to class at night. His bills piled up as he completed the course. Before graduation, I had arranged for him to shadow a man who owned a welding business. When he learned the social circle that working for David would expose him to, he was excited, yet intimidated.

"Wow, I'd be in *that* circle of people?" he asked. It involved Gina's young adult children and their families. This only added to the pressure and a greater fear of failure. Yet it spiked his enthusiasm, too. It was a double-edged sword for a kid in his fragile mental condition.

"Mom, I want to work for David, but I don't think he likes me," he said after meeting him. "The guys that work for him like me, though," he added, perhaps reassuring himself. "But the money isn't enough. I couldn't pay my monthly expenses much less all this debt."

I later learned David *did* like him, was impressed with him and interested in him, and I told Marshall so. But I didn't know how he'd make it financially, either. So we discussed the possibility of two jobs.

Standing on the edge of yet another cliff of opportunity and fulfilling a dream, Marshall was scared, immature, and impatient. He was right there at yet another breakthrough. He was just about to secure a job he'd actually enjoy, one in which he'd *feel* successful. He would have had a great mentor in David, too. Was he afraid he'd fail at this dream? The money, the disappointment, the pile-up of burdens overwhelmed him.

"Baby steps, Marshall," I'd say encouragingly. "How many times did I sit you kids down to tell you there was no financial way out? How many times did I show you the walls, ceiling, and floor of how boxed in we were? How many times did I say, 'This won't kill us, and when we are on the other side, it will be because of God?'" I fired those questions off in rapid succession.

"He will do the same for you. Just one day at a time. Sometimes it's one minute at a time," I continued.

But my words were beginning to fall on deaf ears.

"Arthur and I want to meet with you, Marshall," I continued.

He agreed. We met at the Mexican Inn for lunch. He wouldn't eat.

"I've already eaten," he said.

"Marshall, you have been traumatized. You can't keep stuffing your pain," Arthur counseled. "Remember when I drove you back to your old homes and you faced your father again for the first time after you left?"

He reminisced, sharing with Marshall the details of the scenario. "I never imagined a kid so afraid of his own father," Arthur continued. "You have been traumatized and need professional help getting to the bottom of this," Arthur added, pleading with him to accept professional help.

"We never went back after we left!" Marshall exploded. "That's a lie! How stupid! We would never have returned *there* after we left!"

"Marshall, I personally drove you back *there* twice," Arthur said in disbelief that he really didn't remember as it had only been four or five years since that time. "Yes, we all went back to help move furniture, get a few more items, and help prepare the homes to sell."

"That's stupid," Marshall insisted. "I don't remember any of this," he said tentatively, beginning to partially question himself.

"You don't remember? We emptied the attic in one house and moved things out of the garage of the other."

"I can't believe we would be dumb enough to go back. That's ridiculous," Marshall insisted.

Ridiculous. That's another one of his commonly used words. That, along with, *Seriously?*

"We had to go back to prepare the houses to sell. You have been so severely emotionally traumatized, Marshall, you blocked everything out," I explained. "Honey, you need to accept professional help. You have been traumatized and you have stuffed it way down deep. Please, let's get you help," I pleaded.

"Marshall, that day, I saw how traumatized and frightened you were. Get yourself some help. Please," begged Arthur, "listen to your mother."

"That's how traumatic facing your father was for you, Marshall," I added, keeping up the pressure. "You have suppressed your pain, stuffed it down so far into your 'tank,' you are about to erupt like a volcano inside.

"You need to accept professional help, Marshall," I continued. "The more you stuff down your pain and fear, the larger the monster grows. When you face it and call it what it is, you will realize it's but a little irritating bullying roach, a bottom feeder intent on creating more pain," I continued. "Your fear is harmless until you empower it, so face your fear, Marshall. Make friends with it."

If only he could see it was nothing more than something he could eventually flick off with a finger, stomp with a foot, and end, for good.

"Make friends with it?" He boldly stared me down. "Make *friends* with it? Are you kidding me? That's insane. No way!"

Mom, I need help, Marshall later texted.

Theresa at The Family Place lined up a counselor. Marshall and I went several times, alone, just us two. He eventually concluded that talking just didn't help.

I went to Marshall any time he'd text. I made suggestions. He shut them all down.

"I don't want the stigma of being a mental health patient. It stays on your record," he said, refusing help.

Having called suicide hotlines, hospitals, mental hospitals, a broad variety of programs, and anyone I could think of for help, I discovered no one would help me help him. That was because my son, at the age of 21, was considered an adult. He had to make the call himself. So I left Marshall with a list of numbers. Leaving him, I returned home, alone, to endure numerous sleepless nights of worry and prayer. He stopped answering my calls or responding to texts.

Sick with worry, I attended a women's inaugural event at The Fort Worth Club hoping to somehow soothe my soul. I asked to meet the man who created the "unveiled" logo, explaining to him that I speak and was writing a book about domestic violence.

"I don't know why I'm telling you this," he responded, "but I'm not supposed to be here." He explained how he had recently miraculously survived a suicide attempt, taking enough drugs to kill four men.

"I'll tell you why you are telling me," I said. "My son is home, and he's suicidal right now. Would you please go visit him?"

"It's after nine in the evening," he said, looking at his watch. "Do you really want me to go now?"

After I described Marshall's situation, where he lived, and giving Barry Marshall's gate code and apartment number, he agreed to go.

"Are you going to tell him to expect me?"

"No, please just show up," I instructed. "He may or may not let you in."

Two hours later, Barry called.

"You've raised a fine young man," he said. "You should be very proud."

In pouring over all they discussed the past two hours, what stuck with me was Marshall saying to him, "I don't know if God is real."

To which Barry answered, "Son, you're not supposed to be here, you're a miracle. I'm not supposed to be here, I'm a miracle. You just opened your door to a stranger, a black man you don't know, and we're sitting here on your couch discussing *God*?

"God sent me, son," Barry continued. "What more do you *need*?"

Barely holding on as if floating just beneath the water's surface, Marshall had three life rings floating nearby. *Swim to just one of them*, I'd pray. The life rings were not only Barry and David but also his true Ordinary Angel, Ever, the responding nurse in the emergency room at JPS hospital.

Marshall. Please! Kick and swim, if just to one. Come up for air, I'd beg as he was sinking further from the surface away from me.

His eyes would lock on mine, telling me without words what he was already saying, *Mom, please let me go. You're the only reason I'm still here. Please understand.*

34

Chapter Thirty-Four

You were the hardest goodbye.
—UNKNOWN

Goodbyes are hardest when the story isn't finished.
—UNKNOWN

Like a numb manikin, I robotically smiled, shook hands, and hugged the guests at my 21-year-old son's funeral.

Marshall's struggle was over, but ours had kicked in to even higher gear. There his body laid the baby of four, in his favorite blue blazer, khaki pants, and tie, presented on a puff of white satin on display like a box of fine chocolates. I knew in that moment that shock is our body's gift to us. It protects us from feeling, temporarily anyway. Shock was fueling my every move those days.

My son took his own life. He was only 21. How do I digest this unwanted, rotten pill lodged in my throat? How do his three surviving siblings and I live on without him? These fleeting thoughts warranting a complete emotional breakdown were stifled with duties such as gathering photos; discussions about whom to be sure to inform; creating a program; picking the cast as if we were putting on an entertainment show; and choosing flowers . . . all leading to this evening before the final morning service.

With the planning complete, a funeral director takes over, keeping us following the order of events I faintly recalled even creating. Numb, denying myself the ability to feel, my three children and I enter the room dressed in gorgeous flower arrangements gifted from friends. Those arrangements frame the decorative box in which my son is displayed.

I walk over to kiss Marshall's forehead. It's cool to the touch of my lips. He's not there. It's not him.

It *is* his brown curly hair. It's the hair I cut for years with shears on the back porch. Holding a hand mirror, he'd instruct me: "Can you cut a little more here, Mom?" or "Not too much from there." Because of his hair's bristly nature, he didn't have many style options. Style was simply *shorter*.

It was the same hair his high school graduation cap adorned.

"We've just got to get this boy graduated," his principal would say every time I was called in for Marshall's angry outbursts. "He's a good kid," he'd say. "Marshall's just been through a lot," he'd say, revealing patient understanding.

I flashed back to all the meetings I had with coaches trying to get Marshall involved in sports. The broken arm from horsing around with friends one summer left him on football field sidelines, bored and discouraged. Learning disabilities kept him from making grades to compete in wrestling. Having rejected the ADHD medicines that temporarily helped him focus but left him with unwanted side effects, he'd find solutions in trying a different school. Each new high school year, he wanted to try a new school. Four different high schools later, he finally graduated from a charter school. Not proud of himself as I was, he did it.

"I don't want anyone else coming to my graduation, Mom," Marshall insisted. "Only you," he said.

Sitting alone in the crowd, Marshall walked by looking right into my eyes with that half-crested smile I knew well. He was shyly saying, *I am kinda proud of myself, actually.*

"We can meet after his ceremony to celebrate at a restaurant," Aunt Gaye offered, providing a fantastic compromise. At the restaurant with family all around us, I hear, "Thanks, Mom. I am glad I went through the ceremony," as he gave me a memorable bear hug.

Touching his hair nestled up against white satin, I'm reminded it's also the same hair I caressed when finding him lifeless on his couch in his apartment with a gun in his hand at his side. The peace I saw on his face at that moment, I don't see now. He looks hollow. He doesn't look like how I found him after Winston and his friend kicked open the door. When I found him, he looked peacefully asleep on a red wet blanket.

Falling to my knees onto his big bear chest, I cried, "I love you!" in an agonizing deep guttural groan, a sound I'd never heard from myself before. "Oh my God, I love you, Marshall," I repeated over and over, caressing his hair, kissing his face, holding him as my sleeve sopped up his blood.

Yes, let my sleeve sop up what's left of his life. I want it on me. I want him. I want whatever is left of my son. Let it touch me, get on me. It's his blood that my body gave him when he was in my womb. It's our blood. What came from him is on my sleeve now. I'll keep it. I'll keep it forever.

The police, who had patiently waited, interrupted my grief, saying, "You'll have to go now. This is a crime scene."

A crime scene, my son's death is a crime scene?

As an officer bent over me as I gave my son one final caress, I hear him say, "He did his research. He knew right where to aim."

That would be Marshall. He would do that to make it as tolerable as possible. And before the police ushered us out, Winston picked up a sheet of paper.

"Eviction notice," he read out loud.

It had been taped to his door the day before.

"That would have pushed me over the edge, too," he said, weeping. Marshall had torn up checks that I had given him to help with that.

As I stand over Marshall's coffin, I can't help but think how peaceful he looks. But I'm actually grateful to have seen him then so that the shallow remains I see in this satin-lined box is not my only memory.

As I touch his hands folded nicely over the blue blazer he proudly purchased for himself, memories flood my heart.

* * *

Modeling his then brand new blazer in the mirror, Marshall looked at me in anguish. "I don't know how to tie a man's tie," he said dejectedly

"Let's go to a men's dress shop together and have a sales associate teach you about men's clothing," I replied. The store manager not only gave him a lesson on dressing but hired him part time in sales. Marshall worked through the holidays and, with his extra money, bought himself his first suit and this blue blazer.

"The other sales associates don't believe I really don't know the different types of collars," he shyly reported to me, suffering embarrassment after his first day. "That's why you are there, to learn," I reassured him. "Don't worry about what they think. I'm so proud you are working two jobs as you make money learning what you've been seeking to learn. It takes guts."

He finished out the holiday season with a really nice wardrobe and a new confidence. He knew how to dress, when to button and unbutton his jacket, and was really proud he bought his own suit.

"I bet most people think my parents bought me my suit," he shyly said, smiling proudly one day while I watched him tie his tie. "I'm proud I bought this myself."

He worked hard at pushing himself forward. He had accomplished quite a lot. At 17, he was providing well for himself; had his own apartment, truck, and insurance; and a great start at AT&T as a cable technician.

* * *

Those are definitely his hands, I notice, caressing his hands folded so neatly together. They are the same hands (only bigger) that I held when he was a toddler fidgeting on my lap, wanting to run loose to run wild during his older brother's basketball game. They were the same hands I guided as he learned to tie his own shoes. They were the same hands that reached out to me to hold him when he was unsure about staying in the church nursery. They were the same hands that demonstrated the raw power of his motorcycle as he revved it up. They were the same hands that I held again in the hospital, a month later after his miraculous recovery. They were the hands I loved all his life that gave great, wonderful bear hugs. They were the hands I would forever miss.

People, oh yes, people are here for me to greet. As I turn through the crowd of mourners in black, I saw him enter, making his way to me, bypassing the open casket presenting the human shell that no longer held my youngest son.

How is it that here, at my son's funeral, this acquaintance coming toward me, whom I met only weeks prior, is now one of the most important people to me?

Sweat dripping down his tensed jaw, his eyes locked on mine, he forges through the crowd as if on a mission to stand boldly before me to confess "I failed."

Pausing, bracing himself for my expected response, he waits. I slowly begin nodding my head, wincing to emphatically denounce his declaration.

"Oh no, Barry," I said. "You did not fail."

As tears began to fall, I continued through clenched teeth, holding my fist in the air, "You, Barry, are the sole reason *this* mother isn't shaking her fist at God asking Him, 'Why didn't you intervene on behalf of my son?!'"

With tears streaming my cheeks, I tried to ease Barry's misplaced shame and guilt.

"Barry," I said, "you were right when you told Marshall that God sent you to him. I thought God sent *you* for my son, but He sent you to my son for *me*."

No one could possibly know the thin shredding thread tethering my faith. My hope hung, barely attached, but, yes, attached, because of Barry's conversation with Marshall the last week of his life. In a moment, Barry transformed from a complete stranger to a deep, reliable confidante, a friend of my soul.

And I'd known him all but weeks.

Relaxing his jaw, taking deep, shaky breaths, he receives my message. It obviously resonates with his truth. He knew he wasn't guilty, but he wanted to be prepared should I have considered him so.

Our encounter was bigger than all three of us. It was as if we were part of scripted play. Like genius actors going off script in a production, we observed as we participated. With the star of our three-cast show gone, his remains lying in a box soon to be closed forever, Barry and I agree to later revisit what the original intent and purpose for our meeting was that fateful evening.

Barry left in peace, saying, "I'll see you tomorrow morning."

The following morning, after the sermon, the family photo slideshow set to music, his siblings and cousin reading through tears from his personal collections of essays, the service was winding down to a lovely close. As the funeral director guided his siblings and me to our feet, showing us the way out the door, from across the aisle his father stands to his feet, shattering the flow, stating, "Wait, I have something to say."

"No!" I boldly exclaim halfway to the door, stiff arming with my hand like a traffic cop gesturing traffic to a stop.

"I'm his father and I have something to say," he said. And refusing to follow the protocol of the organized program, he continued to make his way to the podium.

As my two daughters, Winston, and I walk out of the service, Winston says, "Mom, I'm going back in. I want to hear what he has to say about his son."

As I give him a nod of approval, the girls continue with me to the reception room to await the crowd.

People soon begin rushing in. Everyone is agitated, upset.

"Oh my God!" one declares, "You needn't say more. We all saw, with our own eyes, how crazy he is!"

"He's crazzzyyy . . ." is all another says. "I'll call you later!"

"That's the first time I've truly felt fear for my life," another declared. "Sorry, but we are not staying. We're getting out of here. He's crazy."

"Is Winston okay?" asked another. "Seth never talked about his son."

Later, we learned how the crowd got up and started walking out as he yelled at the crowd, "You are disrespecting me!" attempting to regain their attention.

And then Barry comes through the line, speaking in a normal tone as if we weren't immersed in chaos, saying, "I feel like I've known you my whole life. Let's talk soon."

What happened in there?

With Marshall's father, nothing would surprise us. Whatever it was, it confirmed that we made the right decision in not inviting him to a private friend and family graveside service earlier that morning.

Before the service, unbeknownst to his father and grandfather, in an intimate setting, friends and family had already said their farewells, sharing from our hearts, uninterrupted by drama. Marshall had already been properly laid to rest. His friends and family had a chance to share thoughts and memories in a sweet spirit of love without any drama. His father disrupting the memorial service (as we anticipated) only confirmed to everyone how crazy things were for us. This engendered a deeper understanding and respect for my children, especially for how they conducted themselves despite everything their father had put them through. People saw but a mere glimpse of what we had endured. In a twisted way, he did us a favor, revealing himself as he did. We would never have to defend ourselves again.

With Marshall properly laid to rest and all the fanfare (and drama) over, we went to Arthur and Gaye's home where, with certain loved ones, we began a new pain-filled journey of learning to live without our Marshall.

34

Chapter Thirty-Four

Let no man pull you so low as to hate him.
—MARTIN LUTHER KING

It's not mean to avoid people who destroy inner happiness.
It's wisdom to protect your inner happiness.
—ELIZABETH SHAW

Following Marshall's passing, I, for the first time in my life, allowed myself to hate. I hated. I hated my ex-husband and his father and was proud of it.

Hate, I discovered, is a destructive, dark, addictive emotion that took my thought life places it had never gone before. The more I hated, the darker my thoughts went.

And I liked it, wanting more . . . much more.

* * *

"Are you and Marshall still planning to attend—"

I interrupt the call from a Landmark representative.

"Ma'am, Marshall is no longer with us," I said, speaking harshly about the harsh reality of my new life. My mentor and friend Vince Pocente had recommended the Landmark organization as an option for Marshall. Marshall and I were scheduled to attend the following week. After much discussion with representatives, they encouraged me to attend even though Marshall's passing was so fresh. Audrey agreed to join and Winston reluctantly followed. Sophia refused.

Throughout Marshall's struggle, he had remained a strong *maybe* with regard to attending. Representatives from the organization, aware of Marshall's situation, would call him, leaving messages trying to help me get him there. I tried persuading and then taking it away from him.

"This is an investment in you," I'd say. "Don't go if you are going to sit folding your arms, questioning the leaders' character and integrity on whether or not you can even trust listening."

I knew full well that he would not be able to put the leader through whatever "can I trust this person sieve" he creates and runs all people through. He wouldn't have time to size the guy up before listening.

Not wanting to spend my money if that's what he would do, I challenged him.

"Do you think I'm ready for this?" he asked me.

"They say you are. They are the experts . . . so, yes," I replied.

"Yeah, but do *you*?" he asked.

That's the moment I always go back to. What if I had answered differently? Was this a defining moment? Could I have said something that would have kept him hanging on a little longer? We had already been through "I'm out of answers myself, Marshall, but somebody can help us. I'm just me. I don't have the answers to questions you are seeking. But I am only me, Marshall. Someone can help. We need to keep trying."

"Yeah, but do *you* think I'm ready?" he asked the one person he trusted.

What I wish I had said was "I believe in you, of course. I believe you are ready, you got this, man!" Instead, what I said was "Because *they* say you are, I believe you are."

He knew it meant I had doubt. And I did. I did doubt he'd listen.

My God, the hell we put ourselves through when losing a loved one to suicide. We dissect our every move, our statements, and situational responses over and over again. Nightly, I'd sit up straight in bed with *what ifs, should haves*, and *if onlys*.

On the second day, the speaker encouraged us to consider healing any broken family relationships by calling them. With Audrey and Winston flanked at my side, I approached the speaker explaining why this wasn't even remotely possible with my ex.

"Don't forgive him, Susan, offer him grace," he said.

"Grace?" I asked. "How do I offer grace? Let me tell you about this man . . . let me tell you what he did!" I continued spewing my hatred.

"My dad molested my little sister for years," the speaker interrupted. "Our family was divided, broken, and separated because of him. Eventually, we all came together toward the end of his life, never asking him to admit his wrongdoing because he knew what he had done, we knew what he had done, and he knew we knew, so it didn't need to be said. Speaking it was too much for him. We simply loved him unconditionally, and he wept like a baby.

"Finally, toward the end of his life, I had my father," he continued. "This was healing for me. *I* benefitted from it, we all did," he said.

"Offer him grace," he repeated, remaining steadfast.

"I paid good money to be here," I said to Audrey and Winston. "I guess I should try to do what they recommend."

Audrey handed me her phone. On speaker, I dialed Seth's number, holding the phone between us in a huddle.

"Well, hello there . . ." he answered.

"Seth, this is Susan," I said in a curt, angry voice. "I'm calling to forgive you," came forced through clenched teeth.

"Well, praise the Lord! Yes, let's put the past behind us," he said, quickly welcoming the notion of easily passing over all his wrongdoings to a nice, fresh future.

Disgusted, jerking back my olive branch, I redirected the conversation.

"First you have to get right with Sophia!" I said.

Then I began listing all the wrongs he needed to right.

Interrupting and talking over me, he began hollering out my list of wrongs. Like two vicious, angry barking dogs, we were talking over each other in a crazed yelling match, with neither listening to anything.

Click. I hung up on him and marched right back to the speaker with Audrey and Winston in tow.

"How did it go?" he asked. I told him what had happened.

"You didn't call to forgive," he scolded me. "You called with an agenda. Your effort was insincere and phony and your ex smelled that a mile away," he continued. "Grace, Susan, offer him *grace.*"

I marched back out, praying, *Lord, how do I offer this man grace? I hate him. I hate him, and I hate his dad,* I prayed.

Trouble was it felt *good* to hate him.

Help me, I prayed.

We circled up around the phone, on speaker once again. This time, the call went straight to voicemail.

"Seth, I'm sorry," I began. "I was insincere and called with an agenda. So let me try again. I'm sorry, I offer you grace, I love you, and I wish you a happy life. Your relationship with your children is between you and them. I am complete and finished with you. Goodbye."

And just like that, the darkness lifted and sun shone down on us. I smiled. It felt good, *really* good.

As a result of that phone call, Winston felt invigorated and free to seek out a relationship with his father. Winston called him and would regularly text, attempting to rebuild a relationship with his dad. Eventually, Winston broke off all communication with his father, deciding for himself that Seth still wasn't yet capable of having a healthy relationship.

Many people ask me how to get over their Charming Impossible. They long for, grieve, hope, and can't seem to ever let them go.

"How do I forgive and move on when I want them back?" they ask.

To this, I ask them in return: Are you longing for who they are to return to you, or are you longing for the *illusion* they and you created of whom you want them to be? Do you really want them back, or do you want your illusion to return?

In order to forgive *them*, you must acknowledge who they are. Otherwise, you are merely forgiving who you want to *believe* they are. That's forgiving an illusion.

What seems most difficult for people who struggle to move on is that their Charming Impossible never was capable of genuine love. Control and manipulation is not found in genuine, authentic love. One must grieve they never had the love they thought they had and the fact they can never have it from their Charming Impossible. They must acknowledge who the person is, was, and never was.

Then—and *only* then—can they properly forgive. After acknowledging who your Charming Impossible truly is, you will never allow that same person back in your life for one simple reason: That person never existed. If, after you acknowledge who they truly are and you choose to allow them back in your life, you open yourself to who they *actually* are . . . hopefully with proper personal boundaries and realistic expectations firmly in place.

This is the prayer I pray: "By forgiving you, I cut the final string that was hooked, the string attached to potential anger. By forgiving you, I acknowledge you for who you are, for who you never were and for who you never will be. By forgiving you, I see everything you did and everything you didn't do. By forgiving you, I heal."

I pray the same for me.

For some, it is healthy to allow them in, for others it is most healthy to never open that door again. That choice is for each individual to make.

35

Chapter Thirty-Five

Unable are the loved to die. For love is immortality.
—UNKNOWN

To live in hearts we leave behind is not to die.
—THOMAS CAMPBELL

Death, the last sleep? No, it is the final awakening.
—SIR WALTER SCOTT

Throughout the days and grief-filled nights following Marshall's passing, I read through Marshall's text messages. I read over and over again our messages to one another, looked at the timing, and what was going on when this was said or that happened. Finding photos of his high school girlfriend, I contacted her. From her I learned that she had moved five hours away, inviting Marshall to join her when they graduated from high school. He thought about it, she said, but ultimately decided against it.

Asking Sophia if she knew of this, she responded, "Yes, he thought about it but believed it would be best for her if he let her go rather than expose her to all our drama."

Looking over Marshall's big smile with happy eyes in every photo he took with his girlfriend, I grieved. She sent me a photo of a painting he created of the two of them walking a moonlit beach with footprints in the sand. I sobbed, accepting yet more loss. She showed me photos of birthday roses he had given her with a card reading, "Will you accept this rose?" He loved her so.

But due to the psychological warfare and abuse of a Charming Impossible, my son chose to protect the love of his life from his father by rejecting the love he needed, deserved, and that she longed to offer. She was his Ordinary Angel, but he didn't understand that. Ordinary Angels are equipped to walk beside us. We may not like feeling vulnerable, allowing them to see our pain and suffer along with us, but that's part of their journey. To deny an Ordinary Angel their purpose robs them, too. I hope others learn from Marshall's mistake. He should have let her in, opened himself wide, and allowed God to use her and grow her as she helped him heal.

All Marshall's friends and siblings knew of a box Marshall kept locked away from everyone. It was secret, and no one could get near it. He was so protective over it, it became a joke among the gang. After his passing, Sophia grabbed the box. Alone, she opened it to find a box, locked inside a box, locked inside another box that had Kaitlin's cheerleader picture, her love letters, and memorabilia from time they spent together. Sophia also found Audrey's modeling agency photo card and fortune cookie messages of hope and a future tucked inside.

That Marshall pushed away love because of all our family drama broke my heart. Emotional abuser's tentacles are so far-reaching. If only they would let their Targets go when they leave, allowing them space to heal.

Unfortunately, they don't. Like killer bees, they keep stinging until their victim is down . . . and then they eat them from the inside out.

Scrolling through Marshall's phone text messages became more and more a way to feel close to him. No longer was I seeking answers or peace of mind about "what ifs." It was rather my way to hear his voice. That's when I came across an almost year-old text message exchange Marshall had had with Ever, the responding nurse from the emergency room at JPS. Ever was also a motorcyclist. He was with Marshall when Marshall was brought in by ambulance directly following his wreck. They had an immediate connection even before Marshall's miraculous, life-saving surgery. The thought of this man took me back to that day.

From the texts I gathered that Ever had connected with Marshall following his discharge from the hospital. Ever evidently met with Marshall offering to help him sell the cycle for parts or repair it, if possible. Then Marshall suddenly stopped responding.

The final business left for me with what Marshall left behind was this motorcycle. I didn't know what to do with it. My friends in the car business were not interested and didn't know anyone who was. His cycle was in a storage unit with the rent due.

Needing to find it a home, I texted Ever: *I don't know if you remember me, I'm Marshall's mother. I need to do something with Marshall's wrecked cycle. Would you be interested in it for parts?*

Coming straight from work, still in his blue scrubs, Ever met me at the storage unit. When I handed him Marshall's key, Ever unlocked the lock and slid open the metal door. There sat Marshall's "baby" . . . his pride, his shattered dream. Seeing Marshall's shattered dream, I wept. I fell into that deep, dark place of unrestrained pain, loss, and despair.

The last time I had been to this storage unit was the day Marshall was discharged from rehab. I had just loaded his wheelchair into my trunk and folded him into the front seat with his arm in a cast and his leg in a brace.

"Mom, please take me to see my motorcycle."

That was his first request.

Sliding open that metal door of his storage unit, Marshall hoisted himself from his wheelchair, hopping on one foot, to embrace his bike in a desperate plea, asking, "Why, why, why . . .?" it was all he could say, draping himself over his bike, hugging it.

I wondered the same damn thing. *Why? Why can't you give this kid a break? Seriously!* I yelled out silently to God as if this was all God's fault! *Of course, I'm grateful you saved his life. I'm grateful you placed him with the best doctors and staff.*

I continued my quiet conversation with God while Marshall mourned his own loss.

Yes, it's amazing Marshall said he was falling in front of the semi on the highway when he felt a force gently catch him and push him into the grassy median. Yes, it's amazing the policeman happened to be driving by just after Marshall and his cycle rolled, flew through the air, and landed on the median. Of course, it's miraculous he didn't sustain spinal or otherwise debilitating injuries considering the ridiculous speed we know Marshall was going due to his GoPro attached to his bike. I know all the unexplained miracles for his body! I know! But, what about his heart and his will to live? How do I encourage him now?" I silently demanded. *"I'm scared!"*

Months later, there I stood again, this time with Ever in Marshall's stead. Ever looked over the bike, patting it like it was an old friend. We both stood looking, staring, just being for the moment. Then Ever reached up, grabbing the handle to lower the sliding door. He locked the unit with Marshall's lock tucking Marshall's key in the top pocket of his scrubs.

"I have something for you," he said.

Handing me a wrapped gift, he added, "It's from my wife and me. I have an uncle who committed suicide."

When I unwrapped the gift, I found a devotional and card with a beautifully handwritten note of condolence from Ever's wife.

Pointing across from Marshall's unit, he said, "See that unit just two doors down? That's where my bike is stored. I learned about this storage unit from Marshall."

Marshall's bike was an old friend of his, after all. It was more fitting that Ever have Marshall's bike than I realized. Seeing Ever in his scrubs took me back to when Ever would visit Marshall post-op in his hospital room.

"I bought you something, Marshall," Ever said, handing him a metal hand on a stick. "It extends, see?" demonstrating how Marshall could use it to grab things or to scratch when he had an itch inside of his cast.

"Thank you," Marshall said, cracking a rare smile. It was a moment of unasked for kindness . . . thoughtful, caring, and above and beyond nice. A moment so crucial that I have the memory of Marshall's then oh-so-rare smile ingrained in my heart forever. Ever would stop by and sit with Marshall, just because. And now, I'm handing over my son's dream, his everything to Ever. And I'm so grateful someone properly fitting is available to receive it.

Months later, Ever asked to meet with me and the hospital director of trauma, Maryanne. He had a surprise, something very special, he said, he and wanted us to be there for the presentation.

Ever was a nurse, not an event planner, so as he tried to explain to Maryanne and me about how he'd like to make this presentation, we looked askance at one another trying to understand what he had in mind. Not really sure what to expect, Maryanne and I agreed to come, inviting a few others.

"So, what is this, again?" I heard from certain friends and invitees.

"I honestly don't know," I said. "This is a nurse putting on an event for our family, but he can't really tell us about it because he wants it to be a surprise. If you want to come, here's the address."

Ever did share that he created a website titled MRP33.org. It stood for "Marshall Racing Project 33." With what little information he shared, I could tell Ever was putting a great deal of effort in this. I decided to create a t-shirt for those who attended to show support for Ever. With my event planning background, I sensed Ever had a vision for how this should or could go. By the time of the event, we had over 30 people show up to a racetrack on the outskirts of town. None of us had ever been there.

Barry came. I loved seeing Barry in the green t-shirt. We were brought into a crowded room of 100 plus Ninja "crotch rocket" racers.

"Okay, everybody, listen up!" The leader of the group took charge.

"We have a special presentation today, but before we get to that, we have some business to cover."

The leader of the pack went over the regular "drill."

"Safety first," he said, explaining that this was not a race against others but against themselves. He encouraged the seasoned riders to not hesitate to tell a less experienced rider to ease up if they were pushing beyond their experience or training. He led and taught this group of men how to mentor and willingly be mentored. He closed with a prayer asking for safety for all riders.

So this is where Marshall was meant to land. With mentors and "safety first." Ever tried to introduce this to Marshall, bring him into this fold. Had Marshall not had his wreck, he never would have met Ever. This would have been a dream come true for Marshall.

My heart sank at the loss of seeing the joy he would have experienced there. There, he would have had the many male mentors he often wished and longed for. There, he would have lived out his dreams with other like-minded men fulfilling their need for adrenaline in a safe, supportive environment. Marshall would have connected with these guys. He would have been at home there.

The general meeting came to a close. Ever stood, inviting me to the front of the room as he shared about meeting Marshall, who Marshall was to him, and how it came about that I had given him Marshall's motorcycle.

At the front of the room was a motorcycle covered by a sheet. Ever unveiled Marshall's motorcycle, and I fell onto it hugging it, weeping in disbelief and awe. It was painted green, Marshall's favorite color, numbered 33 for Marshall's birthday, March 3. Marshall's name was all over the bike. JPS and Mental Health Awareness logos were beautifully displayed. It was a work of art. It was over-the-top gorgeous!

"I will race Marshall's bike for mental health awareness," Ever announced. "If you or someone you know struggles, come to me. Reach out. You are not alone."

Then Ever handed me a check made out to The John Marshall Foster Memorial Fund, a fund Dr. Haynes arranged after Marshall passed. Their generous donation to JPS, in Marshall's memory, goes to research on the effects of trauma to the brain.

* * *

Sunshine, wind, and fresh Texas spring air was the perfect backdrop for Marshall's bike debut. The crowd, resplendent in their green t-shirts, lined the track and the stands, cheering as Ever drove Marshall's bike around the track at rocket speed. Following the race, a professional photographer took photos of all of us with Marshall's bike and Ever. It was a day of awe. I marveled at who chose to show up. The event is where I met, for the first time, a high school friend of Marshall's. I met the parents of one of Marshall's friends there, too. It also brought Barry and Ever together for the first time.

One friend said that the event was life changing, unlike anything she'd ever attended. She said it was like everything surrounding Marshall's memory was organic, connected, without anyone running it. It was like a live movement without any one person in charge.

It was a beautiful, meaningful way for Marshall's memory to live on.

May he continue to touch people's lives, and may this movement prevent others from making the mistake he made. I only hope his life story encourages those struggling with depression to get the help they need. Through research we are learning how childhood trauma, emotional trauma, and physical trauma affect the brain. The John Marshall Memorial Fund at JPS established by Dr. Jay Haynes will continue to help fund this research. We are discovering new technologies and methods of healing for the brain every day.

* * *

Months following Ever's event, I sat back to absorb how Marshall's life is still impacting us and so many others. This brought comfort but didn't alleviate my struggle of feeling distanced from him. No Scripture, sermon, or affirming words of friends, family, or faith helped me find that peace of mind that Marshall was okay. The despairing cloud hovered over me. *Will this looming dark sadness ever go away? Did his sadness and struggle become mine?* I couldn't see a way out from under it. If only I could crawl in that grave with him became my companion-like thought. After all, a mother isn't supposed to outlive her child. I had lost loved ones. And it hurt. But losing a child is a sorrow all its own. It was a sorrow I wasn't sure I'd survive.

One day, Maryanne from JPS called, asking to meet with me. In response to losing Marshall, Dr. Ghandi, the doctor who saved Marshall, the one Dr. Haynes lauded for performing the medical miracle that spared Marshall's life, began what he and the hospital chaplain named "The Trauma Circle."

"Let's invite the mother of that young man," he had said to Maryanne during a planning meeting. This led to my finally getting to meet Dr. Ghandi.

"I'm Marshall's mother," I told him. "You saved my son's life. You gave me an extra year with my son. I've been looking forward to thanking you! Thank you!"

We were quickly seated in a circle of medical professionals discussing their own trauma.

"We don't even know the questions to ask with regard to trauma," admitted Dr. Ghandi. "I thought who better to start with than us, since we face trauma daily."

Marshall's story had led to the creation of this circle. After I shared my thoughts, Dr. Ghandi said, "I rarely meet my patients or their families. In fact, I usually don't even know the name of the person I'm operating on," he said. "Hearing the aftermath and effects on your family is doing something for me right now that I can't explain."

He doesn't get to see or experience the beautiful results of his work? I couldn't imagine working in trauma, immersed in continual life and death crises, without experiencing the reward of seeing that person vibrant and alive.

"Do you all know Barry?" I asked.

They certainly did, as his recovery was almost celebrity worthy.

"You know him?" Dr. Ghandi asked.

"By saving Barry, you saved the man who last spoke with my son. Barry's conversation with Marshall is instrumental in my not losing faith," I said.

"Do you know Ever?" I asked.

And with that, I told the full-circle story about Ever and Dr. Haynes. What I would have missed had I not looked back to say, "Thank you!"

I learned how rare it is that people ever come back to say those words. It's a privilege to witness another reaping their reward through the powerful act of gratitude. People rarely do things solely for the money or the recognition. They more want to make a positive difference. We, as recipients, rob them of their reward when we neglect to make them aware of how they impacted us. It's simple but powerful. When we hurt, we often want to hide from others. God moves through people. We shut God out when we shut ourselves off from others.

Moving forward, I hope to impact the rapidly growing suicide rate of our society. Hope Squad is an organization that is already successfully making a difference. Schools that implement this program claim remarkable success. Peer-to-peer training is an integral component of this youth suicide-prevention program. It trains the students to recognize warning signs in depressed or suicidal peers and empower them to properly give support and report certain warning signs to an adult.

Brain images are now available that could help us study the effects of habits. Brain images of a video game addict and how that same brain reacts when removed from a technically infused lifestyle effects visible changes. The behavioral, psychological, and attitude changes were as significant as the images of change to that brain.

I also hope to encourage more research on the effects of trauma, porn, video games, social media, music, and different types of music versus playing sports and walking in nature. We have new technology that will allow us to study how our habits affect our brain that can lead to better care for our brains and healing from trauma. "Mental fitness" will hopefully be a common expression, teaching habits with answers for Hopelessly Stuck on how to process and combat attacks from Charming Impossibles. Mental fitness can be our future answer to the child suffering from bullies and mean girls on the playground, for the kind young man married to a Charming Impossible bride, for the wife of an abusive husband, and for the student, church member, or coworker under psychological attack.

* * *

Seeking solace, I open the devotional Ever gave me, randomly flipping to a page with a story of Corrie ten Boom. It was toward the end of her life, where she lived in a home in California that was given to her. A gentleman visitor said to her, "Isn't God good to have provided you this beautiful home overlooking the ocean?" admiring its majesty and beauty.

She said, "Yes, but God was good to me in Ravensbrook, too."[1]

Closing the devotional, I thought about how she lost all of her family in concentration camps. She was a sole survivor, suffering many atrocities I can't even begin to imagine. Looking back on our journey,

I thought about the self-protected me in my youth trapped behind my own walls. As one young high school classmate said, "I see you, but I can't get to you through those glass walls."

He was correct. I was not only untouchable but lacking empathy, having never really suffered. I must say, I do like the me on this side of pain much better. I'm free to love others more deeply and feel joy much more deeply, too.

Marshall is at peace. We will miss him terribly. We will be with him again. Until then, we still have living yet to do. At the loss of all loved lost ones, we choose to remember the good, polishing their halo a bit. It's what we do as humans: Losing a loved one who provided us many loving memories leaves a deep hole never to be filled in this life.

My surviving children are true heroes to me. They have gone through much of what Marshall endured along with their own individual pain, plus the loss of a sibling. I applaud their courage, their dignity and grace. And of all four of them, I'm so very, very proud they maintain beautiful, loving hearts that remain tender towards others.

And just as Corrie said God was good in Ravensbrook, I see that through it all, God was, is, and always will be good.

Yes, indeed, God *is* good.

* * *

To my three surviving children and the too numerous to count other survivors of various abuses, remember: Many great people come from troubled homes and backgrounds. Together, let's choose to continue living our very best until God chooses to call us home.

Afterword

For Those Who Lost Someone to Suicide without Any Warning

Innate in any survivor is self-reflection and blame. We spend countless hours wondering what more could or should have been done. As
survivors, we go through self-recrimination, only to find ourselves at
the same place, with the same unanswered questions, and the same
solution: Acceptance. We simply are left with one solution and that is
to accept their choice, knowing we'll never know the reasons why they
chose the path they did. With suicide and Charming Impossibles, how
can we truly ever fully understand? What I *do* know is, through it all,
the most futile mistake I made was self-damnation and blame.

Throughout the days and grief-filled nights following Marshall's
passing, I read through Marshall's phone text messages. Night after
night, I'd sit straight up in bed in a panic, fretting, "If only I said this
or shared that. . . ."

My grieving heart allowed me no rest, no peace, no restitution.
The yearnings, the longings, the trying to imagine living without him
seemed dauntingly intolerable.

This led to my calling Barry. I asked him to meet for lunch so that
he could tell me everything he could remember about his two-hour
conversation with Marshall.

Barry met me with a life-giving gift. He brought me a typed outline of his conversation with Marshall. Throughout the three hours

we spent together, Barry referred to his outline diligently, assuring nothing was left unsaid from what he could remember. He expounded on how his and Marshall's experiences were similar, different, and unique. Still somewhat numbed by the trauma of loss, I listened, but the information was so precious, *so much.* My broken soul tried to absorb what it could but, eventually, my mind glazed over and began shutting down.

At home, I filed Barry's precious notes in Marshall's box of memorabilia. Weeks went by, and the "what ifs" kept piling up. The same thoughts kept returning. I became convinced that had I shared certain thoughts, Marshall would still be here. I was sure that if only he knew a certain "this or that," Marshall would be here. It was because of what wasn't said, I convinced myself, that Marshall was gone.

It was all about what I left unsaid.

One night, plagued by yet another haunting memory of what had not been said, I paced by Marshall's box and was reminded of Barry's notes. Frantically scrambling through the file for those notes, I discovered Marshall's notes from the Women's Center of Tarrant County next to Barry's outline.

I unfolded Barry's outline. Reading over every word, I learned Barry had gone over every single thought, idea, and scenario I had been beating myself up over . . . the things that I *thought* were left unsaid.

Then I turned to Marshall's notes from The Women's Center. In his own handwriting, he scripted his strengths, weaknesses, and knowledge of his personality type. The Women's Center covered everything I had hoped to cover when Marshall changed his mind and refused to spend the week with me.

He *knew.* He knew everything about himself I hoped he would know. He's the single-most sensitive and rare personality type. These people often feel alone in the world. They are deep thinkers and lovers. He learned these things about himself there. He learned that hurtful words affect his personality type more deeply than others. They covered everything I hoped to cover the week he was to spend with me. Between The Women's Center and Barry's notes, not one subject had been overlooked, not one thought unshared. Barry said it all. Holding those notes to my aching heart, I cried my first tears of *relief.* I finally allowed myself to stop blaming myself. I set myself free. Barry knew God sent him to Marshall. Barry told Marshall so. I believe that is true. If Marshall wouldn't listen to him, he wasn't going to listen to anyone. His mind was made up.

By sharing our story, I hope to bring peace and hope to the survivors still wrestling with *if only.* If onlys and should haves are not options.

Together, let's live our best. Accept other's choice. Choose self-acceptance.

Most importantly, choose *life.*

Acknowledgments

I am my mother's daughter. She provided a safe, secure home so that I could fearlessly explore the great world. Tethered by her heartstring of unconditional love and affirming belief in me, confidence to try without the fear of failure was my norm. Her boundless love empowered me emotionally while my father's steadfast reliability in meeting my practical needs offered a beautiful childhood and upbringing of carefree innocence and joy. For their endless love for my children and for all they sacrificed for them, I am eternally grateful. Thank you for teaching my children character by example.

To my four children, you are the essence of love and every good gift from above. I love you with my whole heart and then some. For your bravery in sharing your story, for your desire to use your pain to help others, for your grace, I respect and admire you.

To my wonderful big brother, growing up with you has provided many laughs and joys. I'll forever cherish the hours listening to records in your room or exploring Grandma and Grandpa's basement and woodworking shop. You became my protector and the protector of my children. You and your family have loved us, supported us, and assisted us through many dark hours. You are a wonderful husband, father, son, and uncle. We could not have moved forward without you and your family. To my sister, your wife, you have given and given. Many women do not accept their husband's family as their own as you do. We truly are family. I love you.

To Gina, your friendship is given from above. There's just no other explanation for the love, devotion, and life experience shared between

us and our mothers. How your family sacrificed all the time you devoted to me is a rare gem I'll forever humbly treasure. There are no
proper words of appreciation for how you walked beside me through
my many valleys. You lived it. Your family suffered your grief for me.
They grieved beside you. It was a great cost of which I am aware and
acknowledge. I would not have made it without you. You are more
than a sister.

To my editor, cousin, and friend, Sandra G Willis, you were with
me in the beginning and stuck with me through it all. Through my
journaling and re-journaling, you have an intimate working knowledge of my stages of grief, anger, and healing unique to most others.
I'm humbled by your selflessly pouring your gift of editing and writing into my many editions, shaping and guiding my work with questions, comments, and corrections. With your help, my storytelling has
improved far beyond where we first began. Moving forward into the
great unknown of becoming a published author, my confidence is ele-
vated knowing you stand beside me. Thank you for your endless hours
of editing and re-editing but most of all for believing in this project,
believing in me, in us. The impact of your assurance and affirmation
far exceeds grammar and semantics.

To Gail Fallen, content editor and my most recent "Ordinary
Angel," you first read and edited my manuscript through your professional eyes with excellence as an editor, taking my writing to the next
level. Then you read my story as a human and, with the patience of an
angel, encouraged me with your personal belief in the importance of
our message, instilling confidence in me as a writer and becoming a
friend. I am humbled and grateful for the enormous amount of time
and passion you put into this book. I will forever be grateful to you.

To Larry Carpenter of Clovercroft Publishing, thank you for your
professionalism, excellence, and availability for calls and questions
along this journey.

To all my Ordinary Angels mentioned in the book, I smile and look
forward to the future when I think of you! You are "framily." I will car-

ry the love and encouragement received from you the rest of my life and beyond. Thank you for being an example of how acts of kindness can move mountains in another's life. Your example teaches the power we all have within to change another's life as you have changed mine.

To the many Ordinary Angels not written about in my book, I acknowledge you and thank you. To the Ordinary Angels of whom I do not know, your impact is known by our creator. I thank you.

Completing my journey and writing this book is the culmination of the collaborative efforts of a great team of people. Bill Wallace, you have stood beside me from early on, encouraging me professionally and personally. Through your personal contacts and Success North Dallas, I made connections that led to securing my jobs. Thank you for your friendship and for recommending me to the National Speakers Association North Dallas where I met a team of professional mentors ready and willing to pour their insights and knowledge into my vision. To Vince Poscente and Chuck Inman, thank you for inspiring and equipping me in public speaking. A special thanks to Cindy Birne, Tammy Kling, and Omar Mediano. Thank you Shahida Arabi for The Smart Girls Guide to Self-Care website. Your informative postings educated me and helped me heal. I hope to meet you some day.

About the Author

Susan E Foster is a mother and first-time author hoping to equip men and women to recognize the narcissists and abusers in their lives. A graduate of The University of Texas School of Journalism, Susan writes a compelling narrative of the insidious, invisible tactics abusers use to render their targets "Hopelessly Stuck." By sharing her personal story of survival and faith, Susan reveals how the web of confusion is spun around abuse, inspiring healthy changes for men and women seeking to overcome and heal. Susan resides in Fort Worth, Texas. To learn more, visit susanEfoster.com.

Notes

Introduction

1. "Statistics," National Coalition Against Domestic Violence, https://ncadv.org/statistics.

2. Ibid.

3. Pierre-Eric Lutz et al., "Association of a History of Child Abuse With Impaired Myelination in the Anterior Cingulate Cortex: Convergent Epigenetic, Transcriptional, and Morphological Evidence," Psychiatry Online, July 28, 2017, https://doi.org/10.1176/appi.ajp.2017.161112.

4. "Statistics," Stand! For Families Free of Violence, http://www.standffov.org/statistics.

5. See Gloria Steinem, *The Truth Will Set You Free, But First It Will Piss You Off!* (New York: Penguin Random House, 2019).

6. See Brené Brown, *Daring Greatly: How the Courage to Be Vulnerable Transforms the Way We Live, Love, Parent, and Lead* (New York: Avery, 2012). See also Dana Staves, "The Best Brené Brown Quotes on Vulnerability, Love, and Belonging," Book Riot, April 16, 2018, https://bookriot.com/2018/04/16/brene-brown-quotes/.

Chapter One

1. Jimmy Carter, "Losing my religion for equality," *The Sydney Morning Herald*, July 15, 2009, https://www.smh.com.au/politics/federal/losing-my-religion-for-equality-20090714-dk0v.html.

2. Ibid.

3. Ibid.

Chapter Three

1. Melanie Curtin, "According to Oprah, All Your Arguments Come Down to These 3 Questions," *Inc.*, June 30, 2018, https://www.inc.com/melanie-curtin/according-to-oprah-all-your-arguments-come-down-to-these-3-questions.html.

2. M. E. Thomas, *Confessions of a Sociopath: A Life Spent Hiding in Plain Sight* (New York: Broadway Books, 2014), 18. 102, 107.

3. See Katie Hurley, "ADHD & Anxiety in Children," Psycom, https://www.psycom.net/adhd-children-anxiety.

Chapter Five

1. "(1982) Audre Lorde, "Learning from the 60s," Blackpast, Aug. 12, 2012, https://www.blackpast.org/african-american-history/1982-audre-lorde-learning-60s/.

2. "Eleanor Roosevelt Quotes," Brainyquote, https://www.brainyquote.com/quotes/eleanor_roosevelt_385439.

Chapter Six

1. Bruce Pulver, *Above the Chatter, Our Words Matter: Powerful Words That Changed My World Forever* (Portland: Multnomah Press, 2003), 5.

Chapter Nine

1. See Lynn Okura, "Brené Brown On Shame: 'It Cannot Survive Empathy,'" Huffington Post, updated Aug. 27, 2013, https://www.huffpost.com/entry/brene-brown-shame_n_3807115.

2. See https://www.catchhimandkeephim.com/.

Chapter Eleven

1. "Global Health Risks," World Health Organization, https://www.who.int/healthinfo/global_burden_disease/GlobalHealthRisks_report_full.pdf.

2. Ibid.

3. See Jerry Mitchell, "The danger of leaving," *The Clarion-Ledger*, Jan. 28, 2017, https://www.clarionledger.com/story/news/2017/01/28/most-

dangerous-time-for-battered-women-is-when-they-leave-jerry-mitch-ell/96955552/.

4. Ibid.

5. United Nations Office on Drugs and Crime, "Homicide and Gender 2105, Heuni, https://www.heuni.fi/material/attachments/heuni/projects/wd2vDSKcZ/Homicide_and_Gender.pdf.

6. National Domestic Violence Hotline, "Get the Facts & Figures," The Hotline, https://www.thehotline.org/resources/statistics/.

Chapter Fifteen

1. See Colleen Walsh, "Winfrey: Failure is just movement," *The Harvard Gazette,* May 30, 2013, https://news.harvard.edu/gazette/story/2013/05/winfrey-failure-is-just-movement/.

2. "Socrates: Know Yourself," The-Philosophy, . https://www.the-philosophy.com/socrates-know-yourself.

Chapter Twenty-One

1. Ellen Hendriksen, "Why Do We Self-Sabotage?" *Psychology Today* (blog), Oct. 10, 2017, https://www.psychologytoday.com/us/blog/how-be-yourself/201710/why-do-we-self-sabotage-0.

2. Ibid.

Chapter Twenty-Three

1. See US Department of Justice, "The National Strategy for Child Exploitation Prevention and Interdiction: A Report to Congress, August 210," https://www.justice.gov/psc/docs/natstrategyreport.pdf.

2. Ibid.

3. See "Impact Report 2018-2019," Children's Institute, https://www.childrensinstitute.org/wp-content/uploads/2019/10/CII19_ImpactReport_102419.pdf.

4. Laura K. Murray et al., "Child Sexual Abuse," Child and Adolescent Psychiatric Clinics of North America, vol. 23,2 (2014): 321-27, https://www.ncbi.nlm.nih.gov/pmc/articles/PMC4413451/.

Chapter Twenty-Five

1. Elizabeth Gilbert, *Eat Pray Love: One Woman's Search for Everything Across Italy, India, and Indonesia* (New York: Riverhead Books, 2007), 164

2. Ibid.

3. Ibid., 165.

Chapter Thirty-Three

1. Wilkinson, *The Dream Giver*, 27.

Chapter Thirty-Five

1. Billy Graham, *Hope for Each Day* (Nashville: Thomas Nelson, 2012), 345.